Old in Art School

A Memoir of Starting Over

NELL PAINTER

A FINALIST FOR THE NATIONAL BOOK CRITICS
CIRCLE AWARD IN AUTOBIOGRAPHY

NAMED A BEST MEMOIR OF THE YEAR BY *TIME*

NAMED A TOP BOOK OF THE SUMMER BY
O, THE OPRAH MAGAZINE

A *NEW YORK TIMES BOOK REVIEW* EDITORS' CHOICE

———————————

"Candid and cheerfully irreverent . . .
Bringing new energy and insight to questions that have long
preoccupied the art world . . . *Old in Art School* is . . . meandering,
pleasingly and profoundly so, as Painter negotiates the artist she's
becoming: not identical with her historian self, but not
running away from it either."
—*The New York Times*

"Painter claims her birthright as an artist, a
black woman, and a woman of a certain age at a time and in
a cultural milieu that ignores all three."
—**CNN**

"While exploring what it truly means to be an artist, this
book asks honest and important questions about how our definition
of identity influences our shared concept of art."
—*Time*

"*Old in Art School* is really a memoir about the meaning of art,
and who gets to determine what art is."
—*Bitch*

"A smart, funny and compelling case for going after your heart's desires, no matter your age." —*ESSENCE*

Praise for

OLD IN ART SCHOOL

"At the age of 64, Princeton history professor emerita and best-selling author Nell Painter decided to reinvent herself as an artist, an avocation she had always longed to pursue but never had the confidence or opportunity to commit to . . . She tells her story with wit, honesty and insight as she learns to see her art, and herself, all over again."

—DIANE COLE, *The Wall Street Journal*

"This tension—between the private, idyllic state of making art and the social and political realities of being an artist—is central to *Old in Art School*. It's very much to Painter's credit that she refuses to become cynical . . . She writes about her experiences with grace and style."

—*The Nation*

"Her memoir . . . is many things: an appraisal of artists living and dead, a hymn to her home state of New Jersey, a meditation on her parents' deaths, a reflection on the travails of leading a scholarly association. It's also a sharp critique of the teaching methods and social environment in M.F.A. programs." —*The Chronicle of Higher Education*

"Painter's memoir presents her as an accessible artist, warm and inviting and keen to share her hard-won insights into her craft."

—*Library Journal* (starred review)

"This is a courageous, intellectually stimulating, and wholly entertaining story of one woman reconciling two worlds and being open to the possibilities and changes life offers." —*Publishers Weekly* (starred review)

"Painter is a personality par excellence; forthright, erudite, and perfectly profane, her voice enthralls . . . Filled with immense insight and presence, Painter's memoir confronts a variety of issues and what it means to shoulder those burdens in the pursuit of art. Essential reading."

—*Foreword Reviews* (starred review)

"A joyous book; a bumpy but unmistakable love story . . . Informal yet passionate, witty yet heartfelt, *Old in Art School* feels like a painting rendered in words; a vivid picture of an experience in time."

—*The Seattle Times*

"Having just retired from teaching history at Princeton and authoring several books on race and identity, Painter is well-equipped to dissect the various forms of discrimination she faces in these programs. And she does it all with a sense of humor, honoring, above all else, creativity, and openness."

—*Literary Hub*

"This is a story of a woman determined to redefine herself, a task made more difficult by the casual racism she faced in school and the increasing frailty of her parents, both approaching age 90 . . . She tells an inspiring tale of an older person pursuing a long delayed passion."

—*Star-Tribune* (Minneapolis)

"Painter clearly enjoys the freedom of being an artist . . . Her memoir captures the adrenaline rush of learning and honing her artistic skills."

—*New Jersey Monthly*

"Painter's memoir, enhanced by her artwork as she progresses, bursts with explosions of self-knowledge as she deals with ideas of beauty, value, and identity in her ongoing journey."

—*The National Book Review*

"This book is so brilliant and, like, delightful. One of our preeminent historians and intellectuals goes back to college and then grad school to study art, with college kids, and has all the confusions and pleasures and anxieties and disappointments and realizations you might expect, but don't expect. I love this book." —Ross Gay, Book Marks

"[Nell Painter] leaves us with a detailed record of her personal art history, a map to understanding her idiosyncratic works and a written means of insuring that her art is not forgotten." —*The Brooklyn Rail*

"Making important observations about age, gender, and looks in the art world, *Old in Art School* tells more than just Nell's story as she transitions from the academic world to the art world. For anyone who needs

a pick-me-up this summer, this memoir will give you hope that it's never too late to pursue your passion and accomplish your lifelong goals."
—*PopSugar*

"As a historian with years of incisive scholarship behind her, Painter is perfectly poised to examine her experience, and the larger art ecosystem, from a more nuanced lens . . . She makes the most of her talents as a writer and offers a story filled with passion, discovery, and, ultimately, her own encouraging triumph."
—*Artsy*

"The book is less about the wounds inflicted over the journey than about the process of becoming an artist—of forging a new identity in the autumn of your life . . . It's that spirit of embrace—of finding new ways to define your worth, and to do so without apology—that makes Painter's story resonate."
—*The Glow Up*

"An alert observer, Painter renders her experience with humor, with skepticism, with anxiety, and in many voices . . . Painter communicates in language which is bodacious and, in moments, color-saturated . . . If you read *Old in Art School*, you will learn, from Nell Painter, what it means to speak in color."
—*Women's Review of Books*

"As one of the most celebrated historians in America, Nell Irvin Painter could've made the decision to write the memoir that was 'expected of her.' The memoir that told the story of how and why she became one of this country's most important scholars on American history; she could've made the decision to write about her life in the past tense, as if it were a eulogy. Instead, Painter opted for the possibility that there was something beyond what others might arbitrarily consider the 'last stop' . . . Though Painter does achieve her goal of becoming some estimation of what she considers to be An Artist, you come away with the sense that her best years are yet to come."
—YAHDON ISRAEL, *Critical Mass*,
The Blog of the National Book Critics Circle
Board of Directors

"If you love art and the creative process of expressing your passion, and if you are of a certain age, you will be inspired by her grit and work ethic . . . Her story has inspired me, as an older reader, to ask myself: What do I want to start after retirement?"
—*Cascadia Weekly*

"Breezy and intimate . . . The heart of this book is Painter's unshakeable dedication to making art. It is ultimately as much a manifesto as a memoir." —*Chapter 16*

"An argument for the necessity of arts education and a critique of it, served up with generous doses of wit and charm . . . Painter allows herself to be challenged in ways that I wish were more common—perhaps it would improve our public discourse about art." —*The Undefeated*

"Bracingly honest . . . More than a fish-out-of-water tale, Painter's memoir testifies to her unusual ambition." —*Harvard Magazine*

"Fascinating . . . That the diligence that was an asset throughout her academic career was viewed almost as a liability in art school is an intriguing tension; so too is Painter's struggle to see art absent of the ideological analysis characteristic of her academic training . . . Painter, at 75, continues to paint, and that's where the book's greatest lesson lies." —*The Christian Science Monitor*

"With her art displayed throughout this deeply inquisitive, involving memoir of transformation enriched by art history, Painter—funny, furious, brilliant, and mesmerizing—celebrates the hard work art requires and the profound freedom it engenders." —*Booklist*

"A candid, captivating memoir . . . The author offers perceptive insights about the meaning of art: the difference between thinking like a historian and an artist; the 'contented concentration' she feels when making art; and the works of many black artists. A spirited chronicle of transformation and personal triumph." —*Kirkus Reviews*

"Bold, brave . . . *Old in Art School* is a fascinating memoir about Painter's daring choice to follow a passion with courage and intellect, even when the odds seemed firmly stacked against her." —*BookPage*

"Reading Nell Painter's *Old in Art School* gave me immense pleasure. Memoirs by black women artists are extremely rare, and this one is so beautifully written, so perfectly formed in terms of its storytelling trajectory, with so many delectable details about art techniques and subject matter, the relationship of the work to her previous projects as a celebrated historian, and her life struggles as the daughter of once-perfect parents, now aged and with health difficulties. *Old in Art School* seems both definitive and unforgettable. The idea that this brilliant woman would move from a field in which her accomplishments are regarded as superlative to one in which she is constantly plagued by self-doubt and the shortcomings of her 'twentieth-century eyes' alone makes it worth the price of admission." —MICHELE WALLACE, author of *Dark Designs and Visual Culture*

"One of our most distinguished scholars of race and racism has written an incisive, surprising, eloquent, and often wry account of what it means to go back to school at 64, the age at which most academics contemplate retiring from it. Along the way, Nell Painter helps us to see the world as art, art as the world, and to understand arduous, creative self-transformation as toil worth the trouble. *Old in Art School* is as edgy as a contemporary work of art: bold in form, assured in line and shape, unflinching in its textured analysis of the ways race, gender, and age color how we perceive the world and how the world perceives us." —CATHY N. DAVIDSON, author of *The New Education: How to Revolutionize the University to Prepare Students for a World in Flux*

"With wisdom, insight, brutal honesty, and flashes of humor, Nell Painter shares her journey to become an artist in this fascinating, original memoir. *Old in Art School* renders both the insecurity and elation of embarking on this path after a long and distinguished academic career. Her courage, sensitivity, and keen observation offer a rare and needed portrait of an older woman determined to live a creative life on her own terms." —FARAH JASMINE GRIFFIN, author of *Harlem Nocturne: Women Artists and Progressive Politics During World War II*

"*Old in Art School* is brilliantly written. A rare reflection of an artist and scholar who combines her voice and vision in this extraordinary work. Painter masterfully weaves a highly personal story into one that situates her art making with her history making . . . It is a book about belonging and longing; expectations and disappointments; beauty and humor. It is engrossing and heroic." —DEBORAH WILLIS, New York University, author of *Envisioning Emancipation*

"Nell Painter's masterful, disarmingly witty, and profound book *Old in Art School* will change your perspective about what is possible in the full arc of a life. Her probing book about [her] art school journey, as sage as it is humorous, revels in the untold magic of exploring how beginnings can happen at all stages of the journey. This book is indispensable nourishment for the creative soul." —SARAH LEWIS, Harvard University, author of *The Rise: Creativity, the Gift of Failure, and the Search for Mastery*

"Nell Painter has courage and intelligence. She reminds us that the only option as we grow older is to grow younger. Never forgetting our curiosity and passion, we are well armed for the challenge." —MAIRA KALMAN, author of *The Principles of Uncertainty* and *Beloved Dog*

"We all dream of starting over, but Nell Painter really did it. This unsparing account of inspiration and the creative process takes on racism, loneliness, self-loathing, the hazards of aging, and bad manners in the art world. Funny, edifying, and always mesmerizing, this book is also about searching for—and finding (most of the time)—happiness." —MARTHA HODES, author of *Mourning Lincoln*

"'There are no second acts in American lives,' the doomed literary charmer F. Scott Fitzgerald famously lamented. Not so says Nell Painter. A distinguished professor of history at Princeton and author of the celebrated *The History of White People*, Painter has done what few academics dare—begin again by pursuing a different vocation: in her case, a long-standing drive to make art. In this lively account, she describes how she started over from scratch by enrolling as an undergraduate art major at Rutgers and then a graduate student at the Rhode Island School of Design. Much like her classmates, Painter's dedication faces competition from 'real life'—in her case, the declining health of her aged father rather than the social and romantic dramas of twentysomethings—but she also extracts important lessons about gender and racial politics in contemporary America that, contrary to the norm in art schools, demonstrate that such complex issues of 'identity' can be addressed in plain but vivid language, even as she gives artistic questions the edge. All in all, Painter makes an invigoratingly affirmative, refreshingly unjaded case—supported by her paintings, drawings, and books—for following one's passion whenever it asserts itself and wherever it leads."

—ROBERT STORR, professor of painting and printmaking, Yale University School of Art

"*Old in Art School* is Nell Painter's journey from famous historian to humble art student at age sixty-four. Along the way, she chronicles her own family history, including a mother who reinvented herself at the same age! Painter blows up treasured clichés about what it means to be 'an artist' and who fits that role, presenting us with comic scenes of questionable pedagogy. This book should have a corrective impact on art education—it deserves to be widely read and hotly discussed!"

—JOYCE KOZLOFF, artist

"Even before a teacher tells her, 'You'll never be an artist,' Painter's story wins us over with its contrarian premise. Among twentysomethings, Painter proves herself a sharp observer—not just of art school partying, pedagogy, and process, but also of generational, sexual, and racial blind spots. Painter has produced a cheerful and beguiling memoir, one that will inspire readers of any age to consider starting again."

—ALEXI WORTH, artist

ALSO BY NELL PAINTER

The History of White People
Creating Black Americans
Southern History Across the Color Line
Sojourner Truth, A Life, A Symbol
Standing at Armageddon: The United States, 1877–1919
The Narrative of Hosea Hudson
Exodusters

OLD *in* ART SCHOOL

A Memoir of Starting Over

NELL PAINTER

COUNTERPOINT
BERKELEY, CALIFORNIA

The Library of Congress has catalogued the hardcover
as follows:
Names: Painter, Nell Irvin, author.
Title: Old in art school : a memoir of starting over /
Nell Painter.
Description: Berkeley, CA : Counterpoint Press, 2018.
Identifiers: LCCN 2017055407 | ISBN 9781640090613
Subjects: LCSH: Painter, Nell Irvin. | Artists—United
States—Biography. | Adult college students—United States—
Biography. | Older artists—United States—Biography. |
African American women artists—Biography.
Classification: LCC N6537.P23 A2 2018 | DDC 700.92
[B]—dc23
LC record available at https://lccn.loc.gov/2017055407

Paperback ISBN: 978-1-64009-200-6

Cover designed by Faceout Studio
Book designed by Wah-Ming Chang

COUNTERPOINT
2560 Ninth Street, Suite 318
Berkeley, CA 94710
www.counterpointpress.com

Printed in Canada
Distributed by Publishers Group West

3 5 7 9 10 8 6 4 2

To the Love of My Life
and the Newark Arts Community

CONTENTS

Old in Art School

Prologue

YOU'LL NEVER BE AN ARTIST

THE WORLD OF THE RHODE ISLAND SCHOOL OF DESIGN and the world of my former academic life rarely overlapped. But some RISD people, like my printmaking Teacher Randa, inhabited both realms and didn't pretend my book didn't exist. Chatting with her in Benson Hall one day after our printmaking class, I seized a rare opportunity in art school to brag about my writing, to wit, my Sunday's morning wonder of wonders, my book reviewed on the front page of *The New York Times Book Review*.

The New York Times Book Review.

Front-page review.

Oh la la la la!

Randa recognized this as every writer's dream, a Once In A Lifetime, a True-to-Life Coup. She ran me downstairs to share my miracle with her teacher colleague Sharon. Passing the printmaking office on our way to Sharon, we ran into Teacher Henry standing outside the doorway of his faculty office, a distraction from wonder, the reminder of a beef.

Teacher Henry had given me an A-minus (bad graduate school grade) and called me "dogged" (a put-down, not an appreciation of persistence). Recognizing an insult, I had called him out over "dogged."

Henry's malevolent magnetic field pulled me off course. Instead of rejoicing over my amazing good fortune with Sharon and Randa, I resumed my fight with Henry. This was stupid of me, now I know, even though I was right, and he was wrong. Henry did not back down. He doubled down. He insisted he had to say what he believed, what he "knew," to be true:

You may show your work.

You may have a gallery.

You may sell your work.

You may have collectors.

But you will never be an artist.

Why not? Because I lacked an essential component, some ineffable inner quality necessary to truly be An Artist. I recognized Henry's logic of "being" as complete, unalloyed bullshit. I said,

Henry, that's bullshit.

I knew it was totally unprofessional of him, a teacher, to say that to me, a student. I knew that from a career of teaching, from a lifetime of knowing teacher-student relations. I knew. I knew. As surely as I was right and he was wrong, I knew. What I felt was something as different as heart from brain.

What I felt was Henry's arrow of condemnation piercing my student's psyche. He hurled an arrow, a dagger, a sharp-pointed weapon into my bull's-eye of a heart, where it lodged among a thousand insinuations, of doubts that in fact, I was not good enough. That arrow-target, the assault and the wound. The target of my self-doubt shape-shifted into an Escher loop of insecurity and self-pity.

Never be An Artist, not good enough, never be An Artist, not good enough, never be An Artist, not good enough

You may recognize this circuit of torture.

Henry cut me so deeply because part of me—while I was in graduate school, the larger part of me—wanted to be An Artist in just that indescribable way. An An Artist artist finds her identity in art, does nothing but make art, and does it all the time, making work of unimaginable creativity. An An Artist artist makes art 100 percent of the time.

I would have loved to devote all my time to art, to pursue each inspiration to its fabulous ends. But I also didn't want to leave book promotion or writing tasks or my dear husband in New Jersey. I wished I didn't always have to cringe when the phone portended parental emergency from the West Coast. But my parents were a part of me I could not even imagine letting down. I could not abandon the rest of me, even when the rest of me overwhelmed my art.

I wanted to be a better artist and make more exciting work with never-before-seen drawings and hitherto unimaginable compositions and color from the ends of the earth. Part of me wanted to be An Artist, without any asterisks. All of me wanted to be An Artist—and yet at the same time to keep my past as thinker and writer. But how could I be An Artist, when "academic" was so poisonous a concept in art and while I had always been academic? The very worst thing in the world you could call someone's art was "academic," meaning sterile, humorless, obscure, unattractive, and old-fashioned. Old.

An Artist's art is ambiguous and ironic, possessing what Teacher Roger called "*right nowness.*" I was doing my darnedest for ambiguity and irony, with mixed results, but *right nowness*? I was too old for *right nowness*.

Teacher Donna faulted me for not being "hungry" enough to be An Artist. I asked myself what on earth is "hungry" if not moving to another state, paying a fortune in tuition, rent, and supplies, working endless hours, and being humiliated on a daily basis? What an art-world fun house of jumbled, upside-down values. Donna's condemnation stung because Henry's resonated, and I was vulnerable to both. Meanwhile, my upbringing, long life's experience, and scholarship had armored me against thinking of identity—racial or gender identity—as something you *are*, or as academics would say, as something ontological. Knowing identity as something people performed in various ways, I was armored against racial and gender "essentialism," as academics would say of something simple and unitary. Yet here I was, falling for essentialism about artists.

Henry's definition of An Artist was ontological (as in "to be") rather than epistemological (as in "to learn") or pedagogical (as in "to teach") or performative (as in "to act"), or even commercial (as in to have a gallery): he was saying that since anything can find its way into a gallery, and tastes vary so widely that just about anything can find a buyer, an inexpressible something, some inward quality of being, hard to pin down and beyond the market, must, therefore, exist on the exciting side of the line separating An Artist artists from inferior beings, i.e., from me.

To be An Artist was *to be* a certain kind of person that you could not become through education or practice. It was a toggle switch between either you were or you weren't. If I was never going to be An Artist, my last few years were a terrible mistake, a waste of time and a great deal of money. If I lacked the essential quality of being An Artist, I was condemned to failure.

My defect was my seriousness, my persistence, my discipline, my goddam hard work. In other realms, these are the foundations of resilience, a positive quality in life, essential for survival. Survival, however, does not figure among the qualities of An Artist. How much more attractive to go down in flames at a young age, like Jean-Michel Basquiat or Arshile Gorky. I remembered skinny white Matt, my skateboarder classmate at Mason Gross, who made awesomely huge, extraordinary imaginative pieces by staying up the night before the piece was due. Totally amazing work, but hardly a routine for the decades. All the better to die young.

Too late for me.

I

HOW OLD ARE YOU?

H OW OLD ARE YOU?" SHE ASKED FROM A SMALL FACE, a small body, a little dress, and Uggs; neutral words. It took a moment for me to detach her from the mass of Rutgers students. Me sweltering at the bus stop on George Street in New Brunswick, anxiously scanning the herd of buses arriving, loading up, and departing, systematically and, to me, confusingly. Had she not spoken, I wouldn't have noticed her, not yet remarking students' individual differences. They in private earbud worlds, historicizing into their or friends' tiny phones, grinning over Tweets or minuscule videos. They roared over towering dramas and hysterically funny incidents. Every experience just born brand-new.

She carried a cell phone, too, but something pulled her out of it and into seeing me. She turned to me to query,

How old are you?

She took a step toward me as if there were simply something she needed to know. She was upholding art-school sartorial drama in bright yellow hair and piercings, art-school fashion statements I was seeing for the first time.

My fashion statement said "comfort." Plain white T-shirt, black pants (I was the only one in long pants), sturdy white New Balance walking shoes, and a baseball cap. Today's cap said New York Sheep and Wool Festival. I may not have been the only knitter in that crowd, but I was the only one wearing it, on this, my second day as a BFA student at Mason Gross School of the Arts of Rutgers, The State University of New Jersey.

How old are you? interrupted the befuddlement of my first encounter with the herds of Rutgers students and buses, red, white, and black. She blurted out her question, no euphemism, no beating around the bush, no aggression, just naked curiosity before telling me her name was Tina:

How old *are* you?

Sixty-four, I answered.

I've never lied about my age, but I'd never been confronted with so bald a need to know.

Tina gasped, mouth open—actually taking a step backward away from me, eyes all amazed, not hostile, just stunned. Sixty-four had turned me into a phantasm, a creature from another planet. Her gleeful next act documented her sighting from the planet of the old:

I've gotta tell my mom about this!

And she did so right then.

It's a wonder she didn't take a selfie with me.

Here was my first experience as an exotic in art school, an exotic on account of age, the exotic old person.

This kid, this girl, made me see myself through her eyes. She had recognized me from the previous day's Mason Gross orientation. Me, then, in the little auditorium among two hundred or more new freshmen, all but two straight out of high school. At Rutgers I stuck out more on account of age than race or quality of attention or personal apparel. Other students were black and brown; they wore T-shirts, shorts, tiny little skirts, the hijab, or preprofessional uniforms. Rutgers isn't like those lame midwestern universities that need Photoshop to multiculturalize their image. Rutgers in its multifariousness is lovable, multicultural New Jersey. Rutgers is in New Jersey, with everyone from everywhere.

The next day I met the other older student from orientation, a man in his forties from South Jersey with tattoos smaller than the kids' and jeans not so skinny. He came out to smoke a cigarette among all the other smokers—every single person but me was smoking—and joined me on the patio in front of the Civic Square Building. We sat to the side of Alice Aycock's *The Tuning Fork Oracle,* a giant steel sculpture—a tipped-up, floating metal table covered with a white marble tablecloth (whitish, actually, on account of New Jersey rain stain), several smoked glass spheres and arrows, a tuning fork in the middle. It's stood there safely since 1997, but you don't feel safe under it so huge and crazily angled. We chatted Jersey talk: Where are you from? What roads do you take to get here, what exit? And he asked,

How old *are* you?

The question still took me by surprise.

Once again, sixty-four.

He said, I hope I look that good when I'm that old.

THE CRUCIAL FACT of my age emerged, not as an incidental, but as my defining characteristic, of how others saw me as a demand to see myself through their eyes. It was as though being old summed me up, not all the things I had done to become a historian—a goddam distinguished historian—not the singular family I come from, not even my fascinating, beleaguered city of Newark in my eternally dissed state of New Jersey. Being seen as an *old woman* added a new way of seeing myself as reflected in the eyes of others.

I was used to juggling my self-perception and other people's views of me as a black person and as a woman, from within and without. But now what I took as *me* seemed almost inconsequential as my essence shriveled to my age. This was something new.

I'm accustomed to being seen/not seen as a black person and as a woman, to the various ways strangers would and would not see me. Some positively refused to see me, the youth who ostentatiously looked away. I knew the pleasant enough half smile of women I didn't know in mostly white places, and the co-conspirator wink-smile of other black women approving my presence and my natural hair, the crinkle-eyed acknowledgment of a sister on the street.

There was also the respectful recognition on the bus or light rail in Newark to say we're all in the same space, but I'm according you both confirmation and privacy. On the street in places as disparate as Newark and Princeton, as Cambridge and Oakland, there was the closed-in-on-itself-ness of people going their own ways.

And there was the approach of the person who has to greet you in some smallish gathering of picked people but who wants to by-pass you for a *really* important person, not you. I was accustomed to all these greetings and un-greetings, of dismissals of me as not sufficiently consequential and of addressing me as someone who might turn out to be useful to their ambition. I was used to crossing paths with all sorts of people I did not know.

I knew standing out on account of sex-race, not because I'm extraordinary in my own right. And I knew disappearing entirely when disappearance isn't appropriate, as in a place where Nell Irvin Painter ought to be seen but she's not wearing her name badge with Princeton on it. This is part of what it means to be a black woman in my country, and I had adjusted to it. Yet I always miss feeling at home. I cherish the times when I'm as one with the people around me—with family, in familiar gatherings, with friends, even with strangers on a train. Solidarity is a feeling I hug when I can feel it.

I knew encounters from the context of race in America. A passage by W. E. B. Du Bois is said often enough to become widely known (like the proverbial literary phrase quoted to you by someone assuming you had never heard it before), but always circumscribed within racial identity. Speaking about black people in America, Du Bois said we see ourselves not only from inside, as ourselves, but additionally, from outside, as objects of other people's disdain.

It is a peculiar sensation, this double-consciousness, this sense of always looking at one's self through the eyes of others, of measuring one's soul by the tape of a world that looks on in amused contempt and pity. One ever feels his two-ness,—an American, a Negro; two souls, two thoughts, two unreconciled strivings; two warring ideals in one dark body . . .

I knew this from blackness, but it really does apply elsewhere, and so now it was with my age, with me as an old woman. It wasn't that I stopped being my individual self or stopped being black or stopped being female, but that *old*, now linked to my sex, obscured everything else beyond *old lady*. Such was other people's gaze turned on me as a query. They didn't know what to make of me as a phenomenon in that place at that time.

There is so much more to me than age. And that *so much more* got me to art school in the first place. With my energy and excellent health, I routinely refute expectations of the older woman, just as over the years I have grown accustomed to soaring above what was expected of me—me as a black person, me as a woman, me as a person of my generation. Why wouldn't I be able to go to art school at sixty-four? Being *able* to go to art school at sixty-four was one thing.

Why I would *want* to go to art school was another.

Answer: The pursuit of pleasure. Concentrating on what I could see gave me intense pleasure, and seeing what I could make with my own hand and according to my own eye was even more satisfying. Mark making and mixing and applying color contented me deeply, just the very processes of putting line on paper, brush on canvas. Art stopped time. Art exiled hunger. Art held off fatigue for what would have been hours as though hours hadn't really passed. Pleasure. Satisfaction. Contentment.

Part of it was freedom from Truth. I know some artists create out of a quest for truth that can't be found elsewhere. Not me. I wanted to create images, to make art that expressed my own mixed-up character, to forge a truer me than one confined by existing categories of sex-race and circulating widely as necessarily true. Yes, yes, I loved all the steps entailed in scholarship, but I reached for more, to take other steps, additional steps, call them side steps, for freedom from evidence-based knowledge of things I could know for sure, things that stood for much smaller as well as larger things, beyond and around the truths of the archive. Fiction. Visual fictions. I wanted to make art. Seriously. And to make serious art unfettered from the mandate that I address larger truths.

Contradiction crouched between my search for freedom and my bent toward serious art. My instincts, my past, drew me toward formal study. And decades in the Ivy League had taught me institutions' role in gatekeeping and networking. I knew it made a difference where you studied that went beyond what you could learn. I knew all too well that the same artifact, the same utterance, would meet widely disparate receptions according to the institutions attached to them. Institutions conferred not simply knowledge, but also the means to be seen.

On one level, I fancied my pleasure in drawing and painting would not require other people's approval. I was at a place in my life beyond regard for approval. Or so I thought. Somehow I overlooked the contradiction between my yearning for artistic freedom and my urge to work seriously, that is, on a professional level.

Seriously.

On a professional level.

What weighted terms.

Seriously and *on a professional level* would mean art school, not merely taking a class here or there and making art for myself and my friends. Art school would mean more than following my own inclinations. It would entail evaluation—judgment—according to already existing criteria. Whose criteria? Other people's criteria. Other people's judgment. An awful discord between freedom and other-defined seriousness that I could not yet see. I had little understanding of the potency of *good* and *better* as applied obsessively to art schools and to art and to my own art in particular.

I had no inkling of how thoroughly art school would instruct me—teach me, challenge my abilities, and question my sanity. I didn't know how much I would learn from the young art students beside me. I just knew I wanted to make art and make art seriously.

2

LEAVING MY
FORMER LIFE

CURIOSITY IN MY REGARD, AND THERE WAS A LOT OF
it, didn't only come from inside Mason Gross, for generally the
kids were cool with whatever. Curiosity came from people of my
generation in my soon-to-be former existence. They regarded my
new life, my adventure, in the words of some, my "journey," with
envy and hesitation. They identified with my break for freedom but
feared their academic or lawyerly selves had already quashed their
inner Beyoncé, that the wet blanket of professionalism had smoth-
ered their flame. They wondered if they, too, could leave dutiful,
controlled professional personas and fling themselves into a new,
hypersaturated, Technicolor—no, RGB color-coded—artistic life
of creativity and apparent abandon. I had yearned like that before
actually walking away. Professing admiration for my bravery, my
friends asked how I did it and hoped I would send back a report.

Why do something different? Why start something new? Why
did I do it? What made me think I could begin anew in an entirely different field from history, where, truth be told, I had made a

pretty good reputation? Was it hard leaving a chaired professorship at Princeton? I didn't think so. No, I thought not. For a long time, my answers, even to myself, were simple—too simple by far.

I said, because I wanted to.

Because I could.

I knew from my mother I could do it.

My smart, small, intense, beautiful, disciplined little mother, Dona Irvin, administrator to author, held the key to my confidence. To a very great extent, she still does. The *so much more* of myself beyond my sex, race, and age that I cherish is rooted in my family, in my father the gregarious bohemian, who had taught me to draw decades ago, but even more in my mother, who, starting over at sixty-five, blossomed as an older woman, transforming herself into a creator in her own right after a lifetime as a shyly dutiful wife and mother. As an older woman she cast off the strictures of a lifetime—well, some of them—and took to wearing red or white with her dark skin and taking the bus overnight to play slot machines in Reno.

My mother had never written a book before sixty-five. She had started her career as a school administrator late, after the civil rights movement opened opportunities for an educated black woman, and she had grown professionally. She overcame crippling shyness whose stutter made the telephone her monster. At a liberating feminist retreat at Asilomar, near Monterey, she reclaimed her own name, Dona, after decades of letting other people correct her. Yes, people tried to correct her pronunciation of her own name, "DOH-na," and talk her into accepting the more easily recognizable Donna, "DAHN-na." At the Asilomar retreat, she put a stop to that and made people call her by her own name. And she started writing in earnest.

·

ALWAYS A TERRIFIC writer of letters and reports, she'd never attempted a book. After Asilomar, she found strength within to pull it off.

She devoted ten years to researching and publishing her first book, *The Unsung Heart of Black America*, about the middle-class black people she knew as close, long-term friends in the United Methodist Church we attended in the 1950s and early 1960s in Oakland, a work the fine and generous historian John Hope Franklin blurbed.

It took me years to sense the bravery, the sturdy determination her metamorphosis demanded, for she was tougher than I could see during her lifetime. I knew she delved deep to express herself with unadorned honesty. Hard for a woman. Doubly hard for a black woman. Triply hard for a black woman of a class and a generation never wanting to let *them* (meaning, mainly, white people) catch even a sidelong glimmer of remorse.

Suppressing doubt and never washing dirty linen in public came naturally to my mother. A public that was black and wore the beloved faces of her friends awaited my mother's writing as an upstanding black person. That public's expectation of her as a black author discouraged her speaking as an individual whose identity exceeded race. She felt that pressure and wrote her first book as a black woman, never losing sight of race in America. Yet there was more to her.

It took her ten more years to write and publish her frank and funny memoir, *I Hope I Look That Good When I'm That Old.* Just pause for a moment and imagine the guts and good humor needed to use that title, to admit to looking good, and to write the word "old" and apply it to herself.

I Hope I Look That Good When I'm That Old.

People used to say that to her all the time, and now they're saying it to me.

In her memoir she went on to claim herself as a unique individual,

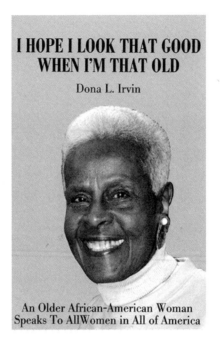

I Hope I Look That Good When I'm That Old, 2002,
Dona Irvin photo by Ron Carter, 9" × 6"

racialized, gendered, but with much more to her than race and gender. She wrote as a daughter of two parents in conflict on the most intimate level. The conflict stayed within the range of ordinary human misbehavior—the usual adultery and betrayal—but talking about that exceeded the vocabulary of race alone. Hard to do in the USA, because it's hard to describe black humanity beyond race and so easy, practically an automatic response, to interpret a claim of individuality as treason to blackness. It's as though individuality, the pride of white Americans, virtually what it means to be white but not a Nazi or Klansman, belongs only to them; as though a black woman speaking as an individual, not speaking as the race, must be backing away from blackness. My mother had to find words to claim both uniqueness and blackness. But find those words she did. Dona was working on a website about vigorous old people of many races when she died at ninety-one, not at all ready to leave. Looking at her, identifying with her when I was sixty, I figured, hell, I could do that. I could do something new in the quarter century or more still before me, even starting from close to scratch. My mother's example made me think I could lay down one life and pick up a new one.

I HAD BEEN a youthful artist, and for years I carried a sketchbook and drew all the time. I drew (but have lost that sketchbook) in Bordeaux, France, on a junior year abroad. I was still drawing when I lived in Ghana with my parents in the 1960s in my early twenties. The three drawings on the following page, pencil on paper, were in my sketchbooks there.

Ghana gave my Bay Area eyes, squinting into a bright blue sky, a whole new palette, a landscape and architecture and people in clothes and rioted textures and colors. Something grew on every surface: bushes, flowers, or mold, or all of it all at once. The California Bay Area that I had left was a beautiful but eucalyptus-gray place, foggy in the morning, dryly sunny in the day, with mostly light-colored people.

In Ghana I moved through a humid world of tropical contrasts and color-wheel hues. The dirt was Venetian red, the trees and grass Hooker's green. White buildings, red tiled roofs. Cadmium red bougainvillea climbing whitewashed buildings and cascading over fences and walls, some topped with menacing shards of broken brown glass or black wrought-iron spikes testifying to class tensions barricading the wealthy against the grasping poor. Together, this colorful landscape and the very black people in white and spectacular clothing altered my vision of everyday life.

Ghana Drawing of Girl, 1964–1965,
graphite on paper, approx. 10" × 8"

Ghana Drawing of Man, 1964–1965,
graphite on paper, approx. 10 ¼" × 7 ½"

Ghana Drawing 3, 1964–1965,
graphite on paper, approx. 7 ½" × 10 ¼"

In Ghana I taught French in the language school and gave the news in French on Ghana Radio for a year. I can still hear the drums

Boom boom boom　**Boom Boom**

announcing, "Ghana calling!" I began graduate study in precolonial African history at the Institute of African Studies before a coup d'état deposing Kwame Nkrumah ended his nascent African socialism and sent us Afro-Americans, including Maya Make (later Maya Angelou), to Egypt, to Europe, and, for us Irvins, home to California. After the first coup d'état in Ghana in 1966, I completed my MA in African history at UCLA. After UCLA, a year of rattle-brained, youthful follies too embarrassing to mention, I ended up at Harvard for a PhD in history. I quit smoking. I wrote a dissertation that became my first book, published by—ahem—Alfred A. Knopf. Many books and professorships at the University of Pennsylvania, the University of North Carolina at Chapel Hill, and Princeton University followed.

I was a whiz kid, tenured and promoted at Penn in three years and promoted to full professor at Chapel Hill in another three. In the early days of my career, I never questioned my ability to do well in my field. I loved history, loved research, loved writing—I still love history, love research, love writing. I published books at a regular pace: *Exodusters: Black Migration to Kansas after Reconstruction* (1976), *The Narrative of Hosea Hudson: His Life as a Negro Communist in the South* (1979), *Standing at Armageddon: The United States, 1877–1919* (1986), *Sojourner Truth, A Life, A Symbol* (1996), *Southern History Across the Color Line* (2002), *Creating Black Americans: African American History and Its Meanings, 1619 to the Present* (2006), and the Penguin Classics editions of *Narrative of Sojourner Truth* and *Incidents in the Life of a Slave Girl*. And there were fellowships (Guggenheim, National Endowment for the Humanities, Fulbright, etc.), scholarly societies (American Academy of Arts and Sciences, American Antiquarian Society, etc.), and honorary doctorates (Dartmouth, Yale, etc.).

I don't want this to sound effortless, for it was all a lot of work, a *hell* of a lot of dedicated work. Good work, I mean, work that felt good to me, for writing history gave me enormous pleasure.[1] Over the years, though, images made their way into my writing of history.

Visual art's gravitational field had renewed its pull decades before my mother had reinvented herself as a writer. Still, I cannot shrug off my change of field as simply a matter of time. It took place step by step, as I was writing history.

My history writing tugged me toward art over the years. I used a photograph I had taken as the frontispiece of my second book, *The Narrative of Hosea Hudson*, and I wrote about the photograph as a meaningful image, not merely an illustration. Then came the "Truth in Photographs" chapter in my fourth book, *Sojourner Truth, A Life, A Symbol*, on Truth's self-fashioning through photographs. Self-fashioning is the ways people present themselves to the outside world—what they wear, how they talk and stand, the props they hold or regard. For Truth, this meant wearing the sober clothing of women who spoke in public and holding knitting or her grandson's photograph in the portraits she had made to sell to her admirers.

I spent hour after hour preparing that chapter in the abundance of Princeton's Marquand Library of Art and Archaeology, where the art books fill four levels and you can sit comfortably for hours with the history and criticism of photography. In Marquand I learned the rhetoric of the image and critical seeing.

I illustrated *Creating Black Americans* with fine art. Though

---

1. If you want to see the whole panoply of achievement, check out my website, www.nellpainter.com, or look at my Facebook page.

it's a narrative history, *Creating Black Americans* gave me an introductory course in African American art history. There was, I discovered, more good art by black artists than I could ever cram into one book, even limiting the art to subjects bearing on history. None—okay, very few—of those artists figured in the art history I would study in art school.

The books I wrote weren't art history, but each one took me beyond text into new visual archives. I loved working with images; I loved learning new history and new artists. This was not like my first undergraduate experience in art.

BACK IN THE 1960s I had studied art at Berkeley, had been an art major and drawn a couple of covers for the campus humor magazine. My art major ended with a C in sculpture, a C I earned by not doing any work. Why should I have to work at sculpture? I reckoned, like the kid I was, that talent should ensure success. I saw talent and talent alone as the crucial ingredient. Therefore exerting myself would make no difference. What kind of reasoning is that? Dumb, kid reasoning. I didn't know how to work on learning sculpture, and I didn't know any professional artists to show me a way. On the other hand, my academic family applauded my writing, not only something I knew how to work at, but also the mastery of one of the hallmarks of a cultured American. This counted in my family's blackness.

There ended my story in art for decades. Except for occasional sketching and knitting, I put down the visual and wrote a very great deal of text. Eventually my books returned me to art, and once back in images, I concluded, Yes, I think I could stay in the world of pictures. Let me test this out.

During my last year teaching at Princeton I took two introductory painting classes. Introductory painting came after my regular teaching and kept me in Princeton to 10 p.m. After that, I'd get home to Newark in the middle of the night. My generous Princeton colleague Valerie Smith[2] often let me stay over at her house and sweetly bought one of my first drawings. At first I didn't know to photograph my work, so Valerie's drawing has disappeared from my files. The office of another Princeton colleague, Edmund White, was next to my painting studio. He bought my very first painting, my attempt to depict a set-up in various surfaces and shades of red and yellow, shiny, matte, opaque and translucent, saturated and toned down. The reflective red hat contrasted with two drapes, one also reflective but mixed with blue, the other with a pattern that

Red Hat, 2003, oil on canvas, approx. 12" × 16"

fractured in the folds of the cloth. The bright yellow shopping bag in front combined a shiny surface and a broken pattern.

In the first Princeton class I painted gray scales and figures and landscapes and learned light sources and perspective, as displayed in these two other early paintings. The gray scale began simply as that,

2. Valerie Smith is now the president of Swarthmore College.

a gray scale, where you alter hue and saturation between black and white. I liked that exercise and added mountains in the distance. It still looks like a gray scale, but with something else going on. The blue painting came from an exercise in creating depth through perspective, shadow, and luminosity. I made both these paintings on manufactured 24" × 18" canvases. I still have a whole pile of these canvases, which I consider beneath me now. My second Princeton painting class taught me how to make my own stretcher bars and to stretch and gesso my canvases, thoroughly enjoyable manual labor.

LEFT: *Gray Scale*, 2003, oil on canvas, approx. 24" × 18"
RIGHT: *Blue Boxes*, 2003, oil on canvas, approx. 24" × 18"

My Princeton painting classes took me to museums, to Philip Guston's cadmium red, ivory black, and titanium white cigar-smoking Klansmen and John Currin's skinny, huge-breasted naked white women the color of supermarket peach flesh. I joined the throng of Guston admirers but never acquired a taste for Currin's virtuoso painting. I still stumble over his skinny, big-breasted women and wonder why his famously rendered Thanksgiving turkey is raw.

•

EVEN BEFORE ART school and with what I look back on as incredible hubris, I toyed with the idea of myself as a professional artist, not a Sunday painter, no *mere* Sunday painter. I might want to go to art school, not just to undergraduate art school, but to graduate art school as well. I might want to work professionally. I might want to be as professional a painter as I was a historian. Well, within reason. What could be the problem?

As I poke into the crevices of memory, I touch another motive for leaving history, a motive that wants to stay beneath the surface, shrinking into its obscurity like a darkness-dwelling troglobite, eyeless and colorless, in the subterranean habitat of my shame. I'm dragging my troglobite into the light, for candor demands acknowledgment of another reason I did not remain in the grooves of academe. Although there was, as always, much more history yet for me to write, there was also a certain sourness I had no right to taste. It is my shame, for any sentiment other than gratitude strikes me as most unbecoming in one whose achievements have been honored with a Princeton professorship, honorary doctorates from the Ivy League and beyond, and the presidencies of the Organization of American Historians (which historians call the OAH) and the Southern Historical Association (a.k.a. the Southern). What could be more annoying (a word I learned to deploy in art school) than a person of privilege whining about what hasn't been bestowed? Nonetheless. Nonetheless, let me whine a little. There was the feeling of limits reached, of disappointment over book prizes not won and books not reviewed. It was as though I had assumed I'd be exempt from the rules of the world, where people who looked like me or who didn't fit an image of how they were supposed to be were never fully seen or acknowledged. For all my lovely recognition, I seemed not properly to fit in.

I've never been a black person easily captured in the idea of a black person—come to think of it, no one is. No person, no black or otherwise person, fits a racial mold. The idea of a black person is a stereotype that shifts its shape in order never to fit anyone real. I've hardly suffered or overcome hardship, can't talk ghetto, won't don a mask of black authenticity or speak for black people as a whole. Too many disparate themes reside in me for coherent recognition: images, phrases, people, and things from the multiple worlds I live in and have lived in over many years of life. The freedom I treasure in art reminds me of walking in Bordeaux in the 1960s and inclining toward the study of history. My mother's dismay at the appearance of aging triggers scattered associations, from the biography of a French theorist to older women artists. Driving down I-95 from Providence calls up a memory of skidding my VW Beetle across a snow-covered bridge over the Connecticut River when I was a graduate student at Harvard. This jumble is not smooth, but its disorderliness is what makes me me. I can't corral my thoughts and feelings within a fence of race.

When I sniveled to friends that I had never received a book prize of import, they pulled me up short, and not just by recalling my honors. They reminded me of the world we live in and the off-kilter nature of my writing. What on earth did I expect? I had enough, I really did have enough in many meanings of the word. Okay, straighten up. Enough in hand, I left history, in the sense of no longer writing scholarly history books as I used to, with honor and fulfillment. History remains a part of me, naturally, and it remains in me even though my relation to history became uneasy in art school.

AFTER MY TWO toe-dipping Princeton painting classes, I took the summer drawing and painting marathon at the New York Studio School on 8th Street in Manhattan. The Studio School started at 9:00 a.m., ended at 6:00, with crits stretching past 9:00 p.m. For me that meant get up at 6:00 a.m., walk across the park, take

Newark light rail to Newark Penn Station. New Jersey Transit to New York Penn Station, that hell of thank-you-for-your-patience dysfunction. The 2 or 3 subway downtown, get off at 4th Street, walk to 8th Street, and arrive before everyone else.

Then the payoff. Stand up and draw and paint for eight hours. I loved it.

I L O V E D I T.

The paper, the charcoal, the canvas, the set-ups, the model, the space, the perspective, the shadows, the colors, the smell. Concentrating hard, I did it wrong, and I did it right. I painted a still life in red and blue that taught me that you can't mix cerulean blue from ultramarine and white oil paints as they come from a tube. A figure painting asked for warm but light browns for skin and an indefinite darker shade for light skin in shadow. This shade has no name, so you mix it out of the leavings on your palette.

Here's the best lesson of all from the Studio School marathon: Staple a 5' × 4' piece of tough watercolor paper to the wall; cover it with a charcoal drawing of the model in the set-up, the very best drawing you can make. Cover the entire paper. This takes hours standing up, drawing in the heat. Sweating. Now rub out your drawing with a chamois. Owwww!! All that work for nothing! Draw it again, only ten inches to the right. Okay. Concentrate. Draw. Sweat. Fill up the paper. Rub it out. Erase it again? Yes. Rub it out. Draw the model and set-up one-third smaller. Draw draw draw. Rub it out. Again.

Lesson learned? *Essential* lesson learned! You can erase what you draw, even what you've spent a long time drawing and sweating over it. You can throw away what you paint and, as I learned to do later, cut it up and incorporate it into a new painting. A lesson to take straight to heart, and not only in art making.

I loved it. Even though I was the oldest by far, I stood up and painted right up until six. Some of the kids came late, farted around,

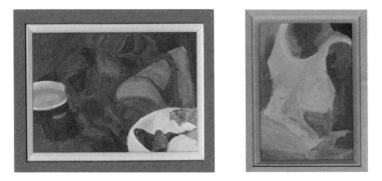

LEFT: *Still Life with Red Pot*, 2004, oil on canvas, 9" × 12"
RIGHT: *Figure with Shadow*, 2004, oil on canvas, 12" × 9"

took two-hour lunch breaks, and left before dinner without washing their brushes. Crit came after dinner break. To accommodate Newark light rail's evening schedule, I would leave crit around 9:00 p.m. Start all over the next morning, five days a week. Okay, I could do it! Let's go!

I applied to Mason Gross School of the Arts at Rutgers with a portfolio of drawings and paintings from Princeton and the Studio School marathon. Rutgers admitted me. What a thrill! What an accomplishment! Admission puffed me up like a kid off to college. My knowing Friend Bill hinted later that undergraduate art school isn't all that hard to get into. Be that as it may, my admission felt like a worthy achievement. I affiliated with Douglass College, the (sort-of formerly) all-women's college, for its feminist tradition, of course, and also for its quiet.

IN THE SUMMER before I started at Mason Gross, Dear Husband Glenn and I attended an art exhibition at the Grand Palais in Paris. You will only hear of Glenn occasionally, when absolutely necessary, because Glenn doesn't want a role in this story, even though

I could not have made it through without him. We were together in Paris, where the Grand Palais had installed a huge show of stirring paintings, abstract and figurative, witty videos ironic and silly, sculpture bright and colorless, and perfectly gorgeous drawings: a feast for the eyes of color and movement and sound. Wait a minute. What in creation was spilling over several folding tables—used ballpoint pens, foil, torn newspaper, doodles, bits of paper, the contents of a wastepaper basket held together with cardboard and brown packing tape. A shapeless mass of faded color and haphazard images. Overabundance splayed out from one section to another without any composition, without coherent color that I could see, as though a drunken do-it-yourselfer had turned over his trash barrel in the lofty Grand Palais. Huh? An art enigma. A mistake, surely. But what did I know? I did not know this was art.

This piece by the Swiss artist Thomas Hirschhorn had won the show's first prize, and Hirschhorn was installation art's shining international star. I hadn't yet heard of installation art and didn't know that in the twenty-first century this was more than any old art; it was good art, excellent art. The best art. With work in the Museum of Modern Art, the Tate, and the Walker Art Center, Hirschhorn had hit all The Art World's high notes and strutted off with its prizes.[3] Clearly, this was art, and Hirschhorn was a major artist. Hirschhorn's work raised the oldest questions in the world of art, questions that followed me for a very long time afterward. What counts as art? Who is an artist? Who decides? Over the course of several years, I learned the answers. The hard way. In art school.

---

3. By "The Art World" I mean the important museums and galleries that bestow visibility and money on selected artists, virtually all white men. Without caps, the phrase means everything in and around art, regardless of sex and race and wealth and prestige.

3

GETTING THERE

FIRST SEMESTER AT MASON GROSS AT RUTGERS UNI-versity in New Brunswick. Four 8:10 a.m. classes, commuting from home in Newark. Yes, I live in Newark, Brick City, bad reputation, scary place of children gunned down in a schoolyard and a riot/rebellion no one ever forgets. Even now, visiting New Yorkers expect wisps of smoke to rise from Newark's rubble. Mine is the Newark of charismatic men: fierce Amiri Baraka and lovable Cory Booker—Newark, where everyone on the street—nearly everyone—is black, brown, or tawny. This scares some people.

My North Newark neighborhood isn't scary, just nice houses, nice yards, and nice neighbors, families gay, straight, black, white, Latino (Puerto Rican, Dominican), and a few Asian (Southern and Eastern). I know most of my neighbors and chat with them about their dogs and what day the city will be picking up leaves.

My block of my street is a little paradise, interrupted only occasionally by a mugging or a burglary or a house alarm (mine) sounding off by mistake. The biggest news was a neighbor in one of the huge corner houses who was posing as a cosmetic surgeon in Manhattan and killed a patient who came into his hands for a cut-rate nose job. He buried her under the steps of his carriage house and ran off to Costa Rica.

Down the hill a couple of blocks is a commercial street, Mt. Prospect Avenue, with a pharmacy, restaurants, a health center, a couple of liquor stores, and shops where you can send money to Latin America and have documents notarized. At a deli takeout counter, the clerk asked about my origins, first in English. I said I'm from California. He switched to Spanish and lowered his voice: "Dominicana? Cubana?" I do indeed fit right in.

Giddily as if off to summer camp, sprightly in the early light, I would set off to Mason Gross from my quiet block at 6:30 a.m., portfolio under one arm, art box in hand. I walked across Branch Brook Park, still late-summer chromium oxide green, later, burnt-umber bare, then, in the spring, the pale green of kitchens in the 1950s.

To get from my house to Mason Gross, I joined New Jersey's national pastime of commuting. At first I thought of my commute as simply getting to art school, as traversing the space between Newark and New Brunswick. I thought of it, no, I hardly thought of it at all, beyond calculating the time it would consume. Over time I came to cherish commuting as immersion in my polychromatic state of classes and nations. Soon I was swimming like a little brown anchovy in a school of thousands of little anchovy-commuters, happily unremarkable, yet singular with my portfolio and art box. Don't ask me to resolve the contradiction.

The everydayness of my fellow commuters left little impression. Invariably someone waiting around the light rail station was complaining into a phone that it's "muy caliente" or "muy frio" or other observations as banal in Spanish as in English. But there were always sparklers, people I'd never see elsewhere or never see again anywhere—the jewels of my commute.

Sitting in front of me on Newark light rail one afternoon were a couple of kids—early twenties or so—listening to music, bumping around in their seats, and talking loud, just exuberant. She was beautiful and spirited, he kind of ordinary to look at. He had the music, but he shared an earbud with her, two heads on one iPod. As she danced in her seat, he did something amazing. He played the subway car partition like a conga drum:

> *DeepDEEP slap stop DeepDEEP slap stop*
> *DeepDEEP slap Deep DEEP slap stop*
> *DeepDEEP slap stop DeepDEEP slap stop*
>
> *DeepDEEP slap stop DeepDEEP slap stop*
> *DeepDEEP slap stop*
> *DeepDEEP slap stop DeepDEEP slap stop*
> *DeepDEEP slap stop*
>
> *DeepDEEP slap stop DeepDEEP slap stop*
> *DeepDEEP slap stop*
> *DeepDEEP slap stop DeepDEEP slap stop*
> *DeepDEEP slap stop*

He pulsated a salsa rhythm on a vertical plastic divider. *Totally awesome!* I was ready for all of us passengers to jump up and boogie down the aisle. I wouldn't have led off dancing, but I definitely would have joined in. What joy in our white and black metal tube of light rail beside Branch Brook Park, a carnival parade on a workday, an outbreak of brotherly love to a salsa beat. Strangers waving their arms and shaking their booties to the music, grinning and singing and looking straight in the eyes of their comrades in commute. But when the pretty girl started clapping her hands to the music, he of the beat shushed her. No dancing in the Newark light rail that afternoon.

The couple had a third-wheel friend across the aisle, a heavyset young woman their age without the couple's brio. No music, no style. To my eye, the trio was dressed like everyday Newark kids, the women in kind of tight, fashionable clothes, the fellow in the ordinary baggy stuff of the streets. Nothing distinguished or classy, or so I thought. I misjudged them. At one point they staked their place in the cultural terrain, agreeing they wouldn't be caught dead in Newark's "ghetto bars." No. They go to Irvington. The fellow imitated Irvington's middle-class (?) white (?) talk, all "dude" this and "dude" that, with "bro" mispronounced in that way of dudes who don't know it's short for "brother" and ought to sound like "bruh." Much to see and hear on public transportation.

IN NEWARK PENN Station in the morning, we'd bolt up escalators (they nearly always work), many heading to track 1 to New York City, others, like me, to track 4 for the Northeast Corridor train going west (meaning south) toward New Brunswick and Trenton. In the track 4 waiting room my fellow commuters massed shoulder to shoulder on long, facing benches, a few traditionalists reading newspapers and books, many, many more bending their heads into their iPods and cell phones. At first I couldn't figure out where the droning came from. Other travelers knew better. They kept to their phones and ignored the evangelist, a Jamaican according to his accent, insinuating *Revelation* at us captives.

With time my irritation subsided and the evangelist became just another character, just another star in the drama of New Jersey Transit. He did eventually depart, and after he had departed, I missed him as this jewel of my New Jersey commute, with its rainbow of voices from the islands of the Caribbean Sea, English and Haitian Creole and Spanish, and Hindi from the East.

I passed through Newark Penn Station almost every day. It has moving sky above the open girders, clouds, and, if you stand aside, the windows of Newark's skyscrapers reflecting clouds and sun. An overload of information on trains and things you can buy and Broadway shows and insurance and travel to other, sunnier places, even Massachusetts. Newark Penn Station has its own perspective, its own light and shadow, its own movement in a rainbow of gray, yet within its overall colorlessness, a beguiling combination of a million yellow-grays that have no name. People all nearby and down the track. I made piece after piece of art on the theme of Newark Penn Station.

Newark Penn Station, 2006, paper collage, approx. 18" × 24"

Newark Penn Station sits between downtown and the northwest edge of the Ironbound section, which used to be the city's poorest, the low-lying East Ward neighborhood of industry bounded by the railroad tracks giving it its name. The Ironbound was always a mixed place of working-class people, an entire neighborhood on the wrong side of every track. Nowadays the Ironbound takes its character, at least that part of its character considered tourist-worthy, from Portuguese, Brazilians, and people from Central and South America. The Ironbound's current fame, such as it is, rests on places to eat too much and to watch soccer games as you drink. Ferry Street's a great place for spontaneous street parades of honk-ing cars and giddy people when your Latin American country wins a soccer game.

The Ironbound's overall complexion tends toward swarthy, its sartorial character unpretentious. One day on my way to Newark Penn Station on Ferry Street, I encountered a young man who com-plimented me on my hair. (People like my gray hair.) His T-shirt rendered me speechless. Across his chest was, "Fuck you, you fuck-ing fuck." Three fucks on one piece of clothing. To my mute aston-ishment, he responded,

Have a blessed day.

EVER OBSERVANT OF my unsurpassed (though chronically under-appreciated) state, I watched it from the window of my Northeast Corridor train. Yes, New Jersey is splendid, its crummy cities testi-fying to lost industrial might, its Atlantic beaches, the little houses with long narrow backyards where people garden and, in good weather and weekends, eat and drink under leafy arbors replicating the old country. I would sit in the train on the east side, passing the time and temperature on the Budweiser factory, Elizabeth's hulk-ing, slot-windowed jail, a gigantic new apartment building under construction by the Rahway station, the accounting companies' be-hemoths at Metropark, where even Amtrak stops occasionally, and the Raritan River at New Brunswick.

The Raritan complicates relations between the Rutgers

campuses in Newark and New Brunswick. Rutgers was founded as Queens College in New Brunswick in 1766, before the American Revolution, "on the banks of the old Raritan," as in the university's official song. The *Raritan* River runs through (then) bucolic (now suburban) central Jersey, emptying into Sandy Hook Bay down by Perth Amboy. The University of Newark joined Rutgers in 1946, becoming Rutgers University–Newark, an urban campus near the banks of the *Passaic* River, the industrial north Jersey Passaic River that empties into Newark Bay beside the Hackensack River coming from Secaucus, the warehouse capital of the world. You could say that these two rivers, the grubby, industrial Passaic River and the picturesque, colonial Raritan River, stand for the contrasts, the tensions, between the haughty flagship campus in New Brunswick and the scrappy urban one in Newark. Hence Newark's river-identified colonial resentment. I was attached at both ends.

NEWARK PENN STATION pivoted me between Newark's light rail and my train to Mason Gross in New Brunswick. But if I wanted to go to New York City to visit The Art World, I'd often take a New Jersey Transit train from the other Newark train station, Broad Street, or, as Newark old-timers call it, Lackawanna Station.

Walking up to the 27's bus stop on Mt. Prospect Avenue on a sunny midmorning, I heard a familiar sound from my long ago, my very, very long ago. An alto recorder. Now there was a sound of my nostalgia. When I was in high school in Oakland, my mother and I played recorders with an amateur early music group. I recognized the sound on Mt. Prospect Avenue without being able to make out the melody. As it ended, I was about to thank the musician, to gush about recorders and say how much I enjoyed his music. But his lurch to the right gave me pause. Was he drunk?

Was he high? Recorder or no, I couldn't engage a man so obviously impaired.

The musician staggered a few more paces along the wrought-iron fence of Bethel Evangelical Church, where a worker was mowing the grass inside the fence. On Mt. Prospect Avenue, the musician was African American, the Bethel Evangelical Church lawn mower Latino. The recorder player faced the mower, looked at him sweetly, and resumed playing in the mower's honor. This time I recognized the air: the prelude to *La Traviata*. *La Traviata* on Mt. Prospect Avenue in Newark, played on a recorder. A drunken musician serenading a man mowing the lawn on the other side of the wrought-iron fence in front of the Bethel Evangelical Church.

That was the first time I'd heard anyone playing a recorder in Newark. But in the late afternoon of the same day, as a party of us architecturally minded, upright citizens were touring the newly empty, faded yellow-ochre Central Graphic Arts Building[4] on McCarter Highway, the son of one of our party pulled out his soprano recorder and started playing while we were on the roof. Two Newark recorders in one day. But only one in my commute.

I'M STILL GRATEFUL for public transportation to New Brunswick, thankful for a visually interesting state of colorful congestion and junkiness and its characteristic sounds—*Revelation*, salsa drumming, *La Traviata* played on an alto recorder, and, leaving every stop, the voice of then Mayor Cory Booker thanking me and all my fellow travelers for riding Newark light rail.

For my final project in painting class I depicted my commute from home to Mason Gross after an art history assignment had

---

4. Now renovated and rechristened "Ironside Newark" in gentrifying fashion.

taken me to the Metropolitan Museum for a report on southern Song Chinese painting. My final painting project reworked that assignment, adopting the style of an ancient Chinese scroll, reading right to left and painted in the scrolls' warm, desaturated colors. I depicted myself as a mounted Chinese warrior in a gorgeous red coat, repeated in the style of simultaneous narration that I had just discovered in Islamic art in art history class. Chinese-warrior-me repeated seven times, starting with leaving my house, crossing Branch Brook Park to the light rail station, to Newark Penn Station, my New Jersey Transit Northeast Corridor line (complete with lumpy Chinese mountains), and over to Civic Square Building on Livingston Avenue in New Brunswick. Traveling on public transportation meant I couldn't carry my piece on the train as it should have been made, twelve inches high and eight

Faux Chinese Scroll, 2006, oil on canvas in two pieces, each 12" × 48"

feet long. So it's in two pieces, with what should be the right side above the left.

My *Faux Chinese Scroll* commemorated my emblematic experience in art school: my commute and my affection for New Jersey camaraderie. A commute anchovy in what I might call Du Boisian oneness with my fellow anchovy-commuters.

4

SO MUCH TO LEARN

U P THE HILL FROM THE NEW BRUNSWICK TRAIN STA-
tion and the Middlesex County courthouse, through the al-
ley beside the George Street Playhouse, careful not to fall into the
ditch running to the stage door, around to Livingston Avenue to
the Civic Square Building, its personality split between left-brained
Edward J. Bloustein School of Planning and Public Policy and
right-brained Mason Gross School of the Arts. The building's two
sides hardly ever interacted. Mason Gross outshines the Bloustein
School with art smacking you in the face as soon as you enter, no,
before you even enter, with Alice Aycock's *The Tuning Fork Oracle* dominating the courtyard. Turn right beyond the front doors to
the gigantic art gallery's regular exhibitions announcing the building's purpose. Visual abundance pours into the halls and all the
floors. To walk around CSB is to be overcome by very good art.

My first-year class in Artmaking met in classrooms on the first
floor, with tables where we drew, cut, and pasted. From the front
door, you walked halls of real art from real artists with roots in
New Jersey, like the sculptor and printmaker Kiki Smith. Professional art on the first and second floors. Student art on the third and

fourth. Some of it—color wheels, images from art history—clearly pedagogical. Some student pieces look fit for Chelsea galleries.

The third and fourth floors house graduate and undergraduate students' studios and drawing and painting classrooms. Graduate students can close off their spacious studios, so you can only rarely peek inside. But you see work in progress during open studios, when graduate students socialize and invite in undergraduates alongside the public. Junior and senior painting students occupy a warren of small connecting studios without doors, an exuberant, overflowing tent city of production and consumption.

Drawing and painting classrooms, large, open white rooms with high ceilings and walls for tacking up assignments, are outfitted differently. For drawing there are traditional art horses, also known as donkey benches, that artists have straddled for centuries or turned on end to draw on while standing. Drawing classrooms also hold eight-inch platforms for the model set-up. During class time, students' drawings, mostly black charcoal on white paper, cover the walls. Painting classrooms are more crowded, with easels and tabourets for paint and brushes and ceiling-high racks for wet paintings. Superabundant color and the acrid odor of oil paint and solvent distinguish painting studios from drawing studios, permeating the painting studios and hallways. The art-school smell of mineral spirits and oil paint always makes me miss Mason Gross and painting in oils.

BY THE END of the first week I had met all my Rutgers classes: two lecture courses in art history (plus section meetings) and two studio classes, all much larger than what I had been used to at Princeton. We were about half women, half men, with only one or two others besides me past their early twenties.

Artmaking class, my early morning playdate, my source of

art fundamentals and artist (re)discoveries, met at 8:10. My train would get me to New Brunswick before our classroom doors were unlocked, giving me time to sit on the floor in the hallway with other first-year students. I could get down on the floor, sit comfortably, and get up by myself. Agility, though, wasn't my generational marker. I showed my age by reading newspapers. The Newark *Star-Ledger* for New Jersey news, the *New York Times* for news of the world. Newspapers! How quaint! Even the very concept of printed-on-paper information was meaningful news.

A second-year graduate student of endearing earnestness, Teacher Carin taught the foundational design concepts of permanent use: color, form, texture, line, and shape. The difference between drawing with charcoal, pencil, or ink. Different papers. What's "tooth" in paper? What's "laid" paper, and why that matters.[5] How to clean up. You'd be surprised by the details of art cleaning-up, like what can and can't go down the drain and into the Raritan River. There was more practical information, often learned from fellow students, like the best kind of eraser. Faber-Castell kneaded eraser for charcoal, Pentel hi-polymer eraser for graphite. Answers vary according to individual taste and how you want your erasures to look—sharp-edged or soft. A chamois for blurriness.

We made color wheels and art according to color. We made symmetrical and asymmetrical art. We made silhouette art. We made inflatables. We researched artists—I reported on Robert Colescott, still my all-time favorite artist, whom no one but Carin had ever heard of. Seriality entered my work permanently. Seriality?

---

5. Paper is one of artists' basic *supports*, the thing you make your image on, such as paper, canvas, linen, and board. Paper is what you use for drawing, the others, for painting. *Tooth* refers to the texture of paper's surface, the more tooth, the less smooth. *Laid* paper has a grid of fine lines in its surface, watermarks from the way the paper is made. *Wove* paper has no such marks.

Basically, something repeated over and over or working in series. Think more than one version of an image, think printmaking, and think repetition.

We newbies gave it our all. Surely this treasury of discovery was what art school was meant to be. With productive undergraduates and an engaged teacher, the crits were eye opening. Mason Gross crits showed me how working alongside serious colleagues with an attentive teacher engendered occupational camaraderie, even pride in skills we were acquiring. Useful knowledge. I did not feel sidelined because of my age.

PAINTING, THOUGH, WAS giving me pause, and I was a painting major. My fellow students knew far less of the world than I—at least of "the world" as I defined it—but they painted better. Jamie, in her mid-twenties, had studied at Middlesex Community College, with its excellent studio art program directed by an experienced figurative painter. She made big paintings (a good thing, right there) of boozy parties in darkened basement rooms that our teacher seemed really to like. Marissa, an androgynous waif fending off self-hatred, painted cartoons like Matt Groening's *Life in Hell* and Charles Addams's *The Addams Family*, working out identity issues through painting. Briana, an incest survivor, hated her parents and painted her raw bodily anguish. Her big paintings seemed to succeed, in the sense that the teacher seemed to approve of them. I found them painful to look at; I thought, mistakenly, they were more self-confession than fine art. Artists routinely paint their anguish as a time-honored approach to visual art as well as trauma. Art therapy is a teaching field, and some of my fellow students painted in order not to lose their minds.

My one clearly preprofessional colleague, Keith, a thin, pale fellow, with a weird tattoo, had studied at Sarah Lawrence. Everybody

praised Keith's work, and not just because there was a lot of it—
at first. He was applauded for being on track professionally, for
talking in class, for knowing his artists, knowing his galleries, and,
in the summer, working in upstate New York as an artist's assistant. There's no such thing as an upstate artist's studio in New
Jersey, which is all a kind of unsung upstate.

Keith and I were the only BFA students regularly attending visiting artists' talks aimed at the graduate students, and we always
asked questions. Knowing the contemporary art world much better
than I, he was the star of our class, though I earned honorable mention for plucky stick-to-it-ness. With a knowing air of assurance,
Keith noted my steady improvement, approval that both patronized and flattered me. Keith had a Yale MFA in mind, and we all
thought that a realistic ambition.

Joseph, who worked at Pearl Paint in Woodbridge (since then
bought up by Blick and, sadly, closed down), was depressed and
medicated but knew a lot about process, that is, about how art got
made, step by step. He had studied for a while, he said, at the Art
Institute of Chicago, but he made the same two paintings over and
over without ever finishing either one. Teachers and fellow students
lectured him for starting only one new painting in his convoluted,
overworked way, and that one not even finished. But Joseph knew
a lot about the properties of paint.

One day, as he talked as usual about pigment, Josh, who had
come from some tony private high school and who suffered from
his own painting blockage, pantomimed strangling Joseph, who
was feeling defensive about Teacher Hanneline's predictable recommendation that he mix his colors instead of using his paint "straight
from the tube," anathema for real painters. This prompted Joseph's
disquisition on how the paints in the tube are already mixtures of
other hues, for example: turquoise = Phthalo green + Phthalo blue +
titanium white. Keith, as coolly knowing spokesman for the class,

recommended that Joseph simplify and clarify his painting, instead of piling multiple ideas onto just one image.

Joseph was also smarting over Teacher Raphael's pronouncement that he painted as though he'd only been at it for six months. True, Joseph's paintings did give that impression, but still, Raphael was cruel to say it so plainly. Teacher Raphael, a performance artist, had a problem with painting in general. Thought, not execution, was what counted for conceptual artists like Teacher Raphael. Process didn't matter, medium hardly mattered. The message made the work. He honored me with a studio visit, informing me I was wasting my time as a painter, for nobody painted anymore. Painting was dead. New media was the thing, and the truly interesting current action was in performance. This lesson he offered me in my studio with scores of my drawings and paintings covering my walls. Openly I demurred; at the time I dismissed his judgment as the prejudice of a performance artist all bound up with meaning.

Nonetheless, there was something to Teacher Raphael's critique of painting in general, and in the case of Jan-Vincent, quiet, intense, and expertly trained in Vietnam. Jan-Vincent possessed amazing skill manifested in expert paintings that sometimes fulfilled the assignment and sometimes not. It didn't matter; he was oh so very good. One assignment had us painting in primary colors with our nondominant hand and our largest brushes. As usual, I followed the rules, so my painting was as awkward as you would expect. Jan-Vincent made a masterpiece with small brushes, thin lines, and a nuanced palette. A handsome painting, indeed, but unrelated to the assignment. The painting teacher loved it.

Jan-Vincent just kept making empty, polished paintings without a clue about concept. Nothing tied his dramatic scenes together, not shared settings or backgrounds, not titles, not even arrangement on the wall. He painted a beautiful woman like a movie star cameo and liked it because it was pretty. I still consider this painting as lesson number one in my continuing art-school education about beauty and why The Art World dismisses it as superficial.

Poor Jan-Vincent didn't get much sympathy from us students, secretly envious of his technique, though the teacher didn't condemn him for disregarding her assignments. His painting was just too perfect for reproach. Later on, still making beautiful paintings uncritically, he applied to the graduate program at the School of Visual Arts and was turned down. He didn't understand why. By then, we other students had learned not to trust mere skill.

SKILL WAS FAILING me in my painting class. Somehow my work now looked stupider than what I had made in my Princeton classes and the Studio School. Teacher Irma* hated my first painting, which was, okay, I'll be honest with you, awful. I didn't understand why it was worse than those I'd made in the past. Was it something in the air in that class? Was I fulfilling low expectations? If so, fulfill low expectations I did. Yet my first painting was visually emphatic.

Irma conceded, You're not afraid of paint.

This is actually important. Amateur painters are often afraid of paint and make insipid images through their tentative colors and timid application of paint.

I wasn't afraid of paint, and I wasn't afraid of color. If only paint application and color were all there were to it. The forehead was too big, the hand minuscule, as though the body parts belonged to two different people. Altogether the work was very badly drawn. Anyone looking at this terrible portrait of a fellow student might conclude I utterly lacked artistic talent.

Talent. Supposedly art's crucial ingredient. That was how I thought about art in the 1960s, when I confused lack of talent with failure of application and quit. But I was thinking differently now, after decades as a historian proving the value of education and hard work. Very quickly hard work turned out to be right as a way to start anew. I worked hard. My drawing recovered, and my painting improved. Keeping at it is a good thing, but it also helps to see appropriately, which early on I could not manage. The culprit? My lying, twentieth-century eyes. I started out ignorant—so wrong, so utterly, completely misguided as to my sense of what art was. I dumbly prided myself on working as a painter while my fellow students, hunkered over canvases in their little corners of the big painting studio, copied other people's photographs and drew cartoons and action figures. Hell, they didn't even look like they wanted to be taken seriously. One pulled his hoodie down around his ears so that his face looked shriveled. Another wore fey little dresses, bragged out loud of being shit-faced, and painted shit-facedness. In my early days at Mason Gross, I reckoned their derivative work surely could not be art, while my bad paintings, as original images, surely were.

False and foolish pride, mine, beguiled by my lying twentieth-century eyes. It turns out that The Art World god Andy Warhol began his fine art career making cartoons, and appropriation of photographers' and anyone else's images is artists' standard practice today. Thinking like a historian misled me as an artist.

Coming out of history, I saw what visual artists call *appropriation* as akin to copying or plagiarism. I was used to scrupulously citing my sources, something artists hardly ever do. This conflict between the two fields' use of other people's work hobbled me in art school. I knew Mark Twain said, "Good writers borrow; great writers steal." Even so, until the 1980s, originality was the hallmark of artistic genius. My eyes were still back there, before copying and reproduction emerged as widely respected ways of making postmodernist art in the "Pictures" generation. I didn't know that.

I've mentioned Andy Warhol. Jeff Koons, the biggest living star in The Art World's firmament, has made his career appropriating existing objects and remaking, or, rather, having them remade on a very large scale. Sherrie Levine, photographing other photographers' photographs. Without changing the images, she made them her own art. Unless you read the captions, you could not tell the difference between a Sherrie Levine photograph of a Walker Evans photograph and Walker Evans's original photograph. Michael Ray Charles inserted stereotypical black figures from postcards—pickaninnies with big red lips, grinning watermelon eaters, natives with bones in their noses—the kind of image normally excoriated as ugly, into his universally acclaimed paintings. Now artists can take an image from advertising or off the web and use it without citation. They can take anything off the street and say it's art—and sell it should it find a buyer. I do that, too, now. But surveilled by my inner historian, I still change the original enough to make the image my own.

Marcel Duchamp, the godfather of contemporary art, made everyday objects—a urinal, a bicycle wheel—into art by presenting them in art venues as *ready-mades*. Feeling my way into portraiture, I inserted a Duchampian bicycle wheel into my *Alternator* self-portrait. I had first encountered Duchamp many years before on a childhood visit to the Philadelphia Museum of Art with my Bucks County cousins. I remember coming up a stair and confronting Duchamp's *Nude Descending a Staircase*, a 1912 painting that scandalized Americans at the 1913 Armory Show in New York. They hated it then. My twentieth-century eyes fell in love with it immediately. I still love it, even if it now seems to me to belong to another era.

IT TOOK ME years in art school to recognize my twentieth-century eyes as my major handicap as an artist, the real way I was old in art school. My eyes hindered me perhaps more than my sex and race. I say *perhaps*, because I can't disentangle old eyes from woman and black, and because I don't want to dwell on my disadvantages. I did come to know that art is fundamentally about taste, and tastes vary; tastes change. My lying twentieth-century eyes favored craft, clarity, skill, narrative, and meaning. My twenty-first-century classmates and teachers preferred everyday subject matter, the do-it-yourself (DIY) aesthetic, appropriation, and the visible marks of facture: drips, smudges, and what in the twentieth century would have been considered mistakes needing to be cleaned up. What I thought of as private intimacy is out in the open, as graphically as possible. Penises and vaginas are commonplace motifs, and nowadays even I contemplate making penis art.

At PS1's "Into Me, Out of Me" show, the aesthetic was completely post-Happenings, where the artist became the artwork. Artists menstruated; artists peed; artists shat; artists copulated; artists cut and tortured themselves and their friends. One sculpture of three drunken young men vomited in the snow. Owwww! My poor twentieth-century eyes! Truth be told, my fellow students' cartoons were better paintings than my earnest efforts toward *art*. Popular culture, cartoons, pornography, imaginary fantasy worlds work now, with faux naive gestures and drips. Mine was the wrong way of seeing; mine were the wrong techniques.

At least I didn't indulge a familiar claim of people my age, that current tastes—in art and in scholarship—can be dismissed as ephemeral fads. This comforting belief remains widespread, whether facing DIY aesthetics or the French theories of Derrida and Foucault as a means of understanding society. I'm remembering a sunny autumn lunch with dear friends in Abiquiú, New Mexico, across the road from Georgia O'Keeffe's studio. I was talking about what I was learning to like in process-centered art, the drips, the DIY, and the shapelessness. One friend waved it away as mere faddishness. It was bound to pass on, she said, presumably leaving real art as we had known it a quarter century ago, as though painters would go back to painting like Georgia O'Keeffe or, as in the New York Studio School, like Paul Cézanne. No such luck. Art keeps on changing. I had to figure out how to see it and make it, as art is made now. I tried to explain to my friends what had changed, even as I cited older artists' work that contradicted my generalizations. I was struggling to define differences between twentieth-century painting and twenty-first-century painting. I was saying that twentieth-century painting favored opaque mediums like oil and gouache. Yet as I said it, I could see the thinned-down oil paint, drips, and splatters of Arshile Gorky's *Water of the Flowery Mill* (1944). In his brief life, Gorky was an Abstract Expressionist stalwart, twentieth-centuryism incarnate. Drips and splatters, even footprints, the essence of twenty-first-century painting, are right there to be seen in famous Jackson Pollocks. So much for simple generalizations. But let these mere facts not obstruct my perusing of categories.

Painters' processes seem more visible to me in twenty-first-century art, almost like the erasure of the divide between public and private and the slender difference separating art and life in reality TV and webcams streaming people's every moments of what used to be private life. Now artwork that looks like real life—uncomposed, unedited—is art. Accidents are to be courted, not cleaned up. In performance and installation art, life, unaltered, pokes through. And digital art, performance art, 3-D art, animation, these many new genres, reinforce the impression that painting is dead. That's an old line by now, but one I heard from my classmates as well as a teacher, even, amazingly, in painting class.

THE PREFERENCE FOR spontaneity sometimes carried over into instruction, with significant exceptions I appreciated deeply. I had to adapt to art-school teaching, less about instilling a curriculum of material-based skills and more about fostering students' creativity. After my three decades of university teaching, this adjustment took more time than I would have expected, had I known to expect the adjustment in the first place. I wasn't exactly gracious in my accommodation.

In art school, you get a teaching gig as an artist by having New York gallery representation and being reviewed in the *New York Times* and *Artforum*, not by imparting the nuts and bolts of image making, patronized as the work of vocational school. For some, teaching can be little more than a badly paid day job. I found little consensus—little discussion, even—about what skills are essential for contemporary art, though everyone agreed that experienced artists make better art than inexperienced ones, that the work of professional artists is more satisfying than the work of amateurs, that viewers can spend much more time with the work of professionals. These are my views, too, and reasons for me to attend art school, not just the occasional art class by a teacher who had certified herself on her own that she was good enough for the job. Though I couldn't express the difference at first, perhaps still cannot do so convincingly, I could see it.

Maybe I couldn't say why I preferred the work of professional artists to that of amateurs because to do so would question my ambition to be a serious artist. If experience and skill measure the worth of what you do, then at my age, I was wasting my time in a new field. As a painter, I feared I could never measure up to myself as a historian because I'd never have enough time to learn to manipulate images as well as I had learned to answer the questions on my mind through research and writing. Is this a reason to stay in a place where you do what you do better than what you can do anew? Does this mean I could never change fields? Well, no. There was no reason on earth why Nell Painter, painter, had to equal Nell Irvin Painter, historian and author. I didn't always know that.

•

MASON GROSS GAVE us students an exhilarating freedom, for there were practically no rules to discourage us. We could paint madly, at least when it came to the formal qualities of our work. On the up side, this was very good at fostering productivity in eager students like me.

On the down side, I had to teach myself a lot, to consult the web to find out, say, how to make a twelve-hue color wheel. Then I had the wrong shade of magenta and had to buy more supplies. Not that I minded spending on materials. Art supplies—paper, ink, paint, charcoal, brushes—are so inviting, so sensuous, like walking into a vagina. The aisles of Jerry's Artarama in West Orange and Pearl Paint in Woodbridge were my vagina-candy store, with so many mediums and colors and the promise of visual, tactile sweetness. Oils, acrylics, dry pigments, and even pastels that I don't use—the possibilities seemed limitless in these voluptuous houses of treasure.

When I compare art supply stores to vaginas and candy stores, I'm not just speaking visually, for there's more to the parallel than brilliant color and the promise of pleasure. You can't eat art supplies, but you can practically taste their scrumptiousness.

In Woodbridge and West Orange, I'd see amateurs and professionals of every level, and parents with children with a natural talent in art. How many parents have gushed to me over their child's ability to draw portraits that look *just like* the subject, taken as the surest sign of a lucrative career as a professional artist.

At Christmastime, especially, parents from all of New Jersey's many races and ethnicities fill Jerry's narrow aisles, as bedazzled by color as their ten- and twelve-year-old prodigies. Cunning with knowledge of their markets, art-supply companies make pastel and watercolor and colored marker sets with twenty-four, forty-eight, sixty-four, and more colors arranged to display subtle differences.

And they package them in arty-looking boxes so you want to buy one for your Picasso-kid at Christmas to encourage his or her natural talent. No one really needs so many different colors, but the display is drop-dead gorgeous, and you're tempted to measure your attachment to your young artist according to how many colors you buy. I admit it; my debit card has sprinted to Jerry's cash register to pay out for this kind of thing, which I don't use but find too seductive to pass up.

At Jerry's, the narrow aisles toward the front overflow with inviting pigments and tools stacked close to you at eye level in beguiling array. Farther back in the store against a wall are less sexy items essential to serious painting, workaday bottles of gesso and solvents and mediums called turpenoid, alkyd, dammar varnish, and a million polymer mediums. No one artist could use them all, at least not at the same time. But these bottles look you in the eye with reproach for not making more art and for not trying more different kinds of materials. It's a good kind of winking reproach, more invitation than reprimand.

Art supplies could make art all by themselves, or so it seems in the stores. Every year new tools come out, making new marks on new kinds of supports, from papers to canvases to boards made of wood and plastic with gesso and clay finishes. Every year brings new ways of putting down line and color, not just spray paint—an old medium—but spray paints of varied levels of opacity and glossiness. Brushes, animal and mineral: rounds, flats, brights, filberts to lay down pigment thick and thin. Oils and acrylics. Paint sticks and masking fluids, heavy-bodied paints and runny, transparent inks. Every time I entered their realm, art supplies reached out to me, slipping their grasp around my readily accommodating debit card. If only there were money enough to buy them all or even just half, or even just the supplies I hadn't known about before. If only there were time enough to use them.

Pearl Paint in Woodbridge, where fellow student Joseph worked and answered my questions, always thrilled me with its abundance—so many art tools there I hadn't even heard of and didn't know how to use. Joseph knew them all. For one assignment, our painting teacher set up two models, a seated woman and a man reclining at her feet. The pale-faced woman sat upright in a closed pose. The suntanned man lay on the floor at an angle. How to fit the whole composition on one canvas? Behind the models was a tall backdrop of bright, translucent drapes of two colors impossible to mix with our limited palette. Just try to make Naples yellow from cadmium yellow without its turning brown.

The composition, the colors, and the drapery befuddled me. Painting Teacher Irma surely set this up to drive us crazy. How to compose the painting with figures going off in separate directions? How to render the drapes' two colors, one on top of the other, without a muddied mixture? How to convey transparency without fading out the hues? Joseph said use an alkyd medium like Liquin or Galkyd to solve my drapery problem, at least. Though we used oil paints in class, Joseph preferred Golden acrylics and recommended Golden's website for technical advice. Very handy to know when you have to find answers yourself. Painting flesh, however, continued to vex me. For years.

All was not self-teaching. Teacher Hanneline taught drawing in a considered way, strengthening the link between eye and hand, between charcoal and paper. She started us drawing bones, for bones contain a multitude of curves, surfaces, and textures. Then she moved us on to human models, first just one, then two in challenging compositions. Trained in Norway, she had a method. For Teacher Hanneline I would draw for days, covering my studio's walls with explorations of composition and color. Not just *could* draw for days; I *did* draw for days, just drew and drew and drew.

At the other end of the teaching spectrum was contemporary art criticism Teacher May,* to me (coming from Princeton, a teaching institution) a total wreck. She didn't give the copy center our course packets. She never arrived at class in time to sort out her slides. She showed her slides out of order, out of focus, badly placed, and uncaptioned. She attracted a coterie of arty young male smokers who smelled like garbage. The crucial matter, which I grasped only gradually, went much deeper than this one teacher. And it spread way out past Mason Gross.

Teacher May wasn't a total mess. No, she *was* a total mess, but that wasn't the point. The issue was meta, not individual; she came from New York, from NEW YORK!

No matter that she came only once a week and kept no office hours in New Jersey. They *all* came from New York. (Okay, Brooklyn.) Teacher May was just an extreme case of the tyranny of New York over art school and over New Jersey. (Don't get me started.) She wasn't really a total mess after all; she was just a regular NEW YORKer coming down to Jersey to dispense NEW YORKness. I never have gotten over it, but I moved on from this matter that was, is, far bigger than one particular teacher and one particular course. Mason Gross was giving me a real art education.

RUTGERS WAS TEACHING me so much I was loving to learn. My commute made me part of the community of my state and gave me a view of New Jersey I loved watching from the train. All this was very good, but, by November, all that was theoretical. In body and therefore in mind, I was spent beyond exhaustion. One morning I became convinced I'd made a series of wrong decisions. I was WRONG to go back to school before I had really and truly finished my book *The History of White People*, which was taking longer than expected to complete. I'd NEVER finish it as it needed to be written; as an artist, I'd NEVER be able to do what HAS to be done to succeed (whatever that means); and further, my art history class was wasting my time. State-university-Rutgers was going down the tubes, taking me down with it.

At Mason Gross we were twenty in each studio class, exceeding the limits of our spaces. Why the increase in class size? To raise more money for cash-strapped Mason Gross, after the state had repeatedly cut its money (I saw it as Mason Gross's money) in order to throw cartloads of money into New Brunswick football. *Football!* Harrumph.

Football, they said, made Rutgers more attractive to parents and prospective students. In theory, alumni would give more if the football team won. Alumni were reputed not to care that at Mason Gross there wasn't enough space in 2-D design class to keep one student's supplies from being mixed up with another's and that one student's wet paint smeared onto another student's art, art made of hours of work and many dollars' worth of art supplies.

If you came late, you couldn't get space at a table. In the painting studio, we bumped into each other, and we couldn't see the models around other students' easels. We painters kept running out of turpentine for cleaning our brushes, and the photocopying machine (this was then) was always out of toner or paper. We were hundreds in art history lectures, and more than thirty in my "discussion" section in contemporary art. Why was I running up and down New Jersey to this dumpy state institution?!

What a fucking imbecile I am to be doing this! I need to have my head examined.

My life wasn't just a grind of Rutgers. There were snarls never ending in the historical association I was president of. New Jersey Transit trapped me twice a day, four days a week. No time, no energy remained for my book, which, surprise! wasn't progressing at all. But no, here I was, scuttling around a big state university, trying to keep up with assignments in other people's courses. Why should

I be rushing down George Street from Artmaking class on Livingston Avenue to art history on the College Avenue campus when I could be spending time in the Adirondacks, doing the work I know how to do at a comfortable pace—

A comfortable pace *at my age.*

How fucking dumb was I?

Totally.

That's what I was thinking, that's how I felt, until it was time for my art history lecture and painting class. Painting the transparent drapery behind the figures, just doing it, just painting, I started feeling good. Painting felt so good, so right to me. Every colored mark on the canvas like Christmas. I was born to paint. The art history lecture was spellbinding. After all my years of Ivy League pampering, my husband Glenn the Rutgers professor joked I wasn't tough enough for Rutgers. He was wrong. I toughened up. I adored Mason Gross. I started feeling good again.

Undergraduate study has a lot in common with youth in its freshness of discovery for the very first time—youth as first-timeness. You aren't expected to know a lot already, so you can learn everything in the freedom from guilt over not already knowing. You can ask questions of teachers eager to help and try things out in innocence. I loosened up (some), tried things out (a lot), and relaxed (a bit) into unknowing. As the weeks passed, my painting hand recovered its abilities.

As my first semester at Mason Gross ended I was making a lot of art, relishing my studies, and learning so much that was new. Hell, I learned a lot just in the last few days of studying for final exams, especially in contemporary art, where I was practically an autodidact. Surely I was where I was destined to be. My eyes were open, art was pouring in, and Mason Gross was where I belonged.

5

FAMILIAR ARTISTS, NEW WAYS

A T MASON GROSS I REENCOUNTERED ARTISTS I AL-
ready knew. But now they appeared to me in new ways, in
new light, and with new meanings—visual meanings. The social
meanings of their work, most important to me before, were fading.
Process was becoming more important to me, how work looked
as well as what it meant politically. Now I could concentrate more
fully on how artists worked.

I had known about Andy Warhol for decades, since I was an
undergraduate art major in Berkeley and he was making his way
as a fine artist—as opposed to a commercial artist—in the 1960s.
His commercial art had caught my eye because he borrowed a style
of line drawing in ink from Ben Shahn, one of my favorite artists
back in the day. Shahn drew with his own fractured line and was
celebrated for it before Warhol picked it up in shoe advertisements.
Both Shahn and Warhol had been graphic and commercial artists,
and both used photography as a basis for their art. It was as though

Warhol was channeling Ben Shahn, but shorn of resolute left-wing politics.

Ben Shahn, painter of social realism, drew, painted, printed, and photographed works of political consequence. Photographs showed him as a man of open countenance, like my parents' progressive friends when I was young. The galvanized working class was his preferred subject, as in his famous depiction of the Massachusetts anarchists, Nicola Sacco and Bartolomeo Vanzetti, martyrs of class struggle. Where Warhol was cool and ironic, an avatar of twenty-first-century art, Shahn was hot and righteous, a New Deal progressive to the end. If Warhol had made art about Sacco and Vanzetti, he would have shown them multiple times and in stunning colors—in the electric chair.

Shahn drew black people, too, as political actors, for instance, his poignant ink portrait of James Chaney in his homage to the three civil rights activists lynched in Mississippi in 1964 at the start of Freedom Summer. Shahn's Chaney faces the viewer strongly, squarely, and straight on, in sharp contrast to the well-intentioned sympathy? pity? of Norman Rockwell's contemporaneous painting *The Problem We All Live With*, a title—who's a "problem"? who are this "we"?—I just could not abide.

Rockwell depicts brave little Ruby Bridges, a six-year-old desegregating her New Orleans primary school, from the point of view of her assailants. Talk about a lack of historical agency! In Rockwell's image, Ruby Bridges occupies only about an eighth of the picture plane, dwarfed by four headless white male officials protecting her from vicious white supremacists. Shahn's Chaney, in contrast, occupies one-third of a page dedicated to him, Andrew Goodman, and Michael Schwerner in 1965, in which Chaney's huge eyes glow with an activist's intensity. Shahn's political art inspired me, I knew that. Less obvious to me was a second route Shahn's work took into my way of making art.

In high school I didn't know to ask my art teacher, the second important influence on my art after my father, about influences on *his* art. Slender and enthusiastic, Teacher Sam Richardson from Oakland was a twenty-three-year-old MFA student at California College of Arts and Crafts (now California College of the Arts), just up the hill from my high school. He was in painting, as I would be much later, but he ultimately made his reputation as a sculptor, with work in several public collections, including the Smithsonian.

In high school I couldn't see how art changes over time and how artists, having learned from those who went before, exert influence on those coming after. Now I can see Shahn's influence in Teacher Sam's squarish, pointy figures, his inky line and desaturated palette. Through Sam's work, Shahn's social realism found another way into my hand as well as my left-wing political heart.

Shahn died in 1969, before I ever met him. But decades later, on an art-school studio visit to Philip Pearlstein, a giant of figuration, I asked Pearlstein if he had known Shahn. Yes. Pearlstein had taught beside Shahn at Skowhegan. I pressed Pearlstein for details about Shahn, my image of a true-blue left-winger, the kind they don't make anymore. I imagined Shahn, cigarette in hand, intensely criting students by day—the youth rolling their eyes at his old-timey techniques and stories (this would have been in the days when the New Left thought itself so much savvier than the Old Left of the 1930s)—Shahn nursing a scotch, urging students politically by night, and, trekking poles in hand, rallying activism in whichever acolytes he could round up to hike around Wesserunsett Lake. Alas, no such thing. Pearlstein remembered Shahn as an embittered drunk, a remnant artist in a slough of crapulent despond.

Even disappointed, I could half understand Shahn's bitterness. He had mounted every step to Art World greatness—to *world*-world greatness, with honorary doctorates from Princeton and Harvard, delivering the Charles Eliot Norton Lectures at Harvard, published in 1957 as *The Shape of Content*, a book I devoured at Berkeley in the spirit of its glowing reviews and heedless of its bitter denunciation of Abstract Expressionism, which, by then, was obliterating his work. In 1954 Shahn had been a featured American artist in the Venice Biennale, beside the Abstract Expressionist Willem de Kooning. Nowadays The Art World reveres de Kooning; Shahn has disappeared. Andy Warhol, inheritor of Shahn's line and crowned king of pop art, survives, bigger and more expensive every day.

Warhol's pop-art glorification of American consumerism ran counter to my left-wing politics in the 1960s. Art, I assumed back then, was about critiquing this flawed world we live in, not putting its tawdry aspects on a pedestal and celebrating them as art. And was Warhol really making *art*? My naïveté doubted. Warhol's blockbuster pop art—silk screens of someone else's photograph of Marilyn Monroe, of someone else's design of Campbell's soup cans, of someone else's Brillo boxes—just seemed like cheating. Just printing and coloring someone else's work, not even doing it yourself. How could that count as really making art?

I didn't then know the identity of the artist who had designed the commercial Brillo Box—I learned later he was an Abstract Expressionist named James Harvey whose day job in commercial art supported his painting. But I knew someone else's work lay within Warhol's *Brillo Boxes*. Until Mason Gross I had never heard the word "appropriation" used approvingly, Warhol's gift to fine art.

Warhol wasn't the only pop artist (Roy Lichtenstein, Richard Hamilton, Jean-Michel Basquiat, and James Rosenquist also come to mind), but he was the one who immediately appeared when you thought of pop art. A hit in 1964, *Brillo Boxes* upended what counted as art. It turned the philosopher Arthur Danto into an art critic. Danto's article "The Artworld" coined that term and moved the definition of "art" from the work of art—the artifact, the thing itself—to the places where it's displayed, bought, and sold. During the years I was in history, Warhol's ways of repeating images, placing images into grids, and using familiar motifs took over contemporary art. In art school, I learned Warhol's lesson of divorcing social meaning from visual meaning, for me, a gradual, step-by-step process.

Before art school, I approached art as though it illustrated social relations and history, upholding or denouncing the political status quo. During my years in art school I increasingly concentrated on visual meaning, on how artwork looked—its composition, its color, its artist's style, as separate from what it said about society. Critics call a preoccupation with appearance that ignores social meaning *formalism*, which carries a negative taint these days when formalism divorces art from the power relations surrounding its creation and circulation.

Coming from the Left, I began as an anti-formalist. But as a maker of art, I moved toward formalism as I sought to discover processes of how art was made, a move prompted by the neglect of the formal qualities of the work of black artists, assumed to be important only according to the degree to which it critiqued American racism. Where Romare Bearden had figured in my mind as celebrating blackness and black Harlem, I now investigated how he made his work, step by step, how he decided what to depict and how to depict it. I was now seeing my father's prized *Sharecropper*, by Elizabeth Catlett, which he bought from her in her studio in Mexico, less as a salute to black workers and more as a masterly lino print. From the opposite starting point, my relationship to Warhol encapsulated my trajectory.

Warhol spoke to me as an artist, even though his personal affect—his spacey talk, his druggy Factory in New York City, his embrace of consumerism, his fascination with beautiful people in popular culture—all that felt alien to me then and still does to me now. And then there was his materialism expressed in a totally un-Marxian way: "Being good in business is the most fascinating kind of art," he famously said. "Making money is art and working is art and good business is the best art." Before art school, I never questioned my prejudice against this artist who seemed anathema in all he said and all he stood for. Then art school sent me in person to see his *Maos*.

Venturing into the oligarchic Gagosian Galleries on West 24th Street for "Cast a Cold Eye: The Late Works of Andy Warhol" required me as a humble little art student to fortify myself. Gagosian operates a string of galleries around the world so expensive that just going through its doors made me feel poor, probably you, too. I was used to galleristas ignoring me, so clearly not a wealthy collector. But Gagosian . . . Gagosian! I needed a makeover just to look around.

I did look around at Warhol's *Maos*. Warhol started silk-screening some two hundred *Maos* after President Richard Nixon went to China in 1972. So Warhol did heed politics, in his own way. In 2015, a staggering manifestation of Warholian materialism sold one—just *one*—silk-screened *Mao* print for $47.5 million. But it wasn't the millions—they were already selling in the millions when I was in art school—that knocked me back at Gagosian.

Eight or ten *Maos* at Gagosian, each about fourteen feet tall, staggered me, almost physically. I backed up, closed my eyes for a moment, breathed deeply to recover. They were breathtakingly *beautiful*—yes, that fraught word came to my mind, and in a good way, with unexpected, out-of-this-world brilliant colors and textures. Each image was different, though each image was based on the same template, a portrait of Mao Zedong from the *Little Red Book*. So again, Warhol was using some other artist's work. But each Warhol *Mao* was original. The *Mao* silk screens turned my eyes around, converting me to Warhol.

NO CONVERSION REQUIRED to the work of Kara Walker, whose silhouettes inspired one of Artmaking Teacher Carin's assignments. I was already familiar with Walker from a decade earlier, when she burst out of the Rhode Island School of Design with room-sized depictions of the sexual depravity of American slavery. Her combination of monumental scale and unconventional style bedazzled The Art World. Silhouettes had been ignored for over a century before Walker showed her work at the Drawing Center in New York, so her technique was not original. Her genius lay in making an outmoded technique contemporary, to depict historical trauma without line and without volume, and to feed The Art World's taste for perversion that I had first encountered as a historian. Phenomenal success.

Research for my own book *Creating Black Americans: African American History and Its Meanings, 1619 to the Present* had taken me into Walker's work and inspired conflicting feelings. One silhouette depicts a quintessential Founding Father being fellated by a black girl while he sits on the shoulders of a naked crouching figure. In another image, an overseer figure sodomizes a naked black girl while pushing her along like a wheelbarrow. An elaborately clothed, moonlight-and-magnolias white courting couple kisses while a naked pair of legs betrays the presence of another person under her skirts. Much cutting off of limbs and raping through various orifices. Walker's revolting scenes—so cunningly made—mash together what was and what might have been, history and fiction.

This art of atrocity can be hard to look at. Before it became a familiar part of American culture and people got used to it, Walker's work dismayed black viewers who saw it as reinforcement of familiar, negrophobic stereotypes. That kind of response had inspired a backlash when Walker received a MacArthur "genius" award when she was only twenty-seven. It looked as though The white Art Establishment was rewarding anti-black art, having snubbed black artists forever. Older artists like Betye Saar, who had been making activist Black Power art for decades—and who had, not coincidentally, been ignored by The Art World—denounced the MacArthur as a reward for degrading imagery.

True, Walker often depicted her characters stereotypically, with rubbery lips, huge behinds, pickaninny hair, and monster penises. But at the same time, this stereotypical imagery was obviously meant ironically, as a critique of the American peculiar institution and made with enormous visual skill, artistic talent, and vision in the literal sense of the word. Knowing the history of slavery, I recognized the truth of that history in Walker's work. After all, slavery was—still is—a pathological institution based on absolute power administered with whips. No whip, no slavery. Without physical violence, slavery cannot be sustained.

I included Walker's work in *Creating Black Americans*, a history book, not an art book. There I was using Walker's work to talk about history (not art history), which it does to perfection. This would change at Mason Gross, where her technique of historico-fictional mash-up fascinated me.

My Artmaking class brought Walker's draftsmanship out from behind the history in her images. Now the lusts and hatreds of slavery, its depravity, even the girlish testament of her writing were much less pertinent to me than her process. Though my undergraduate colleagues doubtless learned something of the American past as they studied Walker's technique, historical meaning hardly counted in Artmaking class as we studied the work's formal qualities: what it was made of, how it was made, how it looked. For the first time I could concentrate on the surface of Walker's art without being captured by its historical import.

I made three different silhouettes: one of a dramatic Alfred Bierstadt landscape, one of Johann Sebastian Bach at his harpsichord, and a third from Thomas Nast's political cartoon of Irishmen rioting in nineteenth-century New York City. I collaged them together for one piece. For another, I collaged the negative pieces left over from the first piece.

LEFT: *Positive Historical Silhouette*, 2006, paper collage, approx. 8" × 10"
RIGHT: *Negative Historical Silhouette*, 2006, paper collage,
approx. 8" × 10"

Now I can imagine creating art by putting Warhol and Walker together, as subject matter or as technique in the freedom of making visual fictions.

I had first approached visual historical fiction in a tiny little way at Princeton in my introductory painting class, where I was free to mingle my biographical subject, Sojourner Truth, and my favorite composer, Franz Schubert, starting with their shared birth year of 1797. I drew them together in a salon, where she sang and he played the piano, and in a Viennese-Austrian–Kingston, New York State courtyard, where they discussed her religion and his music. In colored felt-tipped pens, I drew a map juxtaposing Sojourner

Sojourner Truth + Franz Schubert Territory /
Wein York City and Rivers, 2003,
felt pen and collage on paper, approx. 8" × 8"

Truth's lower Manhattan with Franz Schubert's Vienna, his Danube and her East River.

History would not let me do that. But drawing took me a minuscule step out of my former realm of historical truth into visual meaning.

6

ILLUSTRATION VERSUS
THE CONTEXT OF ART

THAT FIRST SEMESTER AT MASON GROSS SEEMED TO last eons, forever, years, an eternity of stumble, recover, stand, and, finally, stride. I did more than survive. I was ready to paint and paint more. I hadn't formulated exact plans, but looking back, I see now that I really had two goals, one elevated nearly into theory, the other the semester's praxis. My theorized goal seemed obvious: to make work that engaged the eye, because the whole point of painting is visual interest. The work can be ugly, but it must hold the viewer's attention.

You could call this my formal aim, purely about how the work looked. Years later, this is still my aim, and its means of attainment remain the same: make lots of work. One of my painting teachers said 85 percent of what artists make is junk. I spent a lot of my time in that 85 percent. Another teacher advised me not to make so many pieces. I should make less and concentrate on making something really good.

I can't do that. I can't only make something really good. All my work, the 85 percent and the 15 percent, comes out of ceaseless experiment. This meant—still means—time in the studio. Ha! That's easy to say, easier in theory than in praxis. In real life, studio time competes with the need to be present elsewhere, whether at other people's art openings or for tasks like paying your bills and keeping your house and fending off the torrent of email, not to speak of family and friends. And I have to add that keeping an old body in hand is a full-time job. If I wanted to stay cute, I'd have to spend hours every day in the YMCA.

The tension between working in the studio and taking care of everything else never ends, complicated always by the need for material support—in plainer words, the need for money. Fortunately for me, this need did not press, supported as I was—as I am—by Glenn, my husband, my patron. This blessing came with a barb to stick in me and into other older women in art who don't have to worry about money. The combination of gender plus money plus age plays into a stereotype of amateurism, even of inability, as in the impossibility of an old woman with money making good art. This I did not know back then. Or maybe I knew it and rejected the stereotype of a Sunday painter. In any case, and thank heaven for it, at Mason Gross I didn't apply it to myself.

My second goal then and there in my second semester at Mason Gross was solemn, even compensatory. I wanted to paint my friends, my intellectual women friends writing thoughtful books about America. They were to be the meaning of my work—its intention. I was thinking like this: American culture largely discounts my friends, mature women scholars in a society barely interested in scholarship. We do important, original work and write books that enrich society's store of knowledge. Our contributions meet praise in the academic world, but who cares about the academic world? We are not famous or generously remunerated. We dress tastefully in handmade scarves and interesting jewelry. With a tendency toward little jowls, we're rounded of body, but nothing catastrophic. Good shoes. Manicures. Some of us cover our gray; some straighten our hair. While gun-toting, bootie-wagging entertainment rules American screens, we convey the total opposite of drama. Just compare what's paid scholars with what's paid rappers. Of course, professors have longer careers, even longer lives, than most rappers, another reason for invisibility. By the time we have made our major contributions, we're no longer young, no longer cute. My wanting to paint my friends, old like me, also had to do with age. (And here you may be suppressing the uncharitable whisper, Who in the world would want to look at that?) Art history offers relatively few depictions of old people, and very few of those are women.

It sounds very naive to me now, but I wanted my painting to *celebrate* my friends. Now that I know more, I can see how very, very, very naive I was to use that word.

But back then I thought, I will paint my friends in their tasteful studies, next to their computers, writing books worth reading. I will show them alone in thought and together in groups, groups not segregated by color and not prettified in their age beyond the beauty of intelligence. I will respect their singularity and proclaim their community.

I was echoing my mother's hymn to invisible Americans in her book about middle-class black people. Her editor made up the title: *The Unsung Heart of Black America.* I wanted to paint a sort of *Unsung Heart of (Mostly) Black Women Thinkers*, to visualize my little-noticed part of the American world.

WHEN I TOLD Teacher Stephen I wanted to celebrate my friends, he said something I heard as:

No.

As I remember it, perhaps more emphatically than his actual words, he said,

Illustration! You can't do that.

The dismissive term "illustration" leads into a welter of concepts such as realism, figuration, beauty, and boredom, with no clear boundaries between them, themes that run separately and that tangle up together in knots impossible to untie. Realistic painting shows you what you are supposed to think is beautiful, as though you could look through the painting and see the thing—a mountain reflected in a lake, a sky at sunset, a naked young woman. This can be a problem in both figure painting and landscape. In either case, the operative concept is beauty, and beauty, of itself, is boringly insufficient. I thought like that even before Mason Gross. Over the years I have used the word "beautiful" as both a sincere compliment and as a sneering dismissal. So many meanings embedded in that word.

When I say beauty is boring, I agree with my teachers and so many of the artists I know, but not all of them. I part company with a good percentage of the two million Americans who call themselves artists and the millions of collectors who buy their stuff. I met one such artist early in my Mason Gross classes. Soft little Kerry painted pretty horses. I shouldn't call her "fat." My good feminist friends have slapped my hand over my use of that word, but my disdain for her painting sees her in just so judgmental a way.

In crits in our first year, we students, even those who painted cartoon characters or their fellow drunks sleeping it off in dingy basements, knew enough to decry Kerry's horses prancing through fields into multihued dawns and sunsets. They looked like advertisements for mind-altering drugs. Nothing, absolutely nothing under the sun, could be more hackneyed. Kerry stopped her ears and kept painting her horses in their glamour. More crits followed, more of our complaining we'd seen her images a thousand times and were sick of them. We'd already grown tired of them before Mason Gross. She claimed they were beautiful—they *were* beautiful in their banality, like the paintings you can buy online as "gallery quality prints" by "independent artists" to make "decor to adore." She kept painting her horses galloping into the sunset or gazing at the dawn, and we kept telling her they were shit.

MASON GROSS'S PAINTING studios discouraged another kind of painting that thrives in the Adirondacks where Glenn and I spend summers. The mountains foster realistic painting by the picturesque plein air painters in their floppy hats and artists' smocks you see every summer setting up their easels and paints beside breathtaking lakes. Their nature scenes are lovely evocations of an imposing landscape, handsome to behold and widely collected in summer cottages called camps. Every year it's the same beauty. The same pellucid lakes, the same majestic mountains. A juried show in Saranac Lake has been thriving for the past twenty years. Every year eighty artists or more submit mostly paintings but some sculpture, to be shown at the local artists' guild. These evocations of nature hew to the formula known as "Adirondack," as in "Adirondack art." I could even go so far as to damn them as illustrative. Still, I'm more at ease in a room full of boring paintings of beautiful nature than with boring paintings of beautiful people.

In our society of billion-dollar beauty industries and incessant advertisement, personal beauty is a problem. Beauty is a problem for me in history as well, and not simply on account of race, but race is a hell of a lot of my problem. There's also the image of class. I can't repress the distaste too many European aristocrats and churches and castles have stirred up in me over the years. Is it my inner Communist? In Siena, Italy, Glenn and I visited a tiny church museum off the central square. The museum proudly exhibited sumptuous priestly vestments—the cassocks, the stoles, the surplices, the crosses, the miters—and *objets d'art* collected in the church over the centuries, all costly furnishings of very great beauty. Immensely great beauty. Meanwhile, Italy was driving out its starving poor in search of a living wage. Italians immigrated to Massachusetts and New Jersey and Argentina, where some of them became anarchists and got painted by social realists like Ben Shahn. Their progeny became chiropractors and politicians, winemakers, Jesuits, and the pope. This contrast—this contradiction between priestly sumptuousness and popular want—did not seem right to me. I know my response was more ideological than visual. The objects were gorgeous, products of a society in distress. That was my politics talking. But how to disentangle the visual from the social and economic? Even at my most formalist, I see the social and economic contexts that art comes out of. Formalists may argue for art's "autonomy," for its power to transcend the circumstances of its creation and the surroundings where it's exhibited. This does not work for me, for ideology still plays its part in what counts as good art, in Siena, New York, Miami, and New Jersey. No art detaches from its material world.

Becoming a painter reinforced my resentment of beauty in the scenarized abundance of the Metropolitan Museum of Art, a resentment that causes me problems in figurative painting. In the museum, the subjects in those rooms after rooms are rich Europeans—white people—dressed and painted to showcase their wealth. It's enough to turn you—well, to turn me—into a little artist revolutionary.

I'm hardly the first to turn self-righteous and dismissive of highly skilled figure painting, beautiful or not, as retrograde. This is even more of an issue in our era of art-school deskilling, when polish alone can damn a work. How many complaints have I heard from conservatives (mostly) that the DIY aesthetic has ruined painting? Painters can no longer draw, they say, they don't know color, don't know perspective, and don't know how to transfer the look of a body to paper or canvas. But when virtuoso finish just replicates tradition, what's to appeal to a student of painting today? Certainly not the name "figurative." The problem lies in the label as well as the craft.

In fact, exciting figurative painting is plentiful right now, some highly resolved, some advertising spontaneity. Only it's not called "figurative," a term reserved for boring painting. If the painters who paint people are interesting, their approach gets stressed over their subject matter, so that:

Dana Schutz's gestural paintings suffuse history with humor.

Kerry James Marshall's scenes of idyllic blackness draw on his Birmingham, Alabama, childhood in conversation with the history of art.

Peter Doig takes risks in the space between attraction and repulsion.

Whitfield Lovell's tableaux explore history and meaning.

Nicole Eisenman plays with caricature and art history.

Mickalene Thomas riffs on art history, bringing women of color to the fore.

Even Willem de Kooning, whose most famous painting, *Woman 1*, is actually figurative, is classified as a leading Abstract Expressionist, an avatar of the very movement that killed figuration. It's the chain of associations with figurative painting—realism, skill, beauty—that pushes it to the side nowadays, into the scorned category of "illustration."

TEACHER STEPHEN'S OBJECTION, I ultimately figured out, echoed The Art World's prejudice against "illustration" as opposed to "art." Illustration to make a point, illustration for pay, illustration as following someone else's direction—someone with money—illustration as mere design, illustration as hack work, not fine art. In The Art World, illustration is inferior to art on account of serving an end that is not art. Illustration serves subject matter, in my case, my intention to depict my friends. Illustration belongs to the verbal world of meaning, serving verbal meaning's purpose, whereas painting comes from the "context of art."

The context of art?

"The context of art" confused me. It was not Arthur Danto's "context of art" when he called Andy Warhol's Brillo Boxes art, not where art was shown and bought and sold. Was this "context of art" art history, the subject I was studying in Voorhees Hall on the College Avenue campus among hundreds of other undergraduates scrutinizing images from a textbook running to several volumes and no black artists after the ancient Egyptians? Was this "context of art" in the contemporary art world that I was seeing in museums and galleries, art so heavily inclined toward white men, as though white men floated freely above definitions—limitations—related to sex and race? Was this "context of art" to be found in biographies of important contemporary artists, where women are still a minority and black artists are still feeling their way? Did something in the work of women and black artists set it outside the "context of art"? How did these questions affect my work? Where was my place within the larger context of art? Did I, could I, find a place within it?

For the longest time, most art by female and black artists got ignored completely. Everyone will admit to this by now, even the staunchest upholders of the theory that truly great art gets its due no matter who makes it. But maybe more was in play than straightforward, unadulterated discrimination on account of sex and race.

I'm not condoning discrimination here or pretending it did not, does not exist. I'm trying to understand The Art World's unique means of getting notice through the widely accepted distinction between art and illustration. Part of ignoring black and feminist art came out of its widespread dismissal as mere illustration, as mere propaganda. It was as though the work of Faith Ringgold and Alice Neel, for instance, lost its value as *art* on account of carrying strong messages against racial injustice or in solidarity with women and workers. This, beside the prevailing—and continuing—assumption that white-male work is raceless and genderless and innocent of ideological content. Which it isn't.

Of course, much of the prejudice against black and women artists such as I was on my way to becoming was merely because they—we—were and are black artists in a racist culture and female artists in a sexist world. But there's more. Art history's lacunae were showing me that non-black artists who are male also fell by the wayside, thrown over as illustrators. I've mentioned the case of Ben Shahn, beloved in the 1940s, forgotten a generation later in the 1960s. Abstract Expressionism also buried Thomas Hart Benton's American Scene painting. Benton, another leftist, depicted a rural world of honest, hardworking white people besieged by the forces of industry. In the 1930s and 1940s Benton was a Great Artist whose work adorned public spaces. By the 1960s he was as gone from art history as soon would be Ben Shahn.

Was Benton on Stephen's mind when he bridled at my plan? Perhaps. As a teacher of undergraduate painters he had surely endured too many encomiastic paintings of stupendously empowered goddesses and perfectly gorgeous black families. This kind of painting is figurative or realistic or beautiful, and idealized. Patronized within The Art World, it's beloved in the wider world.

Here's an example. The Studio Museum in Harlem gave in to popular demand in 2002 and featured positive-image work in its show *Black Romantic: The Figurative Impulse in Contemporary African-American Art*. And popular demand certainly exists. Idealized, illustrative work by black artists far outweighs and far outsells the black art recognized in The Art World as contemporary art. Black romantic art evokes praise from people who avoid Kara Walker.

No question but that black romantic works' positive images are as pleasing and positive as the white world depicted in work by Norman Rockwell and the Wyeths, all of it long dismissed as illustration. Rockwell and the Wyeths comfort viewers looking for a nicer American world, but artists of the black romantic have an even stronger mission. In a society still propagating stereotype, their work assails negativity. These images contest stereotype and fill a psychic need. Black romantic artists are widely popular among non-Art-World audiences, and they are better known than the few black and female artists I was learning about in art school. Teacher Stephen was probably steering me away from feel-good, positive-image art. I still ask questions, though: Is positive-image art mere illustration? Does it emerge from *a* or from *the* context of art?

The illustration versus context of art conflict is easily resolved when you look at art that is so much message that you lose the image, or where the image doesn't hold the eye. But it's hard to draw the line. What counts as art has changed as tastes have changed. Message art sometimes breaks into The Art World as "conceptual art," art that transmits ideas first and foremost, as in the work of highly regarded artists like Lawrence Weiner and Glenn Ligon (all text, no image) and Barbara Kruger (mostly text, some image).

Conceptual art starts and ends with idea, often expressed in the virtual absence of art made by hand by the artist. In recent decades, what used to be dismissed as propaganda—Soviet socialist realism, Black Panther posters—can be exhibited as fine art, now that their messages have lost their bite. The Obamas have displayed Norman Rockwell's *The Problem We All Live With* in the White House, and the Crystal Bridges Museum of American Art in Bentonville, Arkansas, has mounted a major exhibition of Rockwell's work organized by the Norman Rockwell Museum in Massachusetts. (If you want your work to be seen after you die, make sure surviving family members build a museum in your name. The Norman Rockwell Museum [not Crystal Bridges] owns *The Problem We All Live With*.)

I was studying art at a time when changing tastes meant Art World recognition for artists whose work conveyed clear progressive meaning. Feminist artists like Joyce Kozloff (who began in the outspokenly feminist Pattern and Decoration movement of the 1970s), Judy Chicago (one of the founders of Womanhouse in Los Angeles in the 1970s), and Nancy Spero (who expressed feminism through ancient imagery) were ignored for decades before breaking into what must surely be the context of art. Similarly, black artists, even those who, like Jacob Lawrence, have stated their intent to depict the unknown beauty of their people, now belong to art history. Barkley L. Hendricks's vivid, life-size portraits spent decades exiled from the art history I was studying in Voorhees Hall. Hendricks was painting up a storm in the 1960s and 1970s, producing visually arresting images of his self-confident friends, neighbors, and undressed self, all of whom were black. But he didn't have a retrospective until 2008. Only then could his work be seen as part of American realism and postmodernism, right up there with the long and loudly applauded work of Alex Katz.

It isn't just Barkley Hendricks who has come into his own within the context of art. Other black artists, including black women artists, are now subjects of a multitude of books and articles. Things definitely have changed. But I wasn't thinking about all that early in my undergraduate art career. I just wanted to paint my friends, with a particular painting by a particular painter in mind.

I WANTED TO convey meaning, as in the narrative, figurative work of the French baroque painter Georges de La Tour. The five chiaroscuro figures in *The Fortune Teller* (ca. 1630), probably inspired by Caravaggio's dramatic lighting, always intrigued me, starting with the old gypsy woman fortune-teller on the right who regards a sumptuously dressed young man in the center. She takes a coin from the man, who looks at her askance. His sidelong glance and her animation create the painting's central drama, but much more is going on. Two dark-haired female figures on the left, probably also gypsies, pick the young man's pocket, ready to carry off his loot. More puzzling is the pale young woman behind the man. I had initially seen her as his fiancée, and perhaps she is, even though by cutting his medal from its chain, she also thieves. I aspired to this kind of narrative in paintings celebrating my friends, and a method of learning already existed. The time-honored technique of transcription was to supply my means.

7

TRANSCRIPTION

HOW COULD I POSSIBLY LEARN TO PAINT LIKE THAT—
the composition, the figures, the detail, the touch, the colors?
An impossible chasm of expertise separated *The Fortune Teller*
from my poor inadept hand, a gulf not only of centuries, but also
of skill and sophistication. At the painting marathon at the Studio
School a couple of years earlier, I had bemoaned the amateurish
look of a painting I had concentrated on for hours, maybe for days.
My teacher, sympathetic but factual, retorted,

You *are* an amateur!

True. All too true.

Happily for me, artists had long ago turned to transcription
as means to further their skills through close study of the work of
others. This kind of painstaking labor is no longer common in art
education. Still, beginning and established artists use transcription
as boot camp and as an occasional return to the basics. I could concentrate on the visual in this way, via the work of others.

By gridding another artist's painting into squares and copying
the image onto my own canvas, I could follow and unlock another

painter's secrets, from composition and line to color, right down to denser or thinner paint. This was no new invention. Transcribing masterpieces used to be integral to art education. Jean-Auguste-Dominique Ingres copied—no, *transcribed*—old master paintings in the Louvre, newly opened as a museum in his youth. Henri Matisse transcribed still lifes by Jean Chardin.

Transcription would take me into the details of someone else's painting, centimeter by centimeter. How does this line connect to that one? How much cadmium red inflects that cobalt blue? How close is this figure to that one, and do they overlap to create the illusion of depth? Is paint laid down thickly in impasto or thinned practically into ink? Copying existing works would show me new ways of seeing and applying color. From the Studio School painting marathon, I already knew that painters use tricks like putting a spot of white in the pupil of the eye to convey liveliness and making a muddy mixture of colors for an undecipherable facial shadow. A start.

I would need to learn how to paint people so that bodies looked alive. Face and figure need expression flowing into the body's parts to make them occupy a particular space. They need movement to enliven their poses. Composition would also need a play of light and shadow, perspective, the illusion of space and volume, and the possibility of narrative, of a before and after the scene, all this without slavish realism.

For my purposes, I would also have to learn how to depict dark skin, where La Tour's painting and virtually all the painting in virtually all the museums I'd ever visited wouldn't help. This is not just a matter of using brown paint, because if I didn't use additional colors, reds and yellows, even blues and greens, the brown would look flat and dead. And I would need to capture the reflectiveness of dark skin through contrast. This would be awfully hard for me, because painting dark skin and its reflectiveness weren't taught in my school. I had Mentor Bill to help me with this, but I never managed it as an art student. However, I had encountered transcription at the Studio School.

The Studio School marathon had included an assignment transcribing a Rembrandt drawing. I had continued the exercise the summer afterward with a book of Rembrandt's drawings I pulled off my shelf in the Adirondacks. I had bought the book years earlier and now reread the text. It talked about Rembrandt's life and fortunes, his preferred subjects, including himself and his wife, Saskia, and his most famous paintings, *The Anatomy Lesson of Dr. Nicolaes Tulp* and *The Night Watch*. Before that moment, I hadn't missed information I now sought, but found lacking: how big were these drawings? And, of even deeper import, what kind of paper, which mark-making tools did Rembrandt use? As I prepared to copy Rembrandt's drawings, these were my questions. I hadn't wondered about his process back when I bought the book.

I figure the drawings I copied were made on textured cold press paper with tooth, now darkened, in what looks like walnut ink but is probably black India ink that has faded. I learned later that Rembrandt also drew in red, black, and white chalk, sometimes along with ink and pencil. The 6B pencil I used makes a very different mark from a quill pen. By varying my pressure and using the point or the side of the pencil, I could evoke Rembrandt's line and washes, though, alas, not the sureness of his hand.

Even in pencil, it was a slow process of contented concentration. It's not the same as when I make my own work, though both processes demand submersion in the image and a kind of searching. The search in my own original work feels more open, like standing on Hurricane Mountain in the Adirondacks and looking all around for the next peak to attempt—or, more likely, how in the hell to get back down. Transcription's gaze hones in closely on an existing image that may hold as many secrets as the mountains. Keeping to the metaphor of mountain climbing, transcription focused me on the path immediately before me, its secrets already there but held within.

That contented concentration is what I love about making art. I don't call it fun. My non-artist friends would invariably ask about art school, was I having fun? True, art can feel like play, can actually *be* play. But I'd say *fun* is too frivolous an amusement-park word for the contentment, the concentration, the peace of mind I experience when I draw or paint, even when the work isn't going well or feels unfinished. My friends in California would say I was in the zone. Wherever it was or is, time passes without remark; hunger disappears; fatigue only pounces once drawing ends.

IF TRANSCRIPTION IS to reveal its lessons, it's a meticulous process that takes a lot of time, which I did not have in painting class. Though La Tour's *Fortune Teller* measures only about 40" × 46", it was far too detailed with too many figures for me to transcribe in one semester, even if that were all I planned to paint. Perhaps with more than a few months before me, I would have attempted it. But probably not, for more than just skill separates me from Georges de La Tour. His painting was too much a piece of its seventeenth-century times, too subtle, too close to museum masterworks for me to replicate.

I had many reasons to hesitate before the La Tour painting that intrigued me: the limitations of my undergraduate skills, my times, my in-between-ness as an ambitious student and as a black artist coming out of an invisible art history. Already I could hear the expectation, an unspoken command, that a black artist's subject must always be blackness, that white art history was art history, and a black artist's relation to it could only be confrontational, even though no one was saying this kind of thing to me in so many words. The judgments spoke through the air, wafting toward me unbidden, issuing from mouths I could not see. Even though I always told myself that other people's expectations wouldn't hinder me, disembodied expectations gave me pause.

So there I was, trying to learn to paint people, not just white people, avoiding the trap of too much realism, but wanting to capture likeness and a certain kind of unconventional beauty—beauty as a barbed concept but the truest word we have for excellence. A further conversation with Teacher Stephen brought him around to my choice of artists to transcribe. I leaned toward offbeat images that held my eye with unexpectedness. My choices, based on the formal qualities of their work, were two twentieth-century painters now in art history, the German Max Beckmann and the American Alice Neel. In Neel's case, there was the draw of her ballsy, nude self-portrait as an old woman and a portrait of another woman painter, Faith Ringgold, whose work as an artist and activist addresses injustices in American society. My attachment to them as women and as older women artists was obvious. There was also, for both Beckmann and Neel, the lure of depicting oneself psychologically in time and place.

I FELL HARD for Alice Neel's unprettified, humorous, naked self-portrait at age eighty. I thought the painting was generous in size at 53" × 40", though in light of contemporary art's prevailing huge dimensions, that now seems a modest scale. The work's courage spoke to me first, for this was back when I was conventional-minded enough to fault Neel's draftsmanship. I could never paint myself naked—I cringe just mentioning such a thing, and I could not even have done it in my youth when American history and my personal upbringing dressed me modestly. I admired Alice Neel's spunk, which reminds me of *You or I* (2005), the Austrian painter Maria Lassnig's self-portrait, also naked in her maturity. Neel ordinarily painted other people as she painted herself, naked. In its unflinching depiction of an old female body, her self-portrait is also an anomaly within the long tradition of artist's self-portraits, usually male, usually young, seldom sagging in body or face.

Neel was a leftist early on and never discarded her strong political convictions. She painted a union organizer reading the Communist *Daily Worker*, showing its name, hammer and sickle logo, and the headline "Steel, Coal Strikes . . ." clearly legible beneath his fists. Living and loving in Greenwich Village and working on the WPA in 1933, she portrayed an eccentric writer friend, Joe Gould, undressed, with five uncircumcised penises, three in the center on his own torso, one each on torsos on the sides of the frame. In the 1940s, '50s, and '60s, she painted her working-class Latino neighbors in Spanish Harlem when white artists seldom painted subjects of color. She painted naked women with big, pregnant bellies, children, herself and her lovers, always with genitals strikingly resolved. Sometimes her backgrounds show an interior, but vigorous color more often amplified the emotional impact of portraits that got bigger as time passed, without approaching the massive scale of her Abstract Expressionist contemporaries.

After decades of obscurity, Neel started being recognized in the 1970s. She began painting art-world notables like Andy Warhol and Frank O'Hara that put her in proximity of celebrities. These works came at the same time that feminist art historians and critics were at last making women artists visible through acknowledgment in print, as in Linda Nochlin's groundbreaking 1971 *ARTnews* article, "Why Have There Been No Great Women Artists?" and in groups like Women in the Arts and Women's Caucus for Art, where Neel showed her work alongside Faith Ringgold's. Neel and Ringgold became comrades marching together in picket lines protesting art-world discrimination and the Vietnam War.

Neel's 1974 Whitney retrospective signaled her arrival as a

major artist. I was struck that after so many years keeping at her art, it took the Whitney retrospective to justify her work in her own eyes. "The show finally convinced me that I had a perfect right to paint," she remarked at the time. Reading that statement, I thought it was so like a woman. She was seventy-four years old. So like a woman that it took until then.

I also chose Alice Neel because I felt I painted a little like her, or, rather, if I painted longer and better, I'd hope to paint like her. The way she painted unconventional subjects with a drawing hand free from anatomical punctiliousness made her portraits psychologically acute. Her non-naturalistic color, her expressive line, and her flattened pictorial surface made her my hero. My plan to steal her secrets through transcription settled on her forthright painting of Faith Ringgold.

I had known Faith Ringgold slightly for years and had admired her extraordinary range of work—much on historical and art-historical themes—before attempting the transcription of Alice Neel's 1976 portrait. Ringgold writes as well as paints, and she was the first object of my love for artists who make books. Although a generation younger than Neel, Ringgold was still one of the multitude of women artists whose work was ignored for a long time.

I once asked the painter Pat Steir how she kept working in those many decades of sexist obscurity. How did you persist, I asked. She answered,

Sheer spite!

Painter Howardena Pindell has said she kept working to deprive The Art World the satisfaction of shutting her down. Ringgold kept going by making art that addressed her own personal questions as a woman artist and as a black woman artist. Those questions aren't the same, because racism isn't the same as sexism. It comes on top of sexism and can run off in different directions. Ringgold's work answered in words as well as images, in her own original way.

Ringgold began her painting career protesting American white supremacy and patriarchy. It was this work, she told me, that damned her in The Art World as an activist rather than a painter and her work as propaganda rather than art. In the 1980s she began working on fabric in collaboration with her mother, a fashion designer, creating a series of painted and collaged story quilts that combined text and images. These quintessentially postmodern works create fictional art-historical narratives in which historical figures like Matisse (one of Ringgold's favorite artists) appear beside invented characters. Ringgold was making the free-spirited historical fictions that had drawn me to art in the first place.

One of the twelve story quilts of *The French Connection* (1990–1997), *Dancing at the Louvre*, depicts Willia Marie Simone, Ringgold's fictional African American protagonist, in Paris in her twenties. Willia Marie becomes a muse and model to Matisse and Picasso and an artist herself. Living a life in Paris of extravagant fullness, she speaks for Ringgold and many other women artists:

My art is my freedom to say what I please, *n'importe* what color you are, you can do what you want *avec ton art*.

Out of necessity, she said, Ringgold turned to writing, after complaining of invisibility to her activist lawyer friend Florynce Kennedy.

Kennedy responded, Write your own damned self.

Ringgold wrote *Tar Beach*, a Caldecott Honor Book, based on her story quilt of the same title, and an autobiography, *We Flew Over the Bridge*, describing how she makes her art—more than ninety-five quilts and hundreds of other artworks, including sculpture and public installations like the *Flying Home Harlem Heroes and Heroines* mosaics in the 125th Street station of the New York City subway. I admired her work and her grit at keeping at it over the long haul. Here came inspiration.

In her determination to paint and write her own damned self,

Ringgold shared Neel's dedication to her work across decades of disregard. Having painted so long in obscurity, both worked in their own ways, heedless of Art World fashions. They had freed themselves and their work from The Art World's gaze and persisted. They were seeing their art through their own eyes, not the eyes of others. By now, at last, Neel and Ringgold have won their share of Art World recognition.

Neel's Ringgold portrait is a strong image dominated by the cadmium red of the dress against a cobalt-blue and yellow-ochre background. Neel wanted to paint Ringgold naked, but Ringgold said no, perhaps out of the same black-woman aversion that made me recoil from depicting myself unclothed. Ringgold's refusal of nudity yields a bounty of pattern in the dress, necklaces, and hair decoration against the blue-and-white-striped chair that appears in many of Neel's portraits. This is a thoroughly feminist work that

My *Neel's Ringgold*, 2007, oil on canvas, approx. 24" × 18"

started, and I do mean only started, teaching me how to enliven a portrait and paint dark skin.

Ringgold told me that after Neel's death, she copied Neel's naked self-portrait, adding text that affectionately recalled their friendship.

IN THE MID-TWENTIETH-CENTURY era of Abstract Expressionism, Alice Neel was an outsider whose raw, expressive brushwork and sensitive drawing put her in the company of the German artists of the *Neue Sachlichkeit*, or "New Objectivity," of the 1920s. Like the German painters I was drawn to, she captured the tenor of her times, often with an edge of satirical social realism, though her work never approached the bitterness of George Grosz and Otto Dix or the searing social protest of Käthe Kollwitz. Neel called her portraits "writing history," saying, "I paint my time using the people as evidence," an attitude that spoke to the historian in me. I count her as an expressionist, for her personal style shared the essential spirit of German expressionism.

In art school, I came back to German expressionism via Alice Neel, though I had first encountered it in an exhibition of work about Potsdamer Platz at the Neue Nationalgalerie when Glenn and I were on sabbatical in Berlin. The exhibition showcased this crossroads that had been under the Berlin Wall from 1962 to 1989 and was being aggressively redeveloped after the wall came down. The exhibition centered on Ernst Ludwig Kirchner's *Potsdamer Platz* (1914). On my first view of Kirchner's painting, I thought,

This stuff is really ugly.

Vertiginous perspective, skinny women with green faces and vacant eyes, crazy color, slapdash brushwork. But the more I saw of Kirchner and, especially, the postwar painters of the New Objectivity, the more they spoke to me. Influenced by art from Oceania and

Africa newly arriving in Europe, early-twentieth-century German expressionists made mordant images of postwar German hypocrisy and rejected the naturalism of pretty prewar paintings that I also could not like. I admired this work's critical edge as the perfect antithesis of work like Norman Rockwell's, the black romantics', and the Adirondack plein air painters'. Expressionists rejected sentimentality. And bravo to that.

Here was the style I was coming to prefer, figurative but untethered from slavish realism. Art with an edge of unrest. I chose to transcribe two of the self-deprecating self-portraits of one of the Potsdamer Platz artists, Max Beckmann. Beckmann made large works with multiple figures depicting scenes from mythology before and after a series of sardonic self-portraits. It was not only the life of the painter that attracted me, as with Neel and Ringgold. There was a bit more. Beckmann painted *Self-Portrait with Champagne Glass* in 1919, a year of tumult I had written about at length in *Standing at Armageddon: The United States 1877–1919*. So, yes, once again, something of history came along with the art I was drawn to.

Beckmann was an artistic prodigy from Leipzig in Saxony in eastern Germany who spent time in France and Italy in the very early years of the twentieth century. There he made huge paintings and fancied himself the German Delacroix. From the beginning he painted self-portraits, early inspired by cubism, later more painterly, all expressing his intensely individual focus. He holds a horn or saxophone, wears a red scarf or bowler hat, or masquerades as a sailor, an acrobat, or the medical orderly he had been in the First World War before a nervous breakdown.

Beckmann flourished after the war until Hitler's National Socialists designated him a "degenerate" artist in 1937 and ruined him in Germany. The Nazis confiscated six hundred museum works (he had made *six hundred* paintings of museum quality!)

and sent him into several unhappy years of exile in the Netherlands. In 1947, with the help of his dealer and the head of the Saint Louis Art Museum, he immigrated to the United States to fill in temporarily for Philip Guston at Washington University in Saint Louis. Beckmann died of a heart attack on the corner of West 61st Street and Central Park West in Manhattan in 1950, as his work was being featured in the German Pavilion of the Venice Biennale.

The weird reflections of diabolical others, the off-kilter depiction of Beckmann's eyes and hands, its lack of sentiment, its lassitude, its futile posturing in view of a demonic neighbor, its astringent, grayed-down palette, the chalky white and yellow skin colors, the warmth of the ground, and its strange treatment of the body, all this in Beckmann's besotted *Self-Portrait with Champagne Glass* beguiled me. I transcribed this tipsy self-portrait of the world's weariness. A perfect summation of 1919. A visually satisfying figurative painting.

My *Beckmann's Self-Portrait*, 2007, oil on canvas,
approx. 20" × 18"

More than its connection to history and its era, Beckmann's self-portrait was my artist's version of the French medieval history that had first brought me to the study of history—the freedom to be drawn to the work just because it intrigued me. It is a weird painting whose secrets of weirdness I probed through transcription.

8

LOOK LIKE AN ARTIST

I LOST FIVE POUNDS OVER MY FIRST SEMESTER AT MASON Gross thanks to my commute and climbing the stairs in Civic Square Building. In the fall I spent three days in Birmingham, Alabama, at the annual meeting of the Southern Historical Association's pleasant gerontocracy as I became president for the coming year. People complimented my appearance: I looked so good, they said, so lively, so much younger, that is, slenderer. This came as a gift from the art gods, for five fewer pounds is a very good thing for an artist.

I've never been fat, but there have been many times in my life when I could stand to lose five pounds. Or ten pounds. I inherited my mother's tastes and imported her vigilance into my own never-ending, and I do mean *never*-ending, anti-fat campaign. Weight loss always pleased my mother, she, ever svelte, despite giant Hershey bars and peach ice cream. To our dismay, I inherited my father's tendency toward embonpoint. Over the decades he managed to stay slightly on the winning side of the battle with his belly, but his battle never let up. Once, years ago, my father and I were walking down Route 5 in western Maine. My father never hesitated to speak to strangers, turning every encounter into nascent friendship. This time he chatted up a slender neighbor working in his garden beside the road. My father was looking for tips in his perpetual struggle with abdominal fat.

How do you keep your belly down? he asked.

The neighbor's reply: Cancer.

MY MOTHER SURVEILLED my weight as part of her passive-aggressive relationship with personal beauty in the United States of America. Even though she never had to contend with fat like my father and me, she kept her eye on me—for my own good, of course—to protect me from the fat-black-woman stereotype. A good lefty, she would never criticize working-class women for their looks. At the same time, she could also never forget that American culture casts the fat black woman as a servant, a servant happy to serve. No one ever confused me for the help while I was at Mason Gross.

As an artist, you know, you have to look good, starting with the raw material of your body. You can't be taken seriously in The Art World unless you're slender, or at least not fat. No fat artists allowed. This goes for men as well as women, even though in the regular, non-art world, women's appearances weigh more against them than men's. Come to think of it, this is changing, as men, artists or not, self-fashion for the look of beauty, not just power. Male artists, in particular, govern their allure, in body, face, and costume.

Male or female, you have to dress like an artist. I noticed right away at Mason Gross that artist professors don't dress like professor professors. Artists don't get dressed; they costume themselves in artist-outfit, an undertaking judiciously arranged for *sprezzatura*, for apparently insouciant style. Artists never dress up in jackets or ties. Artists always dress down. Artists wear pajama bottoms and house shoes from Brooklyn to New Jersey. Artists wear paint-stained clothing, for surely they must just have run into the classroom after a long night of painting. I have known artists, really excellent artists, even excellent women artists, who curate their appearance in order to stand apart from collectors. Artists are shabbier than collectors. You can tell collectors by their expensive, billowy, Japanesy clothing and whimsical (and outrageously expensive) eyeglasses. Curators wear hard-to-find shoes from Germany. Artists wear cowboy boots. For several years, even after leaving art school, I disdained cowboy boots as artists' affectation.

Teacher Hanneline would come in from Brooklyn—Brooklyn!—in her cowboy boots as from the great outdoors (Brooklyn). I loved her, but cowboy boots struck me as too posed in central Jersey. That was when professor-professor sartorial habits kept me from donning costume. With time I grasped the point of artist's apparel as costume and began costuming myself. Now I curate my appearance. Now I wear cowboy boots. Now I will swear to you that they really are comfortable. Really, they are.

I came to admire my sister and brother art students' self-presentation, whether in cute little dresses with boots or in Uggs with shorts or in much torn and worn items put together with élan. Art students buy their clothes at Goodwill, or they wear expensive designer things that look like they came from Goodwill, tight clothes in clashing colors—is "clashing colors" still a recognizable concept? The fashion for men looked to me as though everything had shrunk: tight and short.

Undergraduate women, like Tina, who asked my age that first day, wore outfits that I thought made them look like children. At first, stiff-necked second-wave feminist that I was, I inwardly scoffed at girlyness as retrograde, the very response that makes younger women see feminists my age as superannuated fuddy-duddies, stamping out fun, like pornography, which should be enjoyed as an edgy but harmless pastime.

In my own case, experience had already altered the way I dressed over the years. I had moved on from 1970s-Harvard-graduate-student jeans and blue work shirts to careful dresses and skirts as a professor, until a trip to China in the 1980s introduced me to Chinese women professors still in their little blue pantsuits, which they discarded as soon as the Cultural Revolution had safely receded. Plain but extremely comfortable little blue Chinese pantsuits moved me back into pants, where I stayed for years, into and after art school. I'm wearing pants right now. As a woman of a certain age, I placed limits on my accommodation to artist-fashion for a long time. No dresses. Never any shorts. No tattoos, ever. On dresses I have relented. Not on shorts or tattoos.

Another artist's stricture: you have to be able to drink, because there's alcohol everywhere. Legendary artists, like legendary writers, are famous as wets. I always expect wine at art openings, even though Chelsea openings in the summer can stick to bottled water. Wine and beer all the time works for young people, who can carouse all night, drinking, smoking, dancing, and drugging, and still look like the mandatory million bucks. That's hard to pull off when you're over forty, not to mention when you're over sixty-four. I have to eat when I drink. Otherwise, after three glasses of champagne, I'm nauseous. I don't throw up, at least not often, but I feel awful. If I carry on three nights in a row, I look like shit. And when I say "carry on," I'm not *carrying on* all that much. Such a little old lady I'd become in my mid-sixties. How was I going to be an artist if I couldn't drink, or, rather, couldn't drink enough?

I made one enormous concession toward art-school self-fashioning. I straightened my hair for the first time since going natural in Ghana in the 1960s. My mother and I had stopped straightening our hair there out of resignation in a humid climate and pride in a nascent sense of the beauty of natural blackness. For decades, even after Black Power subsided, my black pride kept my hair natural, whether longer or shorter—until I went to art school, with its unspoken decrees on winsome appearance. No one told me my natural hair looked wrong or dated, but I got a message about how to look better. Wordlessly, my natural hair seemed twentieth-century.

So I straightened my hair. I straightened my hair, but I didn't cover my gray. For this I have a very good reason best illustrated by my mother's experience with a cane, which she preferred to call a walking stick, as in the deportment my father adopted in Ghana. Bear with me here.

In her eighties my mother began having trouble keeping her balance, a fact she confided to me hesitantly, as though this were some shameful secret (like, at the other end of womanhood, having your menstrual period) that was her own individual failing. I recognized balance as an older woman's issue. Ever since joining an older women's group at sixty, I had been reading up on what happens to you when you get old. I learned that losing your balance is one of the worst of the many impairments of age. First balance goes, and then it's falls. From falling, straight to death.

I advised my mother, Mom, we don't want you to fall. You've got to start using a walking stick. I knew she'd never go for a "cane."

Dona saw through my euphemism.

She could never heed my caution, she said.

Why not?

Then they'd know I was old, she said, utterly without irony.

Being seen as old at eighty-five was an unacceptable trade-off for stability.

This story ended well. In the online Smithsonian store, my father and I found a handsome cloisonné cane that won Dona over as a fashion accessory. Even better, there came her renewed confidence in walking, for, fearing loss of balance, she had stopped venturing out. With the support of a cane—sorry, walking stick—she walked outside again. In the Adirondacks she walked down- and uphill to the post office. In Oakland she revisited old haunts like Marcus Books. She posted the story on her blog as "My Walking Stick Freed Me." And it surely did free her at eighty-five.

And this is how I get back to straightening my hair in art school, but not covering my gray. As a young comedienne would say, I've passed my "fuck-by date," and a good thing that is, too, even in The Art World. My gray hair frees me to be an older woman with an older woman's release from the ceaseless, expensive, time-consuming, and anxiety-inducing demands of sex appeal. Vanity I have with me still, but I would not try to camouflage or to deny my age, even for art school. Aging is a very big deal; it changes your life, not usually for the better, but there is some better. The better part is emotional; old people are happier and more trusting than the youth. You learn that all that upheaval that used to distress you really isn't such a big deal after all. Just let it go.

The concrete meanings of old age can surprise you. Some of them surprised me, even though they're well known and talked about in the *New York Times*. Up to now for the most part, at least, I've escaped the worst of it in my heart, lungs, and circulatory system. So far the hardest part for me about being old emanated from other people's automatic assumption, back before I started becoming known for my art, that my work, because made by an old woman, isn't interesting, even before being seen.

It's not only women who resent aging, for men, also, despise getting old. Even really smart French men who I would have thought to know better. Jacques Derrida, the prince of twentieth-century post-structuralism, the king of the complexities of this world, dreaded aging. Years ago, Derrida had influenced my writing of history, and French history was a long-standing interest of mine. His biography gave me a glimpse into his experience. Derrida, even

Derrida, hated like hell turning seventy. He had never liked birth-days, but seventy irritated him in the extreme. Derrida confessed to a friend,

More than ever I'm obsessed by age and the desire to un-age. Seventy, you see, is hell.

Derrida didn't make it even to seventy-five. My mother outlived him by a couple of decades, but that didn't make being old easier to face.

Now that I watch women artists my age, I note what seems to be new attention to women artists past seventy, even going up to nearly one hundred. These are artists who've been working for fifty or more years, who, like Faith Ringgold, live by a philosophy of: If you live long enough and you persist, you are going to get recognition; you must stay in the game.

Several of them have stayed in the game to reap the rewards of sustained production.

Women artists continue their youthful practice of costuming, dressing to face down without acknowledgment the passing of time. Lynda Benglis, speaking at the Rhode Island School of Design, wore tight leggings as though she were still thirty-two, in *Artforum* magazine posing naked but for a pair of cat-eye sunglasses and a two-foot-long dildo. Chakaia Booker fashions an original robe flowing from a gigantic turban of African fabrics. Vija Celmins remains comfortable working in my kind of clothes. Echoing T. S. Eliot, eighty-two-year-old Michelle Stuart sums up a conviction I strive toward—with modest success:

I wear my trousers rolled, Stuart says.

It's the philosophy of an older person . . . There's a wonderful freedom in not having to prove anything.

Audrey Flack is still sculpting, with ideas flowing continually, ideas flowing into busts of women from European history. For painters and sculptors like Flack, one's life's work ultimately presents one of the severest tests of age. Unless an artist belongs to the 1 percent who sell out regularly, old age means a lifetime of artistic production piled up around you. What to do with all those paintings, all those pieces?

Inventory, then, not appearance, is aging's burden on old artists—and their heirs. But first, there's making the work that goes into the inventory.

9

DRAWING

IT SOUNDS SO DUMB TO SAY IT SO BALDLY, BUT I'LL SAY it baldly anyway. I love to draw. I can't remember back to before a time when I didn't draw: racehorses in the sports pages, court-room scenes, paper dolls and their clothes. The joy of larkish Saturdays drawing with high school art Teacher Sam and the rest of the multicolored mob of the Oakland Tech High Art Club. Heedless, thankfully, of insurance liability and seeming not to mind our many colors back well before multiculturalism in California, Teacher Sam took us on sketching trips around the Bay Area: to Chinatown in San Francisco, to Marin County, and to Fort Cronkhite, with its battle-gray Cold War military remains, where we connected our eyes to our hands to our ravishing Bay Area.

After I graduated from high school, Sam got his MFA at California College of Arts and Crafts and pursued every artist's dream of New York City fame. Sam did not become a famous New York painter and, like many another local artist, came back home. He became a sculptor and made a career teaching art at San Jose State University. Sam died in 2013. In high school I also took drawing classes at CCAC, where Richard Diebenkorn's memory and the

Bay Area Figurative School modeled the right way to draw. I still feel their influence. Margo Humphrey, my sister student at CCAC, stayed in art and became a prominent printmaker. Two prints she made as an artist-in-residence at the Brodsky Center at Mason Gross hang in our house in Newark.

At Mason Gross I had started with the kind of drawings you make in undergraduate art school, where you learn to make marks, to see by making marks, to trust your line—not to be distracted by color—to align your eye and your hand and your mark. At first it's simple objects, for one goal of this kind of drawing is to reproduce the appearance of things in the world, called *mimesis*. I knew some of this when I was in high school, maybe even all of this I knew. But in my decades as a historian and not drawing, I forgot what I used to know. Now I went back to drawing's history in the way history always captivates me.

Drawing goes way back in human history to scratches on rocks and paintings in caves, to persuade the gods, manipulate nature, entice animal prey, keep notes, and, most basically, to please the eye. So many useful roles for images to play. Art-school drawing, I mean self-conscious *art* drawing, dates to the Renaissance, to the fifteenth-century masters Leonardo and Michelangelo and the sixteenth-century *Accademia del Disegno* of Giorgio Vasari in Florence. *Disegno* you can translate as "design" as well as "drawing." Vasari's *Lives of the Most Excellent Painters, Sculptors, and Architects* is considered art history's foundational text. Intrigued by Vasari as painter as well as biographer, writer as well as teacher of drawing, I bought a paperback copy to check out Vasari's comments on artists' techniques and his admiration of Leonardo's drawing.

Drawing is the fountainhead, the well. Here lie the roots of the master drawings of painters like Dürer and Rembrandt, whose skilled studies of the figure count as fine art in their own right, even though they were made as exercises or sketches for assistants.

Leonardo and his contemporaries conveyed volume with cross-hatch and distance with perspective, so that just browsing Leonardo's voluminous sketchbooks—his studies of people, animals, maps, buildings, machines, and fantastically detailed draftsmanship—might intimidate you out of ever picking up your own pen. And to think that those drawings are simply considered "studies."

Hardly anybody draws like that anymore. Hardly anybody even strives to draw like that, though I know of an exception, the New York Academy of Art. I spent a weekend there learning to draw faces, examining and drawing the actual shape of the human eye. Well, the actual shape of the human eye in art history as depicted in the Italian Renaissance. On the second day we had a Latino model whose eyes were New Yorker shaped. It was a good, useful lesson to look hard at Renaissance-Italian eyes, then to really see non-Renaissance-Italian eyes.

The New York Academy of Art preserves the Renaissance tradition, even down to making écorchés. Literally something flayed, an écorché is a body with the skin taken off to reveal the muscle, bone, and sinew. Interestingly, one of the most striking examples of the rendering of musculature is an etching rather than a drawing: Antonio Pollaiuolo's *Battle of the Ten Nudes* (1470–75), in which every single muscle of the contending warriors is tensed. They look, as Leonardo once said, "like a sack of nuts rather than the surface of a human being, or indeed a bundle of radishes rather than muscular nudes." Leonardo wasn't talking about Pollaiuolo; he was sneering at Michelangelo's figures. But the description still fits. Leonardo's own sketchbooks are full of écorchés of humans and animals. He could have built a person or a horse from scratch. For centuries écorchés were considered the basis of figure drawing. But not anymore, at least not in most American art schools. Too hard. Too time consuming, even where mimetic drawing still plays its role.

All beginning art students in the twentieth century studied mimetic drawing as the foundation of visual arts—until conceptual art began dematerializing art in the 1960s, so that the thought, the concept, mattered as much, maybe more, than the thing, and the artist didn't have to make the art at all. For conceptual art, drawing is passé, to my mind a crucial loss of intense seeing—call it mindful sight. In traditional drawing class, you began by drawing simple forms—spheres, cones—and worked up to the human body. For this kind of pedagogy, the nude was where you honed your skill. Even when drawing was considered an end in itself—not merely as a sketch or basis for a painting or sculpture—it culminated in the nude. In my drawing and painting marathon at the New York Studio School, there was a nude model in a set-up in every studio for every assignment.

BEYOND THE SATISFACTION of making an image, I always liked drawing as a means of slowing down, of really seeing what I was looking at. The singer-songwriter Abbey Lincoln called it looking at what you see, a lesson she took from her own mother. When I'm drawing, I *look at* more; I see more. I still can't draw as expertly as my friend Madeleine, who earned her MFA in Boston in the 1970s, when and where mimetic drawing was still an essential skill. But the ability to make my drawing look like something in the world, like the "motif," has always mattered less to me than the profound pleasure of making my marks on paper. What satisfies me is the process itself, the alliance of paper and ink or pencil or charcoal or any of myriad new markers and even objects like twigs dipped in ink or powdered graphite. My drawings don't further some other project. Tiny or large, they're artifacts in their own right.

Drawing like this feels spontaneous—I see what I have made as soon as I make it. And because of its small scale, it feels intimate.

My paper usually fits on my lap or under my arm. I can carry drawing around to work on at any time. I like to draw on smooth Bristol paper, because paper with tooth distracts my line. I also use Yupo, a slick, synthetic polypropylene paper that doesn't absorb ink or graphite easily and produces unexpected textures from watery mediums like ink. Sometimes I do use color in my drawings, but I like deep black India ink, using the dropper as a mark-making tool. Especially in abstract drawings, I collage torn-up pages of art magazines with their good, heavy paper and vivid color. Gallery advertisements let me quote the work of other artists and sneak in a touch of art history to add more than purely visual meaning.

As I think now about my love of drawing, I confront the underlying reality of drawing's lack of painting's prestige. Drawings are usually smaller than paintings and on paper, communicating the fragility of the ephemeral, as opposed to canvas, especially canvas on stretcher bars that communicate solidity and permanence. A medium of surpassing simplicity, drawing connects the hand directly with the support, without the interference of paint—paint, I mean, as an ennobling medium. Drawings lack paintings' gravitas and are generally considered less important and therefore less valuable— okay, cheaper—than painting. Drawings are to paintings as bungalows are to castles. This can be a good thing. To me—a famously bad painter—drawing seems more accessible and less intimidating, its stakes lower. I can make many, many drawings without exceeding my skills or wasting materials. In this sense, my attraction to drawing is one facet of my low self-esteem as an artist, perhaps even my own low self-esteem as a woman artist. I don't like to think that way, but such thoughts blow in with the atmosphere.

I LOVED AND still love Teacher Hanneline, my Norwegian Mason Gross drawing instructor who didn't have an American prejudice against organization. I like to think my admiration for her grew out of the thoughtfulness of her teaching, her care in connecting vision to image. I admire the tender way she inhabits the world and how she looks, her attentiveness, her sideways smile, her solid, not too thin, not too fat physical presence. I would say she is beautiful, but American capitalism, with its skinny glamour of industrial beauty, has corrupted the concept of physical beauty. Hanneline is more than beautiful. Is she truly as serene about her looks as I thought? I know she "curated" (as we say) her appearance, emerging from Brooklyn in unmistakable artist's costume. She showed me how to look like an artist.

In Hanneline's class we started with charcoal, drawing bones that were one part simple shapes and another part convoluted, textured forms. She moved us on to ink, exposing us to drawings by various artists: the performance artist Joseph Beuys, the architect Walter Pichler, the outsider artist Bill Traylor, the silhouette master Kara Walker, the Romantic painter Francisco Goya, and the Bay Area–Los Angeles expressionist Richard Diebenkorn. I carried her exercise on *pentimento* into work that stayed with me into graduate school. *Pentimento* refers to traces of original drawing that the artist has erased. In the work of someone like William Kentridge, *pentimento* conveys a feeling of a shadowy presence of something that has gone before and remains a memory with visual meaning. All Hanneline's artists were different, so we could see the scope of drawing's possibilities exceeding any one, single, correct way to draw. The trick was to draw a lot, like Vincent van Gogh.

In letters to his brother Theo, van Gogh talked about doing nothing but drawing and drawing and drawing. How I envied him this. He drew before painting for two whole years and still wanted to learn more, particularly about the figure, which to him, as to other artists, stood at the apogee of art. He talked about color, especially the grays, and various drawing instruments. He said that soaking charcoal in oil produced a nice deep black, and that dashing milk over drawings gave them a nice sheen. Nowadays we have compressed charcoal for intense blacks and acrylic polymer gloss medium for sheen. The part of van Gogh's drawing process I adopted was rectangular carpenters' pencils with their cunning little sharpener (mine in cadmium-orange plastic), so they make lines of different thicknesses according to how you hold the pencil. Drawing isn't only about the line. But for me, the essence of drawing is line.

Hanneline's drawing classes challenged me. After bones, we did research. We made drawings based on paintings from art history, imagined images frontways and from the back, before, during, and after the scene in the original. I drew *The Artist in His Museum*, by Charles Willson Peale, from 1822. I knew Peale to be a naturalist who wanted Americans to appreciate their physical world. *The Artist in His Museum* appealed to me as American history set in a particular place, Philadelphia, and as an over-the-top self-portrait advertising a collection of natural history artifacts. At 8' 8" × 6' 8", Peale's painting is larger than life-size. There's a dinosaur skeleton behind the curtain Peale lifts, mastodon bones in the foreground (in 1806 Peale had painted the exhumation of the first American mastodon), a collection of birds, actual and extinct, arranged on orderly shelves in precipitous one-point perspective, and, at his feet, a dead wild turkey, splendid in its plumage. Visitors in the background. On the table behind him, Peale's palette with paints in an orderly arrangement beside his brushes. Peale's stagey gesture of revelation is proudly deadpan, instructing an innocent American public, a Philadelphia of science in its youth, not yet feeling the need for irony. At the time, Peale was eighty-one years old.

My version uses a more simplified palette than *The Artist in His Museum*, and, of course, my pieces are much smaller and on paper rather than canvas. Drawn in ink with only rose as color, my *before*

UPPER LEFT: *Peale Drawing 1*, 2008, ink on paper, 23" × 18"
UPPER RIGHT: *Peale Drawing 2*, 2008, ink on paper, 18" × 23"
LOWER LEFT: *Peale Drawing 3*, 2008, ink on paper, 23" × 18"
LOWER RIGHT: *Peale Drawing 4*, 2008, ink on paper, 23" × 18"

the scene shows a serving woman tidying up before Peale appears. While she works, he naps. There's no mirror or pinhole camera, the devices he would have used to aid his composition. Once the woman's work is done, Peale poses alone for his masterwork.

Drawing for Hanneline fueled my imagination. It wasn't just the images as I drew them. It was everything surrounding the images. As Jacques Derrida would say, there's no beyond the frame; everything, whether you think it belongs in the picture or not, brings meaning to the image (or, in literature, to the text). Drawing for Hanneline reached back into my own autobiography to trace the Bay Area's influence on my eyes.

I grew up looking at territory delimited by mountains, my Oakland horizon bounded by the Coast Range east and west of the San Francisco Bay. I learned to drive on a stick shift on Bay Area hills, at steep stoplights—brake, clutch, accelerator in a careful sequence—without rolling backward into cars lined up behind. My first car was an English roadster I drove around with the top down until the temperature dropped into the forties—rare in Oakland back in the twentieth century. Hills, mountains, triangle-shaped lines cross my drawings, just as they taught me how to drive.

My hand and eye sought mountains as necessary to compose a landscape, even an indoor scene with lamp and easy chair. I needed a bumpy horizon line and drew mountains in charcoal with Hokusai waves and Mount Fuji in the upper left or lower right, a Philip Guston lightbulb above, an easy chair interior, and an ultramarine blue checkerboard to quote Robert Colescott. I drew a lot for Hanneline.

In the last group crit of the spring semester, Hanneline mentioned her Yale School of Art assignment of one hundred drawings. *One hundred drawings.* I could do that. Hell, I could do that right now. A nice round number, impressive in its own right. Make one hundred drawings. One student groaned, a couple of others held

LEFT: *Hokusai Composite Drawing*, 2008,
ink and graphite on paper, 18" × 24"

RIGHT: *Colescott Mountain Composite Drawing*, 2008,
ink, graphite, and colored pencil on paper, 18" × 24"

their tongues. One hundred drawings! How could we ever make one hundred drawings?!

One hundred drawings' intoxication. By the end of the summer, I reckoned, even with *The History of White People* (which I sometimes shortened to *THWP*), the fucking, everlasting Organization of American Historians, and book-prize-committee chairing, I could make one hundred drawings, twice one hundred drawings. No, let me be reasonable and leave the goal at one hundred—one hundred drawings during the summer.

Ink and a new sketchbook launched my one hundred drawings starting on the first day of summer vacation in late May in Newark. Our backyard. New Jersey really is the green and glorious Garden State.

New Jersey spring has flowering trees like in the South, but you don't have to dread the South's day-after-day-after-day of ninety-five degrees, June to October. You don't have to scuttle between air-conditioned home and air-conditioned office. Heat doesn't punch you in the face when you open your car door in the supermarket parking lot. You don't have to sweat absolutely all the time. Sweet spring in Newark, New Jersey. Come outside. Draw.

On such a fine May morning in Newark I took my sketchbook to the backyard with a bottle of ink, a pen, and a brush. I sat at the glass table looking over our tiny, earnest backyard farm with the pretty, vain, fat brown tabby cat surveying his domain.

Ro, 2008, ink on paper, 7" × 5"

All summer I continued drawing, alternating stabs at writing my book and history organization chores. All summer I made small drawings, representational, figurative, and abstract. I called the project *One Hundred Drawings for Hanneline*, though there are really only sixty-seven.

10

I COULD NOT DRAW MY MOTHER DYING

L A DI DA DI DA DI DA, AS CAREFREE AS I COULD BE.
I drew and drew my one hundred drawings for Hanneline,
la di da di da di da.

As the summer was ending, there came a crisis. Another crisis
in Oakland. My parents. My father, weeping, could only hand my
mother the phone. I had to come to Oakland, now. That call—
tears, desperation—not the first such summons to Oakland, nor the
last, not by far, but the first in a last sequence.

My parents were calling from their cottage at Salem Lutheran
Home, where they lived independently in their own little house. Every resident wore a panic button. They had not pressed their panic
button. They had not called the nurses' station for help. Despite
Dona's night of excruciating leg pain, they even waited before calling me for help, Frank massaging Dona's legs to assuage her pain,
inadvertently increasing the risk of moving a blood clot. She howled
in pain; he gave up. Desperation pushed their call to me. Diehard

sense of independence forestalled further outreach. *Independence,* my mother's watchword.

Dona went to Kaiser Permanente hospital's emergency, perhaps for surgery, perhaps to lose a leg, and, unsaid, the ultimate worst possible fate. My poor father, emotionally collapsed from depression, wept over this latest possible loss, but he now wept over everything. My father had not always been depressed and wrecked, quite to the contrary. Over the course of many decades he was loved for his looks, cherished for his generosity of spirit, and profoundly appreciated for his willingness to help others, whether through sympathetic listening—he was the world's most empathetic listener—transportation, or even money in times of need. His were not just ingrained good manners, though he was known for gentlemanliness. When you talked to him, he listened, he responded to what you had actually said. Caring for other people and good listening made my father everyone's hero, even in those times when that good person hid from view. He had been a depressed wreck for years, unable to do more than wait for me to come from New Jersey to fix things. We knew this drill all too well by then, for my parents had already been deteriorating. By the time they reached their late eighties, Glenn and I could see them as frail.

When I say "see them as frail," I have a particular morning in Oakland clearly in the eye of my mind. Before moving to Salem, my parents lived in the hills above the Oakland zoo. A mile or so farther up lay a hilly East Bay Regional park where my father walked his dog every day before depression nailed him to his bed. Usually he walked alone with his dog, Dona only rarely accompanying him, for the hills he walked were too strenuous for her heart after years of smoking. One sunny morning when Glenn and I were visiting, before things started totally collapsing, the four of us walked a flat path in the park.

Most of the path crossed open grassy rolling hills where you could see the San Francisco Bay, San Francisco, downtown Oakland and Berkeley, over to Richmond and Marin County. No question about it—the Bay Area is the most beautiful place in the world. Whenever I'm there, I ask myself why on earth I still live in New Jersey.

That morning Frank and Dona walked a flat path with trees on either side. Glenn and I followed, watching them lean on each other, essential supports for seventy years. They were so tenderly interdependent, so deeply and so lovingly connected! We teared up over the sight of them in the arid California bower, so tottering, so frail, like the figures on a wedding cake, but collapsing. We could see they lacked the strength to live on their own.

It took Glenn and me two years to get them to agree with each other on moving into continuing care in Salem Lutheran Home, a process that entailed an exasperating churn of home health aides. Once Dona and Frank were settled in their new home in Salem's Redwood Cottage, I had started art school thinking my parents

Frank and Dona Irvin at Their Seventieth Anniversary,
Oakland, 2007, digital photograph

were stabilized. (Just as mistakenly, I had thought my book was finished.) But now Frank and Dona were failing. They had been so glorious a couple for more than seventy years, a sane, open, liberal, handsome pair, as welcoming to gays and lesbians as to straights. Everybody wanted them for parents. My parents the paragons. People adopted them as replacements for their own lesser families. My poor parents, for so long a gorgeous, inspiring couple of progressive, intelligent beauties! No longer.

The desperate call from my father at the end of the summer of my one hundred drawings was pathetic entreaty and parental command. This was not Dona's first hospitalization or the first urgent trip to scare me to death. Intense leg pain had sent her to the hospital a year earlier, and low blood pressure had kept her in intensive care. Angioplasty was the remedy then. Now, a year later, my mother was again in intensive care, and my father was once again weeping, commanding, and beseeching me to drop everything and fly to their rescue, his condition as alarming as hers.

We need you now.

I put my paper and ink aside, washed my pen, and flew to Oakland.

Thank heaven I had already finished my book manuscript and sent it off to the publisher. The damned thing had taken so long that I was calling it *My Fucking Book*, *MFB* for short. Of course, it would come back for more tinkering, but it had passed the monumental final manuscript stage. I had made a drawing of the final manuscript sitting on my worktable in the Adirondack screened porch, a block of pages so tall one of my Mason Gross mentors called the pile a sculpture.

For a crazy moment I imagined the trip to California as an art opportunity. Maybe I could meet Mary Lovelace O'Neal, a terrific abstract artist at the University of California–Berkeley whose work made me think of my idol, Robert Colescott. I had first discovered

MFB, 2008, ink and oil stick on paper, 6" × 9"

O'Neal while researching the art that illustrates my *Creating Black Americans*, drawn initially by her brilliantly colored, composed, and titled *Racism Is Like Rain, Either It Is Raining or It Is Gathering Somewhere*, a 1993 lithograph featured by the California African American Museum in a Los Angeles show inspired by the Rodney King disturbances. O'Neal is my age, and she makes the kind of work I find myself attracted to: gestural, abstract, brilliantly colored, full of movement and action, and hinting at figuration. Though O'Neal's work is in public collections, and she holds her share of international honors, she is a black woman painter of the modernist generation who could not pierce the veil of mainstream art history. I hoped to meet her, or even just to tell her she meant a lot to me as an artist. In Oakland I bought some art supplies in case I might continue my one hundred drawings.

Envisioning art in Oakland could not obscure the dismal facts, and the facts were truly dismal. My parents were disintegrating, Frank from depression, Dona from congestive heart failure and from the anxiety of Frank's anger whenever she did anything he wasn't ready to do—which was anything whatever, whenever. His anger consigned her to his paralysis, impossibly hard on Dona, ordinarily the personification of energy. I knew she had collapsed from exhaustion. We had already seen the signs: her increasing confusion, loss of concentration, inability to use her computer to check her email. Worst of all for her, she was stammering again after a quarter century of fluency.

My father said he was feeling "thrown away." How could that be? His misery was so misconstrued, I thought, for his situation was excellent. After decades of walking his dogs in the Oakland hills, his physical health could hardly have been better. He was married, financially comfortable, loved, and well cared for. All for naught. He felt absolutely rotten and spread his naught around. This made no objective sense, kind of like unhappy rich people, weeping in the midst of splendor. But what use was objectivity? My parents were driving me crazy, for I knew they were safe, 100 percent better off than so many their age. They had the finest of health care at Kaiser Permanente and an abundance of friends, some for half a century or more. Depression and congestive heart failure, yes, but no Alzheimer's or dementia, no poverty, no diabetes, no cancer or broken hips. No matter. My father peered into his future and saw only hopelessness. He shook and wept and gasped for breath. He said he no longer wanted to live. Dona feared he was dying. Something had to be done, but his psychiatrist had tried every medication available.

MY POOR LITTLE mother! In the intensive care unit she became delusional, imagining herself on an airplane about to take off, leaving Frank behind. She worried and fretted, trying to get us to delay departure, making us promise to hurry Frank up. He always needed hurrying up, even when he was perfectly well. In the ICU Dona was still confused, but adorably childlike in her half-confused, half-cognizant state. In the morning she was easily distracted. As I fed her some breakfast to make sure she ate, she chased other thoughts. This was the first time I had fed one of my parents. But it was not to be the last. Art school or no, I was in charge now.

Dona had been our family's organizer, our super-duper originator, arranger, instigator, architect, executrix, and producer. Our affairs had run smoothly for so long that I had never felt the need to step into the middle of my parents' (outwardly) sunny existence. I loved them; they loved me; everybody loved them. They had whole new families of friends. I always kept in touch over the years, but not continually, in the way of my fellow Mason Gross undergraduates, constantly chatting with their parents by cell phone about what I overheard as trivia, like what to wear on an ordinary day. Even in my parents' mid-eighties, they were still strong, Dona organizing their next steps in lists of their finances, including account numbers and institutional contact information. She even sent me a document labeled "Body Disposal" with all the information I would need when they died, or, as they preferred to term it, once they "made their transition." Frank was in no shape to appreciate Dona's organization, but I certainly did. Glenn sometimes poked fun at Dona's documentary excesses—she tallied up the attendance at their fabulous seventieth anniversary party before pronouncing herself satisfied.

AS THOUGH THEIR lives drew from a single reservoir, Frank rallied as Dona declined. His depression had dragged her down until she collapsed, then his depression relented. During her hospitalization, he visited her with me and sat with her in her hospital room. I read to them from Barack Obama's first memoir that we pronounced excellent, candid, and sensitively, elegantly written. Frank and I sat transfixed in Dona's hospital room as Obama accepted the Democratic nomination for president, a wondrous thing neither of us had imagined possible within our lifetimes. At this same awesome moment, Dona lay elsewhere mentally, agitated, confused, and hallucinating. She was questioning what we couldn't see on the ceiling of her hospital room and picking at her bedclothes. She drifted off to sleep during Obama's Great Historic Speech, never aware it had taken place.

WHILE WE IRVINS were absorbed in our family drama, the Democrats were making history every night. Michelle Obama was beautiful and touching. The Clintons did right. Joe Biden called on his people—the firefighters and police officers (but not the hospital and childcare workers). Obama was tough and beautifully ethical, balancing talk of unity, purpose, and respect with policy and nice criticisms of John McCain's $5 million/year = middle class, and the Republicans' so-called ownership society, translating it as you're on your own. My father and I savored every momentous phrase, every transcendent image.

I felt proud of Americans' working through hotly contested matters. The Democratic National Committee wrestled with contending delegations from Florida and Michigan and reached compromises without drawing guns. Some time ago I would have taken quite for granted the nonviolent resolution of political differences. No longer. In these days of electoral bloodletting, of slaughter in cinemas and grade schools, in churches and casinos, when contested elections produce ethnic cleansing and everybody carries a gun, I felt, still feel, Americans have done something fine.

I remembered a conversation with a Haitian taxi driver taking me from Princeton Junction to Princeton during the drawn-out settlement of the 2000 presidential election. He kept *All Things Considered* on his radio because, he said, he marveled at the peaceful settlement of political controversy.

•

FOCUSING MY FATHER beyond his misery, the 2008 presidential campaign kept him alive. His attention had not always been so closely circumscribed, for years ago, before passing eighty-five, he had subscribed to the daily *New York Times*, the actual paper, I mean. By his late eighties he could no longer take pleasure in the paper as a whole, but in 2008 his interest in current events revived. He followed Frank Rich, Bob Herbert, and Gail Collins, relishing every report of John McCain's weaknesses, especially after Sarah Palin dirtied up the campaign. In Oakland I read to my father from the *Times* online every day.

Glenn and I helped Dona and Frank fill out their absentee ballots, allowing them the historic gratification of voting for Barack Obama for president of the United States of America. A milestone of milestones, an occurrence that changed American history. For a while, anyway, very much for the good. I credit George W. Bush for making my parents' vote possible, for opening Obama's way. First, Bush appointed two black people to the previously unattainable—even unimaginable—position of secretary of state, one a black woman—a black woman who was not an immigrant or child of immigrants, not even a woman with skin light enough to comfort American eyes. Okay, okay, Bush and his people trashed Colin Powell, and Condoleezza Rice was as feckless and right-wing as the rest of the Bush people. But she and Powell remained black. Had a Democrat tried to appoint black people to so prominent a position, the Republican uproar would still be resounding. I felt any such appointees (and they surely would have been as able as Rice or Powell) would have been Lani Guinierized, shredded by mean-spirited lies. But good-ole-boy Republican Bush did the impossible. With the actual fact of black secretaries of state, the domain of the possible widened. If Powell and Rice could be secretaries of state, maybe a black man—a man, mind you—could be president.

By my lights, Bush's second gift to Obama was a disastrous presidency, early bringing thousands into the streets against the war. Then the Great Recession scared everybody to death in 2008. By that point, things had descended to such a nadir that Americans opened up to extreme measures. Obama was so different from Bush that he could appear as a remedy.

The great fear, of course, was that some American would shoot him, in another tradition aimed at charismatic political figures, especially those who are black. Michelle Obama confronted that threat directly, saying that in the United States a black man could get shot just going to the grocery store. Subsequent events have shown this as literally all too true.

MY MOTHER IN the hospital, I got to live my own life in Oakland for a couple of hours. I searched for contact information for Mary Lovelace O'Neal, that terrific abstract artist at Cal–Berkeley, who was pretty damned well hidden. I finally unearthed an email address that she never used. I visited my friend Anna's studio and gallery in San Leandro, where Anna and I talked about materials and curating, about colors and taste, about the art market in general, about the market for work by black artists, and about making work that fits the pocketbook of black buyers. Anna lamented that most of her buyers were white, because she wanted also to reach black buyers. We pondered our situation as American artists, in which the race of our buyers would seem to matter. Anna was happy to have buyers, and that put her ahead of me.

•

DONA LEFT THE hospital, but not to return to Redwood cottage. She moved to room 107A in Salem's skilled nursing department, a kind of mini-hospital. One day a group of my parents' close friends from the First Church of Religious Science made a prayer circle around we three Irvins, Glenn having departed to teach in New Jersey. The friends prayed and sang over us in a most beautiful and moving fashion that sent tears down my face. They hugged me and let me lean on them. That felt lifesaving physically and emotionally.

A day or so later, two other Religious Science ministers came to talk with us, giving Frank and Dona a Religious Science "treatment" that raised their spirits, Frank's especially. I'm not religious, but the treatment felt good to me, too, as an uncanny infusion of encouragement, a physical embrace. I thought I understood the fact of my mother's impending death, but I had not. I had no idea of the feelings and fears and complications, the pit opening up before me, the loss of the key to my identity. I also had no grasp of the enormous support I enjoyed from my parents' strong network of friends. Thanks to them, I was not going into this alone.

One morning Frank asked me what would happen to Dona. I said the short answer was I didn't know. I really couldn't know what I knew, even though I knew it in a place I could not reach. I admitted the long-term prognosis wasn't good. He shuddered and wept.

One mental image I kept was my frail, nearly ninety-year-old father walking from Salem Lutheran Home, down and back up the hill on 23rd Avenue to the convenience store for ice cream for Mom. He was so vulnerable! He could not satisfy her demands in the angry phase of her mortal illness, a rage that reduced him to tears. He wanted so much to please her. This new ability of hers to be angry with him fascinated me and demoralized my father. He cried,

We've been together for seventy-one years. We're like one unit.

I agreed with him. But when he said he couldn't live without her, I asked him not to go there, to take it one day at a time.

I hated to think it, but I hoped that an end to this long marriage might lift my father out of his depression. Already Dona's breakdown had gotten him out of bed more than in years. Maybe both my parents were suffering from too much togetherness for too long a time.

WITH DONA RESETTLED in Salem's skilled nursing, I returned to Mason Gross. Back in New Jersey, I grappled with my mother's impending death, and not for the first time. It had already come up on account of her mental instability and weakness. Her hold on reality wasn't firm, but her spirits were pretty good, for she didn't understand the gravity of her situation. But whenever I told others she suffered from congestive heart failure, their faces fell. As I told Glenn these things, he began looking at his calendar for when we could return to Oakland. Glenn was teaching every Monday, so any visit on his part would have to accommodate that schedule—somehow. But me, I felt as though I should just go to Oakland for the duration. Fuck it. Just let my semester go.

Let it all go. In the end, I didn't let the semester go, even though there were, what, six? seven? trips to Oakland that academic year.

I managed to keep up with my Mason Gross classes, but my work spoke bleakness. After an evening in the basement drawing and painting, I went to bed feeling oppressed. I couldn't shake Teacher Lauren's adjective for my portfolio of new drawings: "dreary." She came down hard on those pieces, offering a little criticism doubtless meant as constructive, but I couldn't hear constructiveness. "Dreary" stuck most tenaciously, because I was so tired that *dreary* described my being as a whole.

One of my most helpful mentors, Artist Friend Denyse Thom-

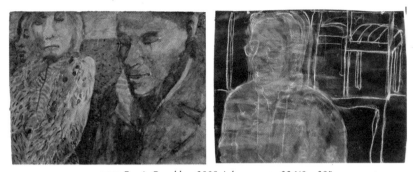

LEFT: *Pan in Brooklyn*, 2008, ink on paper, 22 ½" × 30"
RIGHT: *Ruth Disappears*, 2008, ink and white conté crayon, 18" × 24"

asos, described my work in terms I never could have come up with on my own. She noted my acid tones, my grayed, low-contrast palette, the open spaces, all conveying a sense of isolation and sadness. She said my paintings translated my anguish. After crit, I collapsed on the floor of my studio, exhausted, but unable to nap, my hysterical knee throbbing despite multiple ibuprofens. I was emptied out and queasy, with a canker sore in my mouth. I was so tired, so very tired. And my studies seemed so futile.

My father wailed on the phone that he was close to his breaking point, crying again—he was always crying—back in his all-too-welcoming despair. Depression is definitely contagious, and he spewed depression all over me long-distance. My poor mother must also have caught it over the years and was still now catching it in his hours at her bedside.

One day in New Jersey in my car on the way to New Brunswick, I waited for the light to change at Bloomfield Avenue and JFK Drive to take the Garden State Parkway. Exit 148. The wind blew dead leaves across the intersection, a wave of desolation on a cold, cloudy day. Through the car window I couldn't hear the leaves' clatter. I knew the soundless sound, a dry rasping, "it's over." The worst of my sorrow subsided as I drove up the ramp and onto the Parkway. The deaf graphite rattle of leaves in the wind.

IT WAS THE first day of final crits in Hanneline's class. Only two other students and I were there on time at 8:15. Matt had spent the night in the classroom, another last-minute, overnight wonder. I had seen this phenomenon before in other classes with other students, and I always admired the originality and scale of pieces made overnight. A student who seemed silent and mediocre in class would make a masterpiece, a twenty-four-hour marvel of invention I could never envision. They could do this, the youth, just now producing a huge, handsome collaged drawing, a tour de force that did not relate to any of our assignments. Such unfettered freedom left me slack-jawed in admiration—for the work and for the freedom to disregard what had been asked of us.

The freedom of disregard.

I put my final project drawings up first to claim an entire wall. By the end of the abbreviated class, only six of us had put up work. My friend Madeleine came to give me moral support and loved my final project, my massive, three days' worth of drawing produced in an uncanny, desperate effort following California. She initially assumed it too good to be mine. But in a nice way.

WHEN GANGRENE SET into my mother's leg, I prepared to leave New Jersey at any moment for her death. In BFA thesis class I showed my classmates the four paintings I wanted in the BFA show. They promised to hang my pieces for me, a favor that was welcomed and, finally, needed. Out in the world the news was scary. More firings, unemployment up to 7.1 percent. Republicans still screaming for tax cuts. Obama still trying to accommodate them, even though they wanted to trash his plan to save the American economy. I was hoping his expectation for bipartisanship would work out, though the Republicans were being awfully naughty.

My father was spending nights in my mother's room in skilled nursing under a blanket the nurses gave him for his bedside vigil. On the phone he told me, weeping, that Dona had said—to the room, not particularly to him:

I don't want to die.

This broke his heart again, and it echoed in my ears all night and into the morning. The remarkable thing in her statement and in his repeating it to me was the forthright phrase "to die" instead of their New Age euphemism, "to make one's transition." They were both preparing for the inevitable, though I still didn't have an idea of when, exactly, it would be. Perhaps Frank was expecting "the end" sooner than it would actually occur, perhaps out of grief fatigue.

I was in my lithography class when a phone call from Dona's hospice nurse interrupted the counter-etch of my litho plate. Come immediately, she won't last out the week. That call from Oakland plucked me out of a morass. I had been so sluggish, so emptied out and exhausted, more debilitated than my usual tired. I was living a muddle, struggling through a swamp of slimy, clotted vegetation ensnaring my legs and feet in a bottom I could not see. My actions lacked all meaning. That was how I felt, even though I had not wasted my time. There was a disjunction between my feelings— narcose, lethargic—and my actions—effective and organized. Through the fall's anxious weeks, I had been working on copy-edited *MFB* and took chapters twenty-five through twenty-seven to Oakland with me.

Frank's response intrigued me, for he was unusually composed in those very last days of his vigil by Dona's hospital bed. That vigil carried him to another plane, where he slept better and nearly relinquished self-pity. Would his depression lift with Dona's passing? Glenn saw Frank's depression as a response to her failing health. I rather saw it the other way, that she broke down under the strain of trying to keep him going. Maybe we're both right, as my parents were so intimately connected.

AT SALEM, I returned to what had become my second home, the little no-color, one-room cottage 2C: single bed, bureau with a boxy old-time TV on top, night table with lamp, bathroom, and closet, everything brown and gray and sad worn-out white. The whole cottage was smaller than our bedroom in Newark. The radiator clanked infernally all night. Salem's feral cats yowled outside unceasingly.

Over in skilled nursing, my mother was comatose, eyes 90 percent closed, mouth open, head back, oxygen tube around her nose and neck, its pump both generator and iron lung and sounding like it. A noisy thing, never letting me forget its life-giving function. The time would come, and soon, when it would no longer suffice.

My father was keeping his watch, another night in the chair by Mom's bed. He held her hand, monitoring the relative strength and weakness of her pulse. I watched the faint rise and fall in her throat of her breathing. He stayed in Dona's room, saying he couldn't sleep at home for worrying about her. I believed him.

Dona had many visitors in her last two days, some praying and singing her over. A Religious Science friend sang sweet Hebrew songs to comfort her dying. Even though Dona couldn't register any reaction, we knew she knew we were there. I hoped so; Frank certainly hoped so, wanting so deeply to be with her when she "made her journey."

The process of my mother's dying lasted more than two days,

her face going slack, not just mouth open, but tongue falling to the side, jaw also slumped to the side, and eyes sunken and unfocused. I hadn't thought before of all the muscular effort required to hold the face composed. Except for the obvious exertion required to express emotion, I took muscle tone for granted. But I see now that even a lack of emotion makes muscles work. Dying releases everything, like a stream feeling its way down a landscape, seeking its lowest level.

My mother died at three in the afternoon on a Thursday. My father and I were both there, one on either side, each holding a hand, when she died. Emptiness. Frank summoned the strength to go to Mosswood Chapel mortuary with me to sign her death certificate. Where did he find the power to face this testament of ending? I didn't ask this about myself, accustomed as I was by then to taking charge of my parents' lives and fates. I think now that Dona passed organization on to me in a transfer she had begun years before as part of my inheritance.

Before Thursday ended, the mortician took away what was left of my mother in a small black plastic bag. Though I had been with her as she died and sat with her for a time while she was very dead, the smallness of that package shocked me. A plastic bag contained my entire mother, except for the twenty-one grams of her soul. That small plastic package sealed her deadness. A living person, asleep, might be stretched out on a bed in skilled nursing, but a person still alive could never fit into so small a black plastic bag. It seemed a final insult, the diminution of my beloved mother into a parcel to be carried by hand.

I WAS DOUBTING my artist's bona fides before my mother as a visual spectacle. If I were a real artist, I accused myself, I would have drawn or photographed her dying. I had that thought before she died, struggling to make myself see her as a motif and to draw her.

But I could not draw my dying mother, even to insert her image into my one hundred drawings. I could not take my sketchbook into her room, a gesture that I felt would distance her from me. I tried. I failed. LaToya Ruby Frazier made a poignant series of photographs of her family's physical decline. Annie Leibovitz photographed the fatal illness of her partner Susan Sontag. Roz Chast made an entire, hilarious book about her parents' old age, ending with sober drawings of her mother on her deathbed. I could not do that. Feeling numb, weeping now and then, I loaded my failure as an artist onto my daughter grief.

HOW TIRED COULD a person get? I was plumbing the depths of exhaustion swamp as never before. Lord knows, I've been tired in this life of mine. If my prior experience with exhaustion weren't so extensive, so, well, *exhaustive*, I'd say I'd never been so tired in my life. So I just collapsed in my infernal 2C cubbyhole, with the diabolical radiator clanking all day and night and the goddam cats yowling.

It took weeks to wind up my mother's death and arrange her triumphant "Celebration of Life" at the First Church of Religious Science in Oakland. Even cremated, my mother, from her perch in wherever it is good people go after death, would have been counting up the four hundred and more who came out for her. My father managed Dona's celebration with his erstwhile charm and grace. Once the public appearance ended, he fell back into depression. He left me to deal with everything, every single fucking thing. And then, to all his many friends, he accused me of abandoning him. I was furious, totally furious at his disregard. Finally back in New Jersey, I was a wreck.

•

I RETURNED TO classes at Mason Gross with my hysterical leg—not just knee, the whole fucking leg, groin, thigh front and back, knee all around, calf front and sides and back, ankle all around, all throbbing like hell. Muscle-relaxing pills didn't help. Breathing into the pain didn't help. Three Excedrin didn't help.

One day in lithography class I felt faint.

Sit down! Sit down!

My eyes would not focus.

Sit down! Sit down!

Other students' voices went muffled.

Sit down! Sit down!

I had to sit down, but sitting was too hard.

Lie down! Lie down!

I lay down.

I lay down on the floor behind the press, didn't care who saw me. No one saw me. They were too far away at the other end of the

One Hundred* Drawings for Hanneline, 2008,
mixed media, dimensions variable

room and too absorbed in their own work. I just blotted into the floor behind the press.

Strength and focus returned in a few moments, at least I thought it was a few moments. I stumbled down the hall to the water fountain and drank. My poor old body, my poor old woman's body, just could not manage it all any longer.

My doctor named this *syncope*, passing out. At least it wasn't a stroke. I managed to complete my Rutgers semester, to show some of the sixty-seven, not one hundred, drawings in *One Hundred Drawings for Hanneline*, and graduate. Whew.

11

A BAD DECISION

WHAT COLORS WERE THESE? I COULDN'T NAME them, just a mood—desperate, without clarity to give that mood a name. Those colors were showing up in my paintings, wan, desaturated grays and browns, reds drained of life, blues bereft of light, reflections of my desaturated life. I'm going backward here, for my mother hadn't yet died, but she was headed only one way. We hadn't said "die," but death already overlaid me. Something new was showing up in a shape I couldn't discern. It felt like limits.

I'd never felt the boundaries of my lifetime before, but now, in a new way, unfocused but definite, my years no longer seemed to stretch out before me. At the same time, I didn't feel lifetime boundaries as boundaries on my life. This will sound muddled. I was muddled. It wasn't that I exactly felt hurried, but I absolutely needed to move on. Urgently.

I thrashed about like one of those poor scrawny wild creatures, a wolf, a fox, in a barbed trap whose teeth bit into my ensnared paw. Wolf-me, fox-me, shackled to my fellow undergraduates' fecklessness, tardiness, incomplete assignments, and whiny foot-dragging. Jesus H. Christ!

My fellow students were roadblocks in my way, and now, in-fluenced by art school but unaware, I was thinking in a sort of careerist way, as though I were now on a route to somewhere, and they were standing, sprawling, all over my road. What about their colorful brilliance, their zany humor and stupendous overnight productions?

Forgotten.

What about their endlessly detailed narratives of frustration and delight?

Ignored.

Malaise blotted out my pleasure in their youthful bountiful-ness, for I wanted to bear down, to do, do, do, do more, now, now, now, with time pressing down on me. I sensed their uneasiness with my intensity, for I no longer had the comradeship of ambitious Ma-son Gross Keith. He abandoned me, dropping out on account of "health issues." Even my one graduate seminar left me as frustrated as my undergraduate classes. I wanted to work too much and talk too much about my work, their work, other artists' work, art his-tory, criticism, and society in art and politics. My blah blah blah, endlessly. There must be some means of pushing harder. Approach-ing his retirement on cruise control, Teacher Tom shushed me.

As my mother sank in my transcontinental parental drama, urgency—that's how it felt—urgency led me astray. Instead of spending a fourth year honing my skills as a Mason Gross under-graduate, I decided to apply to graduate school. Where was my common sense? What on earth was I thinking?

How could I not have connected my mother's decline to my irritations with Mason Gross? How did I fail to see the impact of repeated cross-country trips, each time throwing myself up against my mother's destiny and my father's misery? These correlations—so glaringly obvious to me now, so clearly recognizable as the very rea-sons that even internet therapy warns you not to make life-altering decisions in the midst of psychological turmoil—those correlations I failed to make at the time.

Rather than thinking, I felt. I felt irritation at Mason Gross, where my studies and my fellow students had formerly offered so much pleasure. My mother lay dying; I had to get out.

Get out of undergraduate school.

I wondered about graduate school, which I envisioned as a sacred place of intense study and art making. But what did it take to get in? Grades? I had excellent grades, meaning, I assumed, my work was interesting and good. Productivity? I was fuckingly productive. Visual imagination? I had that in abundance, lots of color and line inspired by art history and history history. Hmmmm, maybe the history parts weren't so positive after all. My fellow students drew their content from a well of right-now popular culture that was not my own. Definitely a weakness on my part. But, on the other hand, I could be a great colorist, even when mired in worry. Discipline? My self-discipline could build an ivory tower. Maybe another weakness.

Nonetheless, what more interesting person, what more unique character than me? Who wouldn't want a me among their students, with my ability to think and talk and encourage others? My graduate student teachers asked me for pointers and added that the students were lucky to have me in classes. I had a lot to offer, a hell of a lot to offer.

At the same time, a conviction circulated widely about the impossibility of getting into art school, kind of like a religious tenet or an urban legend. This belief discounted all that I had to offer by elevating the portfolio into admission stratosphere. The portfolio had to consist of exciting, skillful art. Was my art exciting and skillful? Eh . . . it depended on who was looking. One thing was clear: my portfolio would not show drawings of renaissance skill or cutting-edge installations. My strong points were curiosity, thoughtfulness, and extraordinary growth during my two-plus years at Mason Gross. Like every other aspirant, I wanted to go to Yale School of Art, for an excellent art school and for a phenomenal university.

That, I recognized, would constitute an astounding leap for me. I knew of ways to bridge the gap between my current portfolio and a portfolio that would get me into graduate school, programs that function like prep schools. I knew that prep school is about more than building skills. Prep school is also a place to make crucial connections with the people who matter, those artists who decide what counts as art and as art that counts as the right kind of art in the right now. Yes, you learn there, and, in addition and just as important, people who can help you get to know you. That latter point may count as heavily for an aspiring professional artist as what you stand to learn. You can be the greatest artist in the world, but if the eyes that matter aren't on your work, and if the people who count don't speak up for you, you hardly exist beyond your own local circle. I wanted more than that.

I investigated three prep programs. The School of the Art Institute of Chicago Post-Baccalaureate Certificate in Studio was a thirty-credit-hour program for building a graduate school admission portfolio. That sounded perfect for me, but it had one terrific drawback: it was in Chicago, too far away from Newark and Oakland. Maybe if I were a more driven artist, I would have set aside my marriage and my parents. But I wasn't, and I couldn't do that. Then there was the Yale Summer School at Norfolk, Connecticut. For Norfolk, I would have had to be nominated by Mason Gross while I was a junior, which I kind of was. But I had never heard of anyone going to Norfolk from Mason Gross. Was this information being kept secret from me? Or was Norfolk simply not in the Mason Gross orbit? In any case, no Norfolk for me. Then there was Skowhegan, which I'd known about forever, even in California, without knowing more about it than its storied names—Ben Shahn, Philip Pearlstein, and so on.

I looked more closely into Skowhegan, but its rule of keeping you on site for nine weeks put it out of my reach. Had I ever in recent memory gone nine whole weeks without a trip to Oakland? What if I got homesick for Glenn? Norfolk and Skowhegan, especially, seemed too much like adolescent summer camps for me to endure for twenty-four hours a day, seven days a week, for weeks on end. Exuberant young people creating art intensively, expressively in gigantic gestures and series of all-night wonders of solitary and cooperative imagination. Fantastic art. Never-seen-before art. Tattooed art kids bounding around in shorts and flip-flops, day and night, amazed by what was still news to them, annoyed by misunderstood rules, propelled by hormonal surges, drinking and drugging and fucking in the bushes, throwing up in their studios. Exhilarating, yes, indeed, but exhausting. Okay for ten or twelve hours a day, but probably not for twenty-four, not for three months. Not for me.

Clearly, the art summer camps would have done the trick of shaking my eyes loose from the twentieth century and bringing my portfolio into line with current notions of exciting art. No, wait. There was a further problem—no, there was *my* further problem—that much of currently exciting art looked to me like random piles of things: RPT. Surely there was some other art beyond RPT, for I saw other art in magazines and museums and galleries in New York City. There were a lot of different kinds of art around, some I might be able to manage. But at what price? Could I pay it? I needed some expert advice.

I TOOK MY questions to Teacher Irma, who was a visiting critic at Yale School of Art and who wrote trenchantly in the art magazines, even writing against the grain of convention. Her essays were substantive, and she wrote about women and non-white artists before they became hot, something not to be taken for granted, something I deeply appreciated. As a critic she was totally fabulous. I also liked her painting a lot. A special trip to Chinatown in New York City to see her solo show left me in awe. Her blend of abstraction and anthropomorphism reminded me of another awesome artist, the Iraqi painter Ahmed Alsoudani. They both move in and out and between figuration and abstraction with a tumultuous sense of space. He is more drawn (literally) to the chaos of life in our times than she, but they're both great colorists. His paintings are more turbulent than hers, but I find both psychologically postmodern. My student eye for process examined her ravishing paintings from a distance and up close, searching out clues on her scale and technique, her overlapping shapes to convey distance, her color—her absolutely amazing color, bombastic texture evoking collage through paint—and her imagination. Totally fabulous as a painter.

Here was the person to ask about graduate school. I approached her in the painting studio during a long break when no other students were around. I was feeling sheepish asking about graduate school when my paintings left so much to be desired. But I trusted her to cue me in, to help me parse the various qualities that count in graduate admission. I spoke with trepidation, not taking anything for granted. It was guidance I needed, a conversation about my strengths and weaknesses. That's not what I got.

When I asked her about my going to graduate school, she immediately launched a tirade:

You don't need an MFA.

You don't need professional study.

Uh-oh. My ambition as a problem. That had happened to me before.

From what I could tell, her gut reaction came from a place that people sometimes tap instinctively when faced with me: "you don't need it," whatever *it* is. I've heard this oh so many times to say I shouldn't be wanting to do what I want to do. Whatever *it* is I want, I can't have it, because I don't *need* it. (You may have heard this, too.) I had blurted out the name Yale to her as my dream graduate school, a second terrible idea. It was bad enough that I wanted to go to graduate school at all, and, now, worse that I wanted to go to Yale. She had not gone to Yale. Not only did I not *need* graduate school, I, the totally worst possible painter in the whole entire history of art, had no business aspiring to Yale. Ouch, ouch, and ouch. End of this conversation.

But no reason to back down.

I took the matter up with my friend Madeleine, a very good painter, and she talked over my situation with another artist friend, also a much more experienced painter than I. Madeleine and her friend sang me the conventional wisdom of graduate applications: portfolio is all.

Sola fide?

Solo portfolio.

Madeleine cast aspersions on my portfolio: why not take another year to bulk it up? I would have none of it. I would not—I absolutely would not—give up. Even temporarily.

Sitting outside Civic Square Building on a sunny day in the late fall, I told Madeleine why the whole matter of applications burned me so. For years, for decades, discouraging people had been telling me what I couldn't do. Nay-saying didn't apply only to art school. Madeleine could have been giving me the soundest advice in the world. No, it *was* the soundest advice in the world. Only I could not heed her reasoning. I had reasoning of my own that also made good sense.

I told her she was not the person to tell me no.

I told her that telling me no was up to the graduate schools I applied to. If they all turned me down the first time I applied, I'd apply again the next year. I had heard from my graduate student teachers that they had applied twice or thrice before getting in. But I wouldn't close off my chances without even a try.

I was emphatic.

I told her about the Colby College senior I'd met who hadn't applied to a prestigious PhD program because he didn't think he could get in. Well, that's a sure route to not getting in.

I told her with more certainty than I really had that I knew the portfolio must reach a certain threshold, but after that, I insisted, the applicant's personal qualities must kick in, qualities I had in abundance. I doubt I really convinced her. But I did give her pause, and she let up on discouragement.

Recognizing "you don't need . . ." when applied to me, I was still struck by the pervasiveness of the art-school-is-so-hard-to-get-into mantra. I—who as a student applicant got into the University of California–Berkeley, University of California–Los Angeles, Harvard, and Yale and got tenured jobs at Penn, University of North Carolina at Chapel Hill, and Princeton, and served as president of THE association of American historians the world over—had never heard such nay-saying applied to admissions. I was taking the argument all too personally, yet I knew it wasn't aimed only at me. The notion circulates as fact, and it ramped up the significance of application and acceptance.

How did they tell a strong portfolio from a weak one, especially when there's artwork in galleries every day that would not make the first cut in graduate admissions? For one thing, art doesn't appear wholesale in galleries, as in portfolio reviews. At Mason Gross I saw hundreds, literally hundreds of graduate school application portfolios. Seen by the hundreds, expertly rendered model studies reduced skill to banality. Which sank my expert fellow Mason Gross painter Jan-Vincent. For another thing, it actually *is* harder, I learned, to get into an MFA program in painting than to get into

Princeton for a PhD in history, because MFA painting programs are smaller, but similar numbers apply.

I was hurling myself, my old, academic, black self, against the stone wall of graduate-art-school-admission impossibility with a conviction born of defiance. No longer a mere step along the way into painting seriously, graduate school loomed before me like a wall, a mountain, an obstacle test of my personal worth.

This is no way to make a decision, oh, jeez, no.

But I knew enough about the difference institutions can make in evaluating personal worth, and that my personal worth in art, again, my old, academic, black self, would need all the institutional support it could gather. And there was the matter of mortality's corruption of my judgment.

Between trips to Oakland for my failing mother and distraught father, I somehow applied to four graduate art schools with a portfolio that included two paintings inspired by a photographic archive in the Brooklyn Historical Society, a multipanel drawing of the unveiling of the Harriet Tubman monument in Harlem, and a quilt collage I had made out of a drawn self-portrait.

All three drawings were figurative. The two inspired by the Brooklyn photographs were acrylic on paper, 22" × 30", both with multiple figures, both in subdued colors—one using orange and a triangle of yellow with raw umber and sepia, one with diluted pink and viridian. Though they are edited in composition, their origin in photographs is evident, and the figures do not interact. The third, clearly figurative image in charcoal on 12" × 12" paper belongs to a narrative series I had drawn of the dedication of Alison Saar's large sculpture in Harlem commemorating Harriet Tubman. In this drawing, erasures delineated space—the windows of a building, the roof of a tent—around a figure in motion that turns its back to me, the viewer.

The fourth drawing, 19" × 24", took the form of a quilt. It was figurative, but not straightforwardly. You had to look closely to make out the human form. I collaged pieces of a skeletal self-portrait in sepia and black conté crayon onto a burnt-umber ground. Again color, again subdued. The self-portrait fragments extended beyond the ground on the right side and the bottom.

UPPER LEFT: *Brooklyn Beach People*, 2008, ink on paper, 22 ½" × 30"

UPPER RIGHT: *Paper Readers*, 2008, ink on paper, 22 ½" × 30"

LOWER LEFT: *Tubman Memorial, New York City*, 2008, graphite on paper, 12" × 13 ¾"

LOWER RIGHT: *Self-Portrait Quilt Collage*, 2008, graphite, acrylic, and conté crayon on paper, 19 ¼" × 24 ½"

My Mason Gross teachers supported my decision and wrote letters of recommendation. My non–Mason Gross mentors helped me curate my portfolio. Columbia was a very long shot that Artist Stanley and Teacher Hanneline encouraged. I didn't get in there.

No loss. My Mason Gross lithography Teacher Barb wanted me at Mason Gross, which wait-listed me, begging me not to come. Crazy, I know. Maybe as an undergraduate I had already sucked all the juice I could from Mason Gross's painting faculty. My boosters all expected Yale, my first choice, to accept me. But Yale's fiery art school, in a real university that had offered me a chaired professorship in history years earlier and given me an honorary doctorate, turned me down flat. Now, that hurt. And it measured the miles separating the world of art from the world of history. Or was it universe from universe?

I had a solid second choice, the Rhode Island School of Design, with its appealing reputation for intensity and unremitting hard work. What could be more right for me? Perfect, except for the lack of a university attached—but Brown was right up the hill. RISD accepted me, and I was then and am once again deeply grateful for that. RISD's where I went. After three years of undergraduate study at Mason Gross and more personal-intellectual than painterly bona fides, I entered a world of serious art making, full-time art making. I would not be held back by undergraduate farting around. I surely was headed to art paradise. I really did think and feel that. I really did.

12

EUPHORIA

A PRETTY LITTLE CITY, PROVIDENCE, ONCE YOU'VE moved your stuff into your first-year-painter's studio, the curtains are up to block the afternoon sun, and the humidity has let up so you can stop sweating all the time. In the studio like a freshman in your first dorm. Imagine all the passion, all the hard work you came here for, in this space. Providence is so different from Newark, different from anything New Jersey.

A city to savor. Even before you settle in as a graduate painter, you can be a tourist there on the weekend, when, just as it gets dark, there come tonitruous drums, Andean flutes, and Handel's *Water Music*—all mythopoetical past. WaterFire.

WaterFire sends open boats down the Providence River, each with a bonfire, some with a juggler twirling blazing batons. The black-clad people on the boats light braziers stacked with wood along the riversides, a contrast of inky violet and fiery cadmium yellow against the backdrop of night. Smartphones flash. All your feral water + fire instincts kick in, remanding you to millennia before smartphones, before email, before the internet, before houses, before clothes. It's cool enough to wrap up in your bearskin, as your face and fingers protrude into nature's air. WaterFire sticks you back beside the bonfires of summer camp, what they call a simpler, better time. Yes, a fine place to be, Providence.

Providence was too far from Newark for me to commute daily, as in New Jersey to Mason Gross. I took a North Main Street apartment building full of RISD students that overlooked a brook. My place was one and a half stories up from the street, one bedroom, nice and cozy. I walked about twenty minutes to my painting studio in the Fletcher Building on Union and Weybosset Streets. First-year graduate painting students shared studios, meaning one large room divided in two, with one studio nearer the windows—mine—the other without windows but more wall space, next to the hall, Juhyun's. We were the two non-white students in our cohort of nine.

In my first month at the Rhode Island School of Design, I experienced something I scarcely felt during my years of harried parental worry, historical organization presidential torture, and *THWP* chores: contentment. I was feeling so good and so free, so liberated. My mother was safely dead, her affairs wound up. My father had sloughed off the worst of his grief and even some of his depression. He was attending noontime concerts at the University of California–Berkeley, as we used to do before he retired from the university Chemistry Department many years before. My husband agreed to my relocating to Providence, visiting every couple of weeks or so with our two traveling tabby cats. I concentrated on what I could see and the art I could make. I felt so free.

My daily walk to my studio in the Fletcher Building, an un-Jersey commute, no train, no automobile, no parking worries, took me down Main and Canal Streets to Westminster Street over Weybosset and Union Streets. What I saw on my walk was an old city—well, in American terms—with handsome buildings dating from when Providence was a hub of finance (thanks to the Atlantic slave trade, banking, and insurance) and manufacturing (producing machinery, tools, jewelry, hand-wrought stonework), with costly decoration just for the hell of it, names and purposes cut in stone on pediments, now saddened by "Space available" and "For lease" on too many storefronts. Many of the beautiful older buildings were in use as apartments or, in the case of Fletcher, as artists' studios. RISD's soaring Fleet Library at 15 Westminster Street was the renovated Rhode Island Hospital Trust National Bank building.

New-student orientation introduced me to that fabulous library, and I never left—I, who have been carting books home from libraries since time immemorial. Like every other physical space at RISD, Fleet Library is handsomely designed; RISD is not a design school for nothing. The stacks are open, so I could just pull books, any books, off the shelf, settle down on the floor or in an easy chair, and look through as many books as I could carry. Idly browsing the stacks, I discovered a row of books on the French painter–textile artist Sonia Delaunay with knock-your-socks-off color and geometry. I sat on the floor for an hour with her work, no particular goal in mind, just looking. Beyond the books in the regular collection, and of special interest to me, was the collection of artist's books on the second floor, a place I visited often, for I saw artist's books as my own destiny. I could do that, I reckoned, knowing I had plenty of time for learning the craft. I was free.

Fleet Library (55,000 square feet, 155,000 volumes) is bigger in size but smaller in collections than Princeton's Marquand Library (46,000 square feet, 400,000 volumes), a treasure of national scale. But Fleet Library does something Marquand doesn't: it lends books to students. For instance: both libraries hold Mirela Proske's *Lucas Cranach the Elder*, published in 2007, the most recent book on this pivotal Northern Renaissance painter. With the well-groomed Princeton campus outside picture windows, I could read it comfortably in Marquand. I could scan a limited number of pages to download on a flash drive or email to myself. I couldn't borrow it. But from Fleet, I could check it out and take it home. Read it propped up on my tummy lying on my couch. This meant a lot, as I was making my own art inspired by Cranach and Romare Bearden, stretching out my image and my inquiry in Fleet Library's bower.

How I got to Cranach and Bearden is a longish story that has to do with my art and the bounty of a library I could roll around in and borrow from and investigate at leisure. And investigate at leisure I did, perhaps so much at leisure to bore you with the details I pursued in a myth that said so much about spitefulness and lust and beauty and bribery and war. Bear with me again in this spirit of unfettered pursuit in a library where my time was all my own to spend there. I had in mind somewhere down the road making an artist's book on the subject of personal beauty, whose Western history goes back to Greek mythology and the judgment of Paris. I had discovered the erotic dimension of the story many years earlier in Hubert Damisch's *The Judgment of Paris (Le jugement de Pâris. Iconologie analytique)*. All on its own, the judgment of Paris deserves the artist's book that RISD was helping me envision.

Here's the story. The judgment of Paris begins with the gods at the wedding feast of Peleus and Thetis, a pairing that does not withstand feminist investigation. Peleus, king of the Myrmidons of Thessaly, had abducted Thetis, a sea nymph, after Zeus and Poseidon, both of whom were in love with her, had decided to give her to Peleus. To give her to Peleus. She refused Peleus at first, but he bound her up while she slept, thereby convincing her to marry him. This is how making up a woman's mind was done back then.

Was Thetis happy at her wedding feast? Myth does not say or hint at whether that's even a fitting question. Myth does say that Eris, the goddess of discord, had not been invited—understandably.

Eris came anyway. Throwing a golden apple inscribed "For the Fairest" into the party, she sowed her discord. Three goddesses—Hera, wife of Zeus; Athena, Zeus's daughter; and Aphrodite, the goddess of love—struggled over the apple. Zeus, husband and father, recognized an impossible decision. He handed the apple to Hermes and sent him and the three goddesses to Paris, a Trojan prince in temporary employment as a shepherd and presumably free of Zeus's entanglement in these godly family values. Are you still with me?

To win the golden apple, the goddesses bribed Paris with extravagant promises. Hera offered him imperial power over Asia and Europe; Athena offered wisdom and military might; Aphrodite offered the most beautiful woman in the world. Paris gave in to lust. He decided for Aphrodite and for Helen (daughter of Zeus and Leda), queen of Laconia, wife of Menelaus. Getting into Helen's bed necessitated her abduction, the habitual means of securing a female sex partner. Abduction set off the Trojan War.

If you want to know the rest of this part of the story, here it is: Paris killed Achilles, the war's greatest, handsomest, bravest warrior, the son of Peleus and Thetis, with an arrow to his heel. In that same battle, Philoctetes mortally wounded Paris, whose first wife, Oenone (turns out he already had a wife), possessed means to heal him. But Oenone was still annoyed with Paris over his running off with Helen. By the time Oenone got over her chagrin, Paris had died. Oenone threw herself on his funeral pyre. As we used to say in the twentieth century, what goes around, comes around.

What a story! No wonder the judgment of Paris has attracted artists and writers since the ancient Greeks.

Reading up on Romare Bearden in Fleet Library, I made the serendipitous discovery of a print Bearden had made, inspired by the *Judgment of Paris* of Lucas Cranach the Elder. I brought home the book on Bearden to scan the image for my studio wall, next to Cranach and Raphael. Studio walls were for display of what inspired us or what we wanted to borrow from or what we were working on, a kind of rotating art exhibition, our own personal *musée imaginaire.*

Bearden is usually identified as an African American painter and the postwar American pioneer of the use of collage, which is correct, as far, not nearly far enough, as it goes. As an undergraduate art major at Berkeley in the 1960s, I was aware of Bearden's early figurative work, which did not particularly move me—too muddy, too blocky in the style of the times. Give me his later collages. While taking a special interest in African American history and culture and his black artists' community in New York, Bearden never limited his artistic vision, not in terms of subject matter, not in terms of process.

He studied with the German expressionist George Grosz at the Art Students League.

He pursued philosophy and art in Paris. Always interested in art in its broadest international scope, he counted André Malraux's *Musée imaginaire* as a seminal influence.

Bearden's wide range attracted me too, so you can imagine my delight in Fleet Library on finding Bearden's 1969 collagraph on Cranach's *Judgment of Paris*, part of his *Prelude to Troy* series. What on earth is a collagraph?

A collagraph is a print of a collage combining two techniques I'd already been interested in, collage and printmaking. To make a collagraph, you cut out shapes of paper and textiles of various textures and paste them down. The cutting and pasting create an uneven ("tonal") surface. Then you roll ink over the uneven surface knowing that ink will pool in the spaces where the different surfaces meet. Place paper on top and run the sandwich through a press. The ink around the raised portions of the collage creates line, while the uneven surface makes the paint thicker and thinner and, therefore, darker and lighter. To increase contrast, Bearden would have rubbed away and added ink after the plate went through the press. In his graphite gray monochrome collagraph of the judgment of Paris, the two processes of collage and printing produce collagraph's characteristic textures.

The collagraph linked me to Bearden in Harlem. In Harlem, Bearden was a close friend of the writer Albert Murray, who figures in African American literary history. The collagraph also linked Bearden—and, so, linked me—to Cranach the Elder, a court painter in Saxony, Germany, living in Weimar, a close friend of Martin Luther.[6] Cranach the Elder's *Judgment of Paris* is one of the three most famous of scores of works on this theme. The other two are Marcantonio Raimondi's 1517–1520 etching, made in Rome from a drawing by Raphael, and Peter Paul Rubens's 1639 painting, made in Antwerp.

Cranach the Elder depicted in Gothic style a much quieter scene than Raimondi and Raphael. Cranach shows three slender, pale young women, perky of breast and behind, who are nude but for hats and jewelry. Looking at one woman coquettishly holding her ankle and another glancing over her shoulder and flexing her fingers, I'd call Cranach's goddesses adolescent girls. Certainly these are the cutest, youngest goddesses of the three popular renditions. The young women stand beside two male figures, Hermes and Paris, both men in full armor, with a horse tied to a tree behind them and in the distance, a craggy, oxide-green mountain landscape and a pale, cobalt-blue sky. Hermes's orange armor provides the main spot of contrasting color.

The more I learned luxuriating in the freedom of Fleet Library,

---

6. Interestingly, Lucas Cranach's names are instrumental. His family name was Maler, or "painter," and Cranach is a rendering of his birthplace of Kronach. If I lived in Cranach's time and town, Maler would be my last name, too.

the better this story got, with abductions, discord, bribes, the most legendary war in Greek antiquity, female beauty, repeated pictorial treatments. In addition to Cranach the Elder and Raimondi and Rubens, I discovered works by Botticelli, Wtewael, Watteau, Angelica Kauffman, Renoir, Cézanne, Dalí. RISD gave me this. Back home in New Jersey in the perturbation of normal life, I could not have lolled around in these images, painters, and art history. Yes, RISD gave this to me. Thank you, RISD.

Thank you, RISD, for the time to stretch out and follow leads— in the library and in my painting studio. I was euphoric.

Euphoric.

This was what I came to art school for, *exactly* what I sought at RISD. Freedom. I devoted hour after morning hour to the printmaking studio, fumbling with processes, learning to make prints in step by steps of learning. I had time for the details of countless mistakes. Perfect.

One day on Canal Street, a feeling crept over me as an unusual sensation I could not name as I carried out an assignment. In "drawing" class, Teacher Kevin had assigned us a piece he described as indexical. What he meant was an image made by the physical being of the object, not a line drawing. This assignment let me act on my image of Providence. On my daily walk from apartment to Fletcher, I had admired the city's ornate manhole covers, artful citations of companies' cables snaking below, changing names as the utility companies were bought and sold. Kevin's assignment let me make a rubbing of one of Providence's amazingly detailed manhole covers for my indexical drawing.

I found a perfect example on Canal Street, near Park Row at the end of the Roger Williams National Memorial. It was a sunny fall day, warm enough for comfort but cool enough not to sweat. Carrying a piece of 48" × 60" cold press watercolor paper and a stick of compressed charcoal, I made myself understood by the parking lot attendant on the corner, who lent me two orange traffic cones to hold down my paper. I stretched out my paper, anchored it with cones, got down on the sidewalk, and rubbed. It was like building a sand castle at the beach down there on the ground, rubbing and rubbing, never minding the physical effort. The paper's tooth held the grease of the intensely black compressed charcoal, producing an image of high contrast and, in its text, a testament to the history of the city. How I might have looked to passersby or motorists never entered my mind.

Providence Manhole Cover, 2009, compressed charcoal on paper, approx. 36" × 36"

As I knelt on the sidewalk rubbing paper on a manhole cover, the feeling spoke its name: happiness. Yes, again, euphoria. The euphoria of doing physical work on my knees over a big piece of thick watercolor paper and making black marks in the sun, creating a black and white and gray image I had never made before.

This was not quite like the contentment I had felt in my Mason

Gross years before all my commitments crowded out lasting satisfaction. In New Jersey I was daily in transit between home, with my regular life, and art school. This RISD happiness came with the relief that my other responsibilities were behind me. This sense of freedom made it all feel quite new, with freedom the quality I have always associated with art making. I was so happy.

In the drawing crit, we put up our work. Juhyun had blotted her lipstick several times to create a textured monoprint. Collin had channeled Robert Rauschenberg and driven his car over inked paper to make a drawing textured by tire tracks. All very good, very interesting. My turn. Teacher Kevin and knowing fellow student Mike dissed my beautiful manhole cover rubbing as hackneyed.

Don't you know that artists made manhole rubbings, like, back in the '90s?

Manhole cover rubbings are so over.

I rolled up my rubbing and tucked it in the corner of my studio.

IN MY PAINTING studio I spent hour after hour in the afternoons making drawings that ranged from interesting to boring. Though flopping around visually, I was feeling at home, just taking the time to do what I was doing. My apartment's dining table, my all-purpose table, incidentally the spot where I ate, was a work space for classroom assignments, covered with work and the leavings of work: paper, ink, colored doodles, knives, adhesive, and paint. With no one else to accommodate, my art supplies took over my space, boundless in color and texture. These were the things I lived with. In the evening I drew and painted and monoprinted smaller pieces on my dining table. In my apartment-slash-studio, art making never stopped. It didn't have to. Freedom.

One evening, after a day of painting all day in Fletcher and a salad and a glass of red wine at Tazza, I returned to the apartment.

At my table, I made a piece. No, the piece made itself. The piece made itself from paper scraps left over from my other work.

My eyes moved my hand.

My hand moved in its old familiar writing rhythm, left to right. Horizontal lines.

The movement of some other hand, the hand of Omar Khayyam's "moving finger." The moving finger of the *Rubáiyát*, having writ, moves on. Like in writing rhythm, but not the same. Not writing history; no facts, no events. This hand untethered from the past. Drawing at my table, my hand freed of intention. The "moving finger," not of Omar Khayyam, but of Len Barry's pop song from 1967. (How did you remember that?) Barry quotes Khayyam and instructs you:

> Today is history,
> don't let it
> give you misery.
> Forget it.
> Just remember me.
> I said it.

My kitchen table's moving finger, no discursive meaning. No word, no figure. Having writ moved on, only the meaning of what can be seen: color, composition, texture, shape, and size, like cloth woven on a narrow loom in Mali or India or Providence, Rhode Island.

Out of six leftover pieces of paper about 6" × 12" each, there came a long narrow drawing, colored ink on paper, reaching across horizontally. A scroll whose narrative—it is a narrative—cannot be read. The sections don't quite line up. The wet-into-wet painting looks unstable. Against unjustified lines of pale, iridescent primary cyan, burnt sienna, and burnt umber, it collaged bright little colored shapes cut from other drawings. Tiny saturated quotations from who knows where. The lines flowed beneath the collage, unhindered by disparate colors and shapes. Where is this thing going? I don't know. The drawing process took over; I could not stop. I had to stop. Going on past 11:00 p.m., I pulled myself up short and went to bed.

The piece is abstract, tempting you to read it. But it makes no sense whatever. A second coming of my one hundred drawings for Hanneline. Same abstract spirit. Its name? Only the noncommittal *Long Piece*, not the useless *Untitled*, but the next thing to it.

Long Piece, 2009, ink and paper collage on paper, 71 ½" × 6"

Long Piece lacks subject matter, utterly. It was the most popular piece in my midterm crit.

I GUSHED TO a couple of friends, "I've learned more in a week and a half at RISD than in my whole undergraduate education!"

That's an exaggeration—a gigantic exaggeration. But I did learn a very great deal at RISD in just a few days, so quickly it felt revolutionary. How I learned:

In my first crit with Teacher David, he identified himself by field:

My bailiwick is formal properties of painting, such as color and composition.

He asked me to talk about the composition of Cranach's *Judgment of Paris* on my wall, which I really couldn't do, so he explained about sight lines and movement through the piece, how it's divided in half and quarters, and the diagonals moving through the painting. He contrasted the movement through the Cranach with the looping squiggles of the Rubens.

Then Teacher David wanted to see some of my work. I showed him the black-and-white gestural drawing from my admissions portfolio.

This drawing points in the direction my work will be moving in, I said with a measure of pride. The 24" × 18" charcoal drawing inspired by a model's pose contrasted emphatic mark making with passages of smudged gray. It was clearly figurative but not totally mimetic. I thought it possessed a nice feeling of movement and a hint of abstraction.

David looked at it:

It's a beautiful drawing, and well made. Nice gestural marks, good sense of depth, great line quality. But it's very twentieth-century. It reminds me of Arshile Gorky.

Arshile Gorky or no, I recognized mid-twentieth-century as not a good thing.

Twentieth-Century Drawing, 2008, ink and graphite on paper, 24" × 18"

Then I showed him another piece of mine I also liked, the series of charcoal drawings of the Harriet Tubman memorial dedication. This is more contemporary, he said. I like its raw and primitive character. Nice flattened space.

Raw and primitive. Skipping over "raw" and "primitive," I heard flattened space as something I'd been scolded about at Mason Gross. But with Teacher David, this was not a problem; to the contrary, it was a mark of contemporary style. He added,

Today most artists draw from photographs—plein air painting is dead. Photographs flatten space.

Whoa! Wasn't that a relief. Voilà! No more need to feel apologetic about painting from photographs and producing flat spaces.

Teacher Irma (same Teacher Irma as at Mason Gross) came for an auspicious crit in the afternoon, offering to give me a tutorial on acrylic paints a week later. She approved of my beauty project, provided it not become a straitjacket. I said my goal would be to make one hundred paintings of all sorts: figurative, abstract, and all between. Irma agreed—what I would need to do is produce masses of work. You have to make a lot of work, she said, because 85 percent of what artists make is junk.

This comforted me, to the point that I later quoted it back to her. (Maybe not a good idea.)

The evening's "drawing" class had no drawing in it. It was show-and-tell about embarrassing experiences and songs, funny videos, and other ways of getting acquainted. We showed videos, and Anna's, the last and best, was a *Saturday Night Live* skit, "Dick in a Box." Highly recommended.

When my turn came to play a piece of music I was embarrassed to admit liking, I played Pat Metheny's "James," so soft and orange-ly feel-good. But even if I didn't want to own it, "James" fit my euphoria, my happy, sappy mood those early RISD days.

I WAS ENJOYING an interdisciplinary course outside the Painting Department: AD Colab, for "Art and Design: Interdisciplinary Collaboration in Theory and Practice," taught by a painter and a textile designer. It embraced the increasing interrelationship between art and design, which made a lot of sense to me, with artists now using design tools and designers embracing complexity and contradiction, approaches traditionally associated with fine art. Students from various disciplines would read and discuss key texts and collaborate in joint projects to stretch our imaginations. We would visit New York artists and designers working at the intersections of the two fields. Even better, Duhirwe, a printmaker, my sister African American, was also in the course. A beautiful thirty-two-year-old who felt older than her twenty-something peers, she was originally from Rwanda and had attended Spelman College. We became and remain friends.

In AD Colab I saw all kinds of student work, some fitting into the students' home departments, some not. Duhirwe the printmaker was making sculpture and paintings. Kai, a German architecture student, presented a labyrinthine video in our initial slide night. We visited artists and design-oriented companies like Printed Matter (artist's books) and Dieu Donné (hand papermaking and collaboration with artists). With a stimulating breadth of intellect and process, the class ranged far beyond painting.

On one New York visit, AD Colab class met with the hot (youngish) artist Paul Chan, whose then current project looked like porn to me (with my lying twentieth-century eyes) but which he defended as an homage to the Marquis de Sade, whose thought, Chan reminded us, encompassed more than sadism. We had a good Q and A with Chan, during which he maintained that art isn't a thing but an idea. Given its status as objects that are marketed for sale, I disagreed. Later, on the subway to Pentagram Design, I had a rewarding talk with Teacher Brooks that began but did not end with his agreeing that the marketing infrastructure around art seals its status as material objects.

Swaying in the moving subway train, I told Brooks that reading for class had proved very useful to me, caught as I am between art and design, as in my book projects, books being considered part of design, but at the same time, my belonging to the Painting Department, the heart and soul of the fine arts. I started telling him about a book project I envisioned about a trip across Canada that Glenn and I had recently taken.

When we started our trip, I said to Brooks above the subway clatter, I was taking photos of Glenn and me in memorable tourist settings: Here we are in front of a soaring mountain in the Rockies. Here we are before a dramatic waterfall. You know, usual vacation photographs.

Once I decided to make an artist's book about our trip, my strategy changed:

I switched my photo documentation to the everyday objects that characterized Canada, like electric line pylons, traffic signs, and roads.

Brooks interrupted,

You have shifted your attention from the *figure* to the *ground*.

Lightbulb went off over my head right there in the subway car.

In his field of textile design, he explained, the ground is as important as the figure, because in textiles you can't just leave any space unattended.

So here was yet another moment of learning on a theme I'd heard in Mason Gross crits. I now saw that my Arshile Gorky drawing neglected parts of my composition, the ground, and concentrated too exclusively on the figures that claimed my attention. Ground makes a scene; it's what gives an image local specificity.

MY STUDIO MATE Juhyun was from South Korea. At the barbecue for first-year painting graduate students hosted by Teacher David, Juhyun assured me she was a serious student, not a typical rich Korean girl, and not just because she was nearly thirty. She was my suite mate, but not for long. By late fall she got married in Korea. Pregnancy forestalled her returning for spring semester classes.

That early evening at the barbecue, Juhyun said the RISD undergraduates were so heavily Korean because the families swore by the *U.S. News and World Report* rankings that put Yale and RISD at the top for art schools. RISD was getting a very select group of young Korean students.

My experience with Korean undergraduates came in a typography course recommended by faculty aware of my interest in text. Like all RISD undergraduates, the typography students were very skilled, and, unlike me, they were used to the software we used, the diabolical Adobe Illustrator, an instrument of torture with hooks and chains. Illustrator works off vectors, not pixels like Photoshop, which did not snarl me nearly so much. The undergraduate typographers generously showed me that most of the tools I needed from

Illustrator I could find in Photoshop. The kids were great, even though, like the undergraduates at Mason Gross, most of their preferred imagery came from popular culture, especially from advertisements. Too much pinkly Hello Kitty for my taste. But a source of inspiration in design.

Moving into my apartment and into my studio, I had already discovered that RISD was very heavily Korean, with the undergraduates mostly immigrant and some of the graduate students Korean American. Black students, immigrant or native, were awfully rare. I found one friendly young man in textiles, an undergraduate, so I didn't see much of him. There was my friend Duhirwe the printmaker, and Rubens, a second-year painter, from Brazil, with a Brazilian awareness of the African diaspora. Rubens wasn't black, but he carried a social consciousness drawn from many years' residence in the United States.

I couldn't help feeling that the presence of so many young immigrants—wealthy young immigrants, because RISD offered next to no financial aid—tipped the atmosphere away from social engagement, away even from social awareness. Fostering immersion in the visual, art at RISD seemed to exist in a sphere apart from the tensions of American society.

This came initially as a relief. How fortunate I was, I felt, how grateful was I for the chance to devote myself single-mindedly to my artwork! For the most part, American politics, especially American race issues, did not distract me from my work at hand.

13

GRIEF

THE GOOD PART WAS THE WORK, THE *WHY* I WAS there. Hours alone in my painting studio in Fletcher, hours nearly alone in the printmaking studio. I'd go to Benson Hall to the third-floor printmaking studio in the mornings, long before other students were ready to face work. I spent the whole of one day in the printmaking studio on lettering across Michael Jackson's face, painting the ground, outlining the lettering in pencil with a stencil, then filling in with red oxide flow acrylic. Another day, Apollo Belvedere, translucent paper on a dark ground.

Hours in the printmaking studio produced minimal results in screen-printing, where I had no experience and the liquid photo emulsion proved recalcitrant. The studio helper got the fucking red stuff out of my wretched screen, leaving me back where I started. I spent so much time over the weeks wrestling with the processes in printmaking that I hardly reached a place where the distinctive characteristics of printmaking—the textures, the contrasts—emerged in my images. Just one snarl after another, hour after hour after hour, week after week. Actually, it wasn't all that bad, engrossed as I was in the process.

Jackson and Belvedere, 2009, hand-colored screen print,
approx. 24" × 48"

Wrestling with the silk screen, I placed Apollo Belvedere, the very quintessence of classical male beauty, next to Michael Jackson, whose remaking of his physical image into a collection of the most conventional traits of (female American) beauty has fascinated me

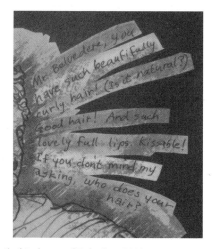

LEFT: Left detail of *Jackson and Belvedere*, 2009
RIGHT: Right detail of *Jackson and Belvedere*, 2009

for a long time. In my prints, they were talking to one another, complimenting each other on their appearance and asking who does their hair—Apollo Belvedere with curlier locks than Michael Jackson. The piece fell flat in crit, but I enjoyed playing with two figures of beauty from different historical eras. I amused myself in the print shop, working steadily and at my own pace alone, listening to *Afropop Worldwide*, *Deutsche Welle*, Cassandra Wilson, and Abbey Lincoln. Sometimes the other students played their music out loud.

During one of my printmaking marathons, another student played a song I recognized; usually their music was all news to me, a twenty-first-century education in sound. This time the song was "Try a Little Tenderness," one of my mother's favorite songs.

> *She may be weary*
> *Young girls, they do get weary*
> *Wearing that same old, shabby dress.*
> *But when she's weary*
> *Try a little tenderness.*

I always heard it with sadness, even before her death, as an evocation of the days when my parents were first settling in Oakland and didn't have much money and their native Californian relatives looked down on them for being from the South—Texas being the South. I imagined the song's meaning in two ways, as my mother's wishing my father, her husband, had tried more tenderness, and, in a sunnier version, as my mother's appreciation that even though they didn't have much money then, he *had* tried tenderness. In the print studio I teared up for my mother, her regrets in life, the disappointments she carried to her death. The song ended, my silk screen no farther along.

In light of my silk screen's withholding, I had to resort to the unusual step, for me, of working in the print shop in the evening. I often lost track of time while painting at Fletcher, staying into the night, but printmaking at night was something new. I climbed one hundred steps from Main Street to Benefit Street and up to the third floor of Benson Hall. The printmaking studio was nearly empty, just a printmaker or two and a student monitor. As I came in, the student monitor stopped me.

Are you taking a class?

I had been so carefree going around RISD, so "moonshiny" (to use a word from *THWP* that was Thomas Carlyle's dismissal of Ralph Waldo Emerson). The printmaking monitor caught me totally unawares. Concentrating on my work in a protective bubble, I had let my guard down. I had closely focused my gaze on my art and narrowed the peripheral vision I normally shared with the animals of the forest that are prey. I had lost sight of how others, strangers, might be seeing me. My guard was down, way down.

Am I taking a class? Why else would I be up here on the third floor of Benson Hall in the night? Wait, come back to the regular American world, where that isn't so much a question eliciting information as a hurdle to be overcome. In a second, I was remanded to my country, where race counts all the time. I don't know what was in her mind at that moment, didn't know what *she* meant. It didn't matter what she meant, what she might *really* have meant, because her question went straight into a tradition that I recognized, a demand for justification.

I heard her question as: This is America, and you are black. You don't belong here.

I heard: You are out of place here. Explain yourself before you can gain entry.

I hadn't been looking at myself through the eyes of others. I hadn't been looking at myself at all. If I had, I would have seen an older woman dressed casually—still in my white-T-shirt-black-pants outfit from Mason Gross (but having learned from art-world observation that the white New Balance walking shoes would have to go)—not as someone scoping out the place to steal things, an interloper against whom RISD needed protection. Did I look like a thief, like someone who didn't belong there? Did I look strange? Or did I just look black?

Before my RISD-induced swoon of art-concentration euphoria, I kept at my ready disposal a counter for inappropriate statements. As though I had not understood, I would ask the speaker of ugliness to repeat what had been said. Making an offensive speaker repeat or elaborate would usually clear the air. It's a tactic that you can use, too. Once at a swanky dinner in the Berkshires next to the drunken lawyer husband of a member of my older women's group, I ramped up my technique. He had assured me of my great good luck of having ancestors who had been transported to North America in the Atlantic slave trade. Wasn't I grateful for having escaped Africa!

Oh? As if I had not understood.

Tell me more.

In a kind of nuclear option, I asked him which places were my ancestors lucky to have been delivered from, which one(s)? I dragged the offender through an examination of the current situation of every single fucking country in West Africa, one after the other in geographical order. Country by country around the coast of West and Central Africa, from Senegal right on around the Bight of Benin to Angola. I took him on an excruciating tour through his ignorance, a pitiless examination that left onlookers not simply astonished but totally aghast.

The printmaking studio in Benson Hall did not merit a bomb. Had I been on my usual guard, however, I would have asked the monitor, a young white woman, to repeat her request and clarify it: what kind of proof did she wish to see? Should I pull out my RISD

ID? A class roll? But in those early RISD days, in my bubble, I had laid down my bomb, my sword, and my shield.

My guard was down, and all I could say was:

Yes.

She recognized the uselessness of her initial query; unless I really were carrying a class roll around with me or my ID as some kind of pass document, some necessary form of proof for the likes of me, how was she to ascertain I really was taking a class? She began explaining at hapless length that *they* had to control access to the print shop. Which was practically empty.

Was such policing the regular thing in the print shop in the evening, her question addressed to each person coming in? I don't know. I do know that such questions routinely serve to inform people that they're considered out of place, that they need to pass an additional test—are you taking a class?—before being allowed in.

So RISD wasn't paradise after all. I put on my apron and looked in the drying rack for the print I had been toiling over.

Gone.

My print was gone. Someone had emptied the drying rack. My print was nowhere to be found. Was this all a conspiracy against me? To hell with trying to figure that out. Start over. I ran one hundred steps down to the RISD store on Main Street, squeezed in moments before closing, bought another pad of paper, and ran back up the one hundred steps to the printmaking studio to repeat the endless job of tearing paper and placing registration tabs.

ONCE RISD'S SPELL on me had broken, once my all-art-all-the-time bubble burst, other annoyances appeared, some really quite minor. One evening I trudged up to Woods-Gerry for the opening of a student-curated show. It had more curators—nineteen—than pieces of art.

A gigantic painting dominated the show, a life-size, 6' 7" × 11' 9" copy of the Russian artist Ilya Repin's 1881–1891 *Reply of the Zaporozhian Cossacks*, which Clement Greenberg's classic 1939 article "Avant-garde and Kitsch" had used as its example of kitsch.[7] You had to know the back story, a totally obscure back story, to understand the painting's meaning. The undergraduate painters were free to evoke art history and history history and to come away from it with praise. How cunning of them, how clever. But this was the kind of history-based work no one wanted me, the former historian, to make. Talk about a double standard.

The rest of the show presented a hodge-podge: a large video installation of the ocean projected behind bunched-up plastic, three found paintings (one actually bought, a charming nineteenth-century seascape with a spouting whale), and sound-art and sculpture. There were nineteen different press releases. Total incoherence. Totally approved.

I was such an old fuddy-duddy among the frolicking youth, a twentieth-century relic, a repository of useless knowledge, of experience no longer interesting, a fogy wanting art to be artful.

More incoherence confronted me in the AD Colab class that had so delighted me. Collaboration—"Colab"—was a crucial part of the course, and I, always on time, always organized, always ever so disciplined, was working with young people with—how shall I say—dissimilar work habits. Yes, I was a tight-ass. Three of us planned our collaboration: a white architecture student named Greg, a jewelry maker from Taiwan named Lisa, and me. We talked and talked and talked and talked and talked. I thought

7. In case you want to know, in 1676 the Zaporozhian Cossacks, having defeated the Ottoman Empire's sultan, sent him a letter full of profanity. In the painting, the uncouth Cossacks revel in their crude insults to a highly civilized sovereign.

we were talking in circles. Like heedless children in a playground, Greg and Lisa romped around in ideas impossible to materialize. Their suggestions would require enormous expenditures on materials, or we would have to photograph or video a performance involving an audience deeply committed to our project. Such was the incoherence. Oh, hell, I thought, what a proud ignorance of narrative and skill, naïveté proffered as cute innocence. This was so hard on my sense of clarity, but I tried to talk myself out of crankiness.

We finally produced a paper sculpture embodying the changing state of disintegration through writing in black ink on paper left out in the rain. Not so bad after all. Even better, I learned a lesson I badly needed to learn.

Letting their imaginations ramble, Lisa and Greg were absolutely right. I was absolutely wrong to focus from the outset on how we might actually pull the piece off. My AD Colab collaborators helped me unwind some, to let go and let up. I took a step away from how Glenn and I as scholars had thought for years.

Before this class, with its collaborative projects, I would have agreed with Glenn wholeheartedly that,

What isn't coherent is bullshit.

How very twentieth-century.

How so not true.

Thanks to Lisa and Greg and AD Colab, I was losing my reverence for coherence. It was hard for me, oh god excruciatingly hard for me, to let go of reasoning that had been mine for so long. But I had to move on and adjust. I had to adapt to the DIY aesthetic prevailing at RISD and in The Art World generally, where mistakes are to remain and accidents are to be embraced.

Here were two solvents diluting my commitment to coherence—one solvent social in nature, calling up past experiences as a black American, the other solvent related to my personal proclivities, my history of thinking like a scholar, and, most likely, the organization-man leanings of my Silent Generation. Incoherence and disorganization seemed liked a test; "are you taking a class?" reminded me that RISD was as seeded with snares as life beyond art school.

So what the hell else is new, you ask.

Of course! You should have known better than to think you could escape.

Right. But I confess to have been bopping along naively, wordlessly assuming myself in a protected realm of art.

Another AD Colab experience plopped RISD smack in the middle of life in America. Once again, it was my architect collaborator, but now it was his refusal to engage with our only reading by a black author, "An Aesthetics of Blackness: Strange and Oppositional," bell hooks's 1990 essay on art and beauty.

hooks's essay has three main parts. The first and third, on her grandmother's aesthetic, open and close the essay. The central portion explains and critiques the Black Arts Movement of the 1960s. This middle section invites a discussion beyond the white mainstreams of art and design that had been our class's subject matter up to that point. You could say that part would only interest some people. I'm trying to be generous here. I wouldn't be one to say that, of course, because I consider black art an integral part of American art, that if you want to think about American art, you have to include black art. That's what I think.

Be that as it may, the first and last sections of "Aesthetics of Blackness" raise obviously fundamental issues of class and consumerism that affect everyone, no matter their race or their interests in art. hooks says consumer capitalism has corrupted most Americans' concepts of art and beauty, turning art into a commodity to be possessed. She says her poor, unlettered, quilt-making grandmother taught her "to see," and that way of seeing reveals the connection of art to inner well-being. hooks concludes that beauty should have a purpose, to foster critical social engagement and the experience of pleasure. Quoting John Berger and Hal Foster as critics offering useful guidance, she doesn't limit her wish to black people or black art. In AD Colab, Greg, the architecture student, didn't see things that way.

He wouldn't read the piece, he said; he couldn't relate to it, because the author was black. (Gasp!)

I responded in a very, very, very even voice that did not judge my student colleague.

This isn't an unusual response among Americans, I said, because racial difference often seems like an unbridgeable chasm.

Phoebe, a British student, joined in with, I've noticed that about Americans and find it shocking. In the UK, she said, all Britons are Britons, no matter their race or ethnicity.

I did not reply, Just try to tell that to black Britons.

I said the refusal was regrettable, because hooks was making useful observations about the art of people without formal education. So in addition to not pulling his weight in our collaborative project, the architecture student was a narrow-minded little twit.

I started feeling relieved not to be young in that environment, where you have to pretend that art is above material concerns, above race, class, and gender, things we didn't talk about. I pined for a university. I wished I could have gone to Yale.

WORKING EVENINGS AT painting and printmaking, I was often eating in RISD's imaginatively designed dining halls, a smaller one in the Fleet Library building, the larger one called the Met up the hill. These dining halls' high ceilings magnified their importance, and the student art on their walls was engaging. Like museums that proclaim their artiness through audacious architecture, RISD's eating halls belong to a school of design. They reminded me that I was within an artists' realm, a place where I was starting to feel out of place.

Day after day after day I ate alone among undergraduates laughing uproariously and commiserating dramatically over what was Technicolor red-orange hilarious and what was acrylic cyan-green catastrophic. Everything new. Everything just born. Drama, always. Undergraduates' lives were so vivid. I, on the other hand, was living in a shadowed realm in ink—black, gray, walnut. In their arty costumes and fabulous tattoos, they nuzzled one another, arms on shoulders, kisses on cheeks. They laughed some more. They chose their vegetarian meals together, paid up together, sat down together, fed off each other's plates, and left together arm in arm. Everything mattered so deeply. I heard one man ask a woman why she was alone. The people she had eaten with had just left, she explained. She wasn't essentially alone.

I was essentially alone. At the Met for my dinner after cleaning up and preparing my silk screen, I sat by myself, knowing no one. I always ate and did everything else by myself. I was starting to get tired of being so much alone, so different from everyone else in so many ways and so always alone.

NO MORE BUBBLE. I was now firmly back in America, where vexation accumulated. Teacher Kevin brushed off my query about Adam Pendleton, a black conceptual artist who made paintings and used text and might be helpful to me. Teacher Kevin, shifting around his Nicorette gum and rolling up the sleeves of his artfully worm-eaten cardigan, said he'd heard the name, then let it drop with a verbal shrug as though to say,

This is of no interest.

The shrug from Teacher Kevin, who could append to every

noteworthy artist (to him) the name of his (usually *his*) gallery. What counted as interesting? Not what I thought was interesting.

And there was my exchange with Mimi the Canadian photographer over Lawrence Weschler's profile of the Los Angeles artist Robert Irwin, a love letter to Irwin and Irwin's 1950s LA car-culture art. I mentioned the gendered dimension of Irwin's story. Mimi accused me of "attacking" Irwin and Weschler.

That was the word she used: attacking.

Sure, sure, this was a small contretemps, but it widened the space between me, probing a reading, and my youthful counterparts, resisting too critical an approach. I was once again out of place and dismissed as aggressive.

In painting I was groping, my work of no interest to others. The lack of concern for what I was groping toward, for what I was trying to do, deflated me. My mood seemed part of a shared discontent. Daniel, a rich Columbian second-year painting student, pronounced RISD "annoying," so annoying that he had run off to Miami and the Bahamas with his boyfriend for a week in the middle of the semester. Even Anna, whose work Teacher Irma fulsomely praised, said she just wanted to go home. I didn't think her dismay or Daniel's impatience could equal my funk, but I, too, just wanted to go home. But I couldn't just go home now, because home was feeding my wretchedness.

THINGS AT HOME—at home with my father in Oakland, I mean—were degenerating. My father, his jaunty musical outings to the university at an end, had retreated to his bed. He was driving to distraction his circle of caring friends. They would try to visit him at Salem, but he wouldn't let them come up to his apartment. Distrusting taxis and car services, he would ask his friends to take him to his doctors. They would volunteer to take him out, but after they rearranged their schedules to accommodate him, he'd break every date, just staying home feeling sorry for himself. In our telephone conversations, he would rail and weep and pity himself as totally alone. He was not alone. He was extremely well cared for by an army of people, paid and unpaid. No one was more beloved. No one had so many people attending to him. I called him every day. All to no avail. No one could be more wretched.

Like a tapeworm traveling through the feet to the gut, like a virus jumping from one stranger to another in a subway car, my father's depression-tapeworm-virus penetrated through the phone. He hadn't infected me lethally, but his funk deepened my purple pall. Abbey Lincoln sang to me as I painted,

> It wasn't always easy learning to be me . . .
> Being me, I guess, to be myself alone
> It was lonely, sometimes, sometimes it was blue . . .

There in my painting studio, Abbey Lincoln's "Being Me" brought on a tearful migraine and transmogrified all I was going through at RISD into grief over my mother.

My god, how I missed my mother! My mother had done what I was trying to do, my brave little mother who had reinvented herself as a writer against her husband's obstructions. How courageous she was to come out from behind the veil of respectability to write openly and honestly about her life. I balled up my mother and Abbey Lincoln and myself into self-pitying confusion; I wept for us all—older women, older black women—in this alien place. I was wretched.

It made no objective sense, of course. Abbey Lincoln was a singer, composer, actress, and civil rights activist who shared little beyond black female beauty with my mother, who was more than a decade older and darker skinned. Lincoln had endured some hard times, harder, I think, than my mother's. Certainly Lincoln's entertainment-world glamour of movies and music remained distant from my mother's local identity, which reached no farther than brief appearances with my father in *Essence Magazine* and *Oprah* as attractive, long-married elders.

I knew my mother had painstakingly reinvented herself as a writer, a vocation my father frequently undermined even before depression embittered him. She persisted, through physical illness and with the burden of an unremitting struggle against my father's depression. I was thinking about my dear mother, and how brave she was to reinvent herself as an older woman. How hard it must have been.

My father's complaining, so constant, so unreasonable, pushed me into resentment. I railed to Glenn that the wrong parent had

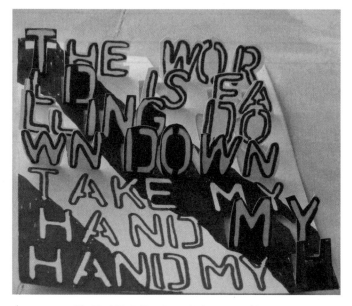

The World Is Falling Down Take My Hand, 2010,
ink on paper collage, approx. 15" × 18"

died, even that my father's depression had killed my mother. Why had she been the one to go, she who had so much to live for, who wanted so much to live and to do. Which one had survived? The angry, depressed one, now wasting precious days in bed, now complaining about his situation and every single person seeking to help him.

Glenn and my Dear Friend Thad knew both my parents well and disagreed. My mother died at age ninety-one of congestive heart failure, they said, and that was certainly true. Death at ninety-one is not premature death. But I know depression poisons life. An Abbey Lincoln song's plea inspired my *World Is Falling Down*, a print in graphic design class, still in subdued colors. It felt like me, the motherless, oldest person of all.

The motherless oldest person in this whole goddam world, eating alone, living alone, feeling alone. I hated fucking RISD, and I knew RISD fucking hated me.

14

PEERS

D ID I HAVE PEERS IN GRADUATE ART SCHOOL? GOOD question, and one that didn't come up at Mason Gross, where undergraduate art majors didn't model professional behavior, where peers and teacher-mentors didn't play so crucial a role in our future. As undergraduates, we were fated to be little more than Rutgers alums, maybe wearing little red *R* pins in our lapels or sticking blocky red *R*s on our cars. But a future in art most likely meant commercial art—work for other people. Graduate school was something else again, where we immediately learned in orientation that as visual artists in our own right we were forming bonds to sustain us forever, and that we would learn more from each other than we ever could from our teachers. Our RISD painting cohort would anchor our identity as artists. It would be like belonging to a very select club. No, not *like* belonging. We *already* belonged to a club whose roster had closed.

As we made our first acquaintance sitting with drinks around a large table at Tazza, one fact united us immediately: Yale School of Art had turned every single one of us down. We were all ambitious; we all aimed at professional careers and art-world visibility. But we all had to overcome this initial falling short. We all came to RISD to work hard and intensely for two years. We all came to learn, perhaps not so much to learn technique, but to learn how to be artists in today's Art World.

I can see that now, though I'm not sure I could see that back then, for I had not examined closely why I was in art graduate school. I just assumed I could not be a serious artist without art graduate school, just as I had known I could not be a serious historian—a publishing historian, a scholarly historian—without history graduate school. For history graduate school, I went to Harvard. For art graduate school, I went to RISD. All nine of us shared some version of that kind of reasoning, if not in so many words. We took for granted RISD's importance in our art without stripping our assumption down to its careerist essentials, without looking hard at the assumption.

We didn't examine one another's family background; at least, I never came to know the details. Maybe they were more forthcoming with one another. Three were from professional New York City families, and, of the New Yorkers, one had gone to Princeton, drove an Audi, and had worked as Philip Pearlstein's assistant, all signs of excellent connections. Another of the New Yorkers came from a family of lawyers, another from a family of doctors. There were two stocky white male Texans, one married and from a modest background. The other Texan's father was a doctor. At first I had a hard time telling them apart. Then there was one from Maryland and another from Chicago whose backgrounds I never discovered. The one from Korea was evidently extremely well off. But for Juhyun and me, all were white. Besides me, two others—Anna and Keith, the two I got friendly with—were over thirty (them, barely) and feeling old among the twenty-somethings.

•

AFTER GET-ACQUAINTED DRINKS at Tazza, I got to know my peers through their work. Anna's theme was memory, its telling and withholding, but always memory of a personal nature, not as history. She tended to work on a small scale, often in trompe l'oeil drawings that looked like photographs but that weren't photographs, and for that they usually garnered high praise. She showed one piece listing her daily activities, hour by hour, day by day, starting with her morning oatmeal. These lists Teacher David dismissed as banal. They were banal—boring as hell. But endorsed as steps along the right way to make art now.

Keith (a different Keith, not the one at Mason Gross) took his cues from *arte povera*. After painting motifs from his son's toys, he reversed his paintings to show the structures and supports, an exploration, he said, of the "objectness" of painting. He worked according to the irregularity of the handmade, creating a personal version of still lifes. His wooden lattices were praised according to their shapelessness, the more distressed ones succeeding the best. The more he made them, the more I thought of the shaped canvases of an artist I liked a lot, the late Elizabeth Murray.

The work of three of my peers seemed unrelated to their individual identities. Of course, that was not true, for even the seeming lack of personal involvement makes its own statement of self-regard. Collin worked in pure abstraction, with color and texture as his themes. He seemed so correct, so conventionally prosperous and successful, that I could not focus on him very well. Katie, the youngest and the star of our class and the only other straight out of undergraduate school, began the semester in representation, with paintings of trash bags and a disheveled apartment kitchen, always in a very wan palette. Later she moved on to abstract three-dimensional pieces made of used building materials with a blazing success that has not abated. Corydon, a physically small person, painted huge empty landscapes based on stock suburban photographs that everyone applauded. Her compositions intrigued me, not because they were unusual in their lack of figures, but because they belonged to a way of working I saw often at Mason Gross and at RISD: a landscape with no people in it. It was as though painting people—what I was valiantly striving to do—was kitschy and old-fashioned. Emptiness was favored, as in Teacher Jessica's "deadpan abstraction" and "deadpan representation," both, evidently, very good qualities. This quality of deadpan was not mine.

Collin used spray paint and brilliant color to make what he called "virtual vacancies," abstract pieces that used texture and negative space to convey a sense of depth as in landscape. Teacher Irma censured Collin's abstract painting for being too "decorative," that is, for being too good looking, like work you'd see in a hotel, she said, where the work has to be pleasing to the untutored eye. "Ambiguity" would have been better. I agreed with her, though the work looked ambiguous enough to me. Did she want images that seemed to incorporate mistakes? I never found out and felt that as a weakness on my part.

Field explored the effects of physical forces like gravity and inertia, which made her a process artist. She spoke little in crit, but the faculty loved the impressions she made by mashing coffee filters and swinging a pendulum over her paper to leave oval tracings. Teacher Holly liked the "trustworthiness" of the process. Even so, the teachers urged Field to take a second step after the trace of the pendulum in order to turn the drawing "into something else."

Juhyun made detailed, abstract installations in the corner of her half of our studio and a video that played on the South Korean fascination with farts. The video needed too much cultural explanation to work in our context as anything other than slapstick. In mid-semester, Juhyun left to get engaged, to get married in a lavish ceremony in her father's factory, and to have a baby.

Of the eight of us remaining, Mike looked the most like a

stereotypical RISD artist, tall, lanky, cute, blond, and lopingly relaxed in apparent self-confidence and awesome professionalism. Mike built his stretcher bars from scratch, using scores of screws (not the ordinary nails or staples like the rest of us) and special quarter-round molding to finish them off. The stretchers alone were goddam things of beauty. He photographed his work painstakingly, balancing reflected lights with multiple readings of a light meter.

I LEARNED A great deal from my peers, from how to talk about painting to what processes could lay down color and line to new drawing techniques. I adopted Collin's and Mike's use of a projector to scale up images to trace or paint from whatever source we wanted to take them. They told me about David Hockney's book *Secret Knowledge: Rediscovering the Lost Techniques of the Old Masters*, on artists' use of pinhole cameras to produce images of previously unimaginable verisimilitude. Collin's and Mike's instruction helped me gain an insight on drawing, one initially prompted by Teacher Judy's drawing exercise.

In one class Teacher Judy told us to draw her as she struck a series of quick poses as an exercise to loosen us up and open our eyes. We were to draw the old-fashioned way, with charcoal on paper, like undergraduates.

I cringed. Uh-oh, here would be my undoing.

One of my RISD teachers began every studio visit with the mater-of-fact declaration that I could not draw, and I could not paint. Like the ninny I was then, I flinched every time, believing the statement surely to be true. Now Judy was going to reveal my disability before all my peers. Anxiety. Fear. Dread. Trepidation. Palpitation.

Judy posed. We drew. After eight or ten poses, we pinned our drawings on the wall. Tensed against disclosure, I compared my drawings with the others'.

They were just as good.

My drawings were no worse than theirs.

I drew just as well as they did by hand.

Aha! My alleged inability to draw and paint was not about any failings of my hand or my eye. I just didn't have techniques such as tracing and projection that other artists used all the time. And not just my classmates. Gerhard Richter, for example, one of the most renowned of contemporary artists and German besides, used projection as his means of creating paintings that looked like fuzzy photographs, the very paintings that established his reputation and the outsized reputation of German painting in the museums of New York City.

I finally figured out that the ritual of belittling my technique related to how art is made now. As I learned from my peers, artists commonly trace and project. All sorts of art finds its audience somewhere, no matter how—or how expertly—it is drawn or painted. The teacher's ritual of belittling my drawing and painting meant I didn't draw and paint the way I was supposed to. I was too stuck on subject matter. I didn't make piles of things or paint shower tiles or empty landscapes.

Graduate school did not bind me very closely to my peers, even though they were usually quite correct toward me. I sensed they saw me, when they saw me, which wasn't all the time, as someone inconsequential and apart from them. I never felt animus from them, just an assumption of my inconsequence and, sometimes when they focused on me, their inability—a good-natured inability, it must be said—to say very much about my work. My work walked off the beaten track. Before learning better, I thought my own autobiography made for interesting art.

I misinterpreted the "embarrassment" assignment by making a big drawing of myself as a person who was embarrassed by being the wrong kind of black person because I was comfortable financially.

I made a collage I called *Embarrassment of Riches*, reflecting my embarrassment over being an un-poor black American. I have never felt totally, authentically black within American society, because real black Americans, authentically black Americans, are supposed to be poor, or at least formerly poor, and to have good stories to tell about overcoming adversity. I could never do that. In some ways, my inability felt like a personal shortcoming.

Laughing at myself in contradiction, I combined a ridiculous number of repeated images of consumer items of plentitude: multiple cars, candies, perfumes, cameras, and houses, along with a drawing of myself repeated three times. The piece was about two feet high and four feet wide, charcoal on paper, with colored objects. I left the drawings of myself in gray to contrast with the blues, greens, yellows, and oranges of the articles of consumption.

With its repetition and unnatural use of scale it certainly stood out as different from what others produced. It was dismissed as an example of illustration, *illustration*, a naive, unironic, straightforward, and downright twentieth-century notion. You could say that it was a work of illustration because I was visualizing an idea: one of my sources of embarrassment, my identity as a middle-class black American expressed visually in material terms.

My predicament as a black American wasn't a theme that

Embarrassment of Riches, 2009, ink and acrylic paper collage, approx. 24" × 48"

engaged my student cohort or my teachers. Well, then. Time for readjustment. In my delirious early RISD days, I thought I could let down my guard and make art in perfect candor. I was mistaken. I was wrong to think this would be seen as art. My peers and teachers were not curious about my embarrassment. Did it seem more sociological than purely personal, when the purely personal was called for? My definition of personal, my sense of myself as an individual, was too tied up in notions of blackness for the others to care. One aspect of my autobiography, however, interested them.

ONE AFTERNOON, MONTHS into RISD, I was painting away in my studio wearing a yellow German T-shirt that says "*Ich bin mit der Gesamtsituation unzufrieden*" (I'm unhappy with the whole situation). This was very much my thought when I bought it in Dresden in the early 2000s, when George W. Bush was president. I still have it, still *unzufrieden*. Right at that moment it summed up my mood in my studio, when Field, who hardly ever noticed me and never visited my studio, burst in to ask,

What year were you born?

Like Tina on George Street at Rutgers, Field had disconnected from the students' gravitational field to enter into mine to let me see myself through her eyes. She spoke without preamble or context. No setting me up with small talk. This was not a conversation; it was a quest. How long had they wanted to know? Had they been curious, like Tina at Mason Gross, since we first met?

I imagined a student committee had deputized Field to carry out the mission, perhaps because she had gone to Princeton and we had Princeton in common. The question belonged to our art milieu, for we were professionalizing in graduate school, and the question came from the familiar formula for identifying an artist:

Name (date and place of birth). Their curiosity demanded of me, as an artist, essential information.

She only asked once.

I answered, 1942.

No phone call to Mom this time, but, info secured, an immediate departure, a return to the committee in another studio breathlessly awaiting my birth date. Who won the antiquity wager? I never heard. Why didn't they invite me into their studio to talk about our generations? Or just figure it out by themselves from the dates on my website? They told me early on they'd looked me up. How to make me feel like a specimen, to remind me I was an outsider! *Ich war mit der Gesamtsituation unzufrieden.*

With the exception of Anna and Keith and Mike a little bit, they seemed largely to have felt as detached from me as I from them. I did form a bond with Anna, who, like me, felt significantly older than the others—she was, what, thirty-two, as was Keith, another thirty-something old-timer. Bit by bit through speaking with Anna, I glimpsed another system of art professionalization, one as crucial as crits.

I learned that Anna and (perhaps) other painters had received multiple studio visits from visiting art stars like Nina Katchadourian.

Oh . . . ?

Nina paid studio visits to us painters?

Anna also had a crit from visiting artist Richard Meyer and from mega-critic David Hickey, though Hickey's visits turned out to be more sexist insult than critical enlightenment. He had asked Emilia, a favored student in printmaking, her bra size. I further learned quite by chance from Anna and Mike of the existence of independent study classes with various faculty, like Dawn Clements, that I did not even know were available, and of conference calls I had been left out of.

What I saw as preferential treatment did not necessarily feel good to the colleagues I thought had been favored. One afternoon as I was stretching canvases in my studio, lanky arty Mike—the very image of the New York–Brooklyn artist—came into my studio to talk, ostensibly to thank me for taking his work seriously in my paper on Johanna Drucker for art criticism class. I didn't kick him out, so he settled down to moan about his paintings' reception. We students bitched everlastingly about the narrowness of his repertoire and the thoughtless sexism of his images. Which were superficial. In the extreme. Teachers were much less harsh, finding pop art and irony in Mike's work.

I was mistaken, it turned out, to see favoritism in Mike's independent study with Teacher Kevin. Teacher Kevin, exquisitely attuned to appearances as well as practices of up-to-the-minute New York art, seemed totally uninterested in me and my travails. Mike, in contrast, seemed to me to literally embody Kevin's kind of artist. I assumed Kevin was taking care of Mike as the promising artist he favored, more grooming for success that left out Duhirwe and me.

I was wrong.

True, Mike was taking the kind of independent study I had missed. But Kevin wasn't favoring Mike. Kevin disapproved of Mike's painting and would only drop by on the fly to hector Mike to do more and better work. In fact, Mike was not Kevin's pet. I was wrong, and not only in the case of Mike and Teacher Kevin.

Anna really *was* the teachers' pet. They praised her, granted her studio visits from all the hot artists and visiting critics, lined her up with people who could ensure her success. What more could she ask?

She could ask for meaningful crits that addressed weaknesses as well as strengths of her work in terms she could understand and actually implement. When she and I had dinner together in a small, obscure restaurant on the other side of the river from RISD, she asked me for advice in getting through life—what? The star pupil looking to the class dumbbell. She said I seemed to live life knowingly, parrying RISD's blows and deflecting its arrows, balancing all the various parts of my life. And she asked me how old I was. Was I feeling old? Not so much right then, but orphaned, ending the first whole calendar year without my mother. Bereft. Alone. As in the disconsolate Negro spiritual, like a motherless child.

LIKE ME IN painting, Duhirwe in printmaking learned of multiple instances of being passed over for opportunities to work with prominent artists like Pat Steir. The system seemed to work like this: each department's faculty chose its favorites, who got to meet distinguished visitors. Duhirwe and I weren't on the lists. Emilia was on the printmaking list, Anna on the painting list. They got everything; we got nothing, even though Duhirwe was a presidential fellow, which supposedly opened The Art World to minorities. The Painting Department's presidential fellowship went to a white male artist who knew how to draw. How it worked was how it actually worked.

Duhirwe and I were excluded from this patronage system. Lacking crucial contacts, we entered The Art World at a relative disadvantage, for personal contact with senior artists is essential to professional success. The patronage system that bypassed us disturbed Duhirwe more than me, because I had already seen it—though in attenuated form—in my previous life as a historian.

So it turned out that studio visits and crits were just the visible portion of graduate art education in a system by no means limited to RISD. An entire network of preference, favors, and connections grew up apart from classes, separating out who counted, the sheep from the goats. I figured faculty favoritism cued students into whom to consider a peer and who did not belong. This classification emerged as we eight painters were taking our class photograph. We convened in the second-floor crit room to be photographed. I was present at the appointed time, spoke to people, and set out a plate of Oreos for everyone. Then nothing happened. More nothing was happening. With things to do in my studio, I asked to be fetched when they were ready to take the photograph. I went to my studio for a moment. In that moment, they took the picture. Back downstairs, I expressed my displeasure. Vividly. They took the picture again.

A few years later I discovered a different version of the class picture on Facebook, one I was not in. My peers, my so-called peers, managed to capture their sense of themselves—without me.

15

CRIT

CRIT: THE QUINTESSENCE OF ART SCHOOL. IN CRIT your work gets taken seriously by knowledgeable and experienced teachers and thoughtful peers, people with sophisticated eyes who examine your work intently. They relate it to art history and the work of relevant contemporary artists. There might be disagreements, but all the viewers, teachers and fellow students alike, look at your work long and look at it hard. Crits are why you go to art school instead of just asking your mom and your friends how they like your work. At the end of your crit, you emerge knowing more about your art—maybe even more about yourself—with a sense of your work's strengths and weaknesses and where it belongs within the long, wide world of art. Crit is art school's sacred space for learning.

That, at least, is the theory.

Crits hold a hallowed place in art education, and rightly so. Starting out, I thought of crits as art school's main event.

Crits, I learned in practice, could be just about anything. More exactly, they were the visible fraction of artists' formation. Mason Gross crits had introduced me to the form.

Mason Gross undergraduate crits took place in the same rooms where we drew and painted. These crits were straightforward, usually with only the one teacher who had taught the class. With only one teacher, the criteria for success and failure were pretty clear.

Even when undergraduate art was thin or hackneyed or students clammed up on the ground that their art "speaks for itself," thoughtful teachers like Hanneline, Stephen, and Barb talked about the work's formal and conceptual qualities, finding ways to insert vocabulary we needed to know. When a drawing looked unfinished, parts remained "unresolved." When colors lacked nuance, mixing in their complements could "unify the canvas."

In undergraduate crits I was one of the hardworking, dedicated students who had grappled with assignments. I wasn't the only one talking—Joseph talked, and Keith did more than his part, mentioning artists "to look at," identifying them not only by name and style, but also by their galleries. Wow! I was impressed. I didn't know the galleries or where they stood on the scale of coolness. I didn't even understand how important it was in Art World eyes to belong to the right gallery. Showing in an uncool gallery was like wearing stodgy clothes.

We hard workers filled in for reluctant and silent others. I fulfilled and overfilled my undergraduate assignments, and I talked about them sitting on the floor with the kids (preening myself silently for my suppleness). One time I did a little tap dance to demonstrate my piece for the "mistake" assignment by converting a tape dispenser (one of my favorite objects to draw, with its snail-like curves and negative space) into a *tap dance* dispenser.

We used pushpins to attach our work to the wall, but there were never enough pushpins. After too many crits delayed by pushpin searches, I bought a box of one hundred pushpins at the little convenience store on George Street. Seven of us painting students were milling around, amusing ourselves while waiting for Teacher

Stephen. With nothing better to do, I started sticking the one hundred pushpins I had bought into the wall, mystifying my fellow students.

Why are you doing that?

I continued sticking pushpins into the wall.

Because we always need pushpins to hang our work.

The others warned me, But people will walk off with them.

I kept sticking pushpins into the wall.

That's okay. They're here for the taking.

Mystification. Somehow pushpins seemed more valuable and hoard-worthy than the $1.39 I'd paid for a box of one hundred.

Joe, looking at my increasingly pushpinned display, noticed a change on the wall. The box that had held the official Notice of Occupancy was empty. Following the artist's impulse to mark every blank surface, he began handwriting a Notice of Occupancy.

How do you spell "occupancy"?

Silence. Nobody could spell occupancy.

Pushing pins into the wall next to him, I spelled out in his Jersey accent,

E-C-C-A-P . . .

There came a pause, as everyone reprocessed the question and recognized the ridiculousness of my answer. We all laughed and laughed. I laughed so hard tears ran down my face. When the hilarity subsided, Joseph wrote, "Occupancy limited to 3."

Teacher Stephen ambled in with his coffee cup (eating and drinking expressly prohibited in the studios) and house shoes, Brooklyn fashion for entering the world as an artist. Our crit began.

Joseph disparaged Diane's earnest paintings as the pretty pictures in travel magazines. Lesson learned about sophisticated imagery: don't do pretty; also don't do glamorous. Jan-Vincent's dramatic landscapes and beautiful figure paintings, all surface gorgeousness from a how-to book on painting, got thumbs-down.

On the other hand, Jason's faithfully rendered, empty scenes of the Civic Square Building's interior architecture earned appreciation. Keith led the applause for a "biography of a wall." Jason's two realistic stairway paintings succeeded, whereas Jan-Vincent's lovely woman and detailed street scene failed. JT put up figurative scenes copied from a random selection of photographs from the web, lacking titles, narrative, and concept. JT was advised to work more thoughtfully. My transcriptions of Max Beckmann portraits were duly noted, but their art history origins bored the others. The twentieth century—*my* twentieth century—was just too long ago to seem relevant (to use a twentieth-century word).

Undergraduate crits were also tests of basic skills, a main purpose of undergraduate art education. And there were recognizable assignments, usually a given number of drawings or paintings on a theme or technique. No problem for me, because I loved making art and was exceedingly productive. For one painting crit, my work covered a nine-foot wall. Another time I put up eighteen drawings. With that much to look at, some of it was bound to work out. Graduate crits, on the other hand, were more choreographic.

CRITS AT RISD assembled several teachers and many students in specially designated crit rooms, one on the second floor, one on the fourth floor of the Fletcher Building. A student would put up many weeks' work and prepare to talk about it. Faculty and students would dribble in and walk around the room, inspecting the pieces with showy intensity. Then everyone would take a doughnut and an orange drink and sit in rows, faculty in front. The teacher running the crit would set a cell phone timer on thirty-five minutes to make sure everyone got the same amount of time, an excellent practice.

Timer started, the student would present the work, then teachers would talk about the work, then other students would speak up. Though plotted out as theater, the discussion had no firm rules; teachers often conversed among themselves about whatever was on their minds. For our first crit in our first semester we first-year painters gathered as for a master class. There was the expectation—an eagerness, really—for wisdom to endure for ages and improve our work for good. Thoughtful little Corydon volunteered to take notes and send them to us afterward, a gesture of solidarity we all greeted with deep appreciation in anticipation of its fruits. As the teachers talked, Corydon typed into her laptop. Afterward she sent us lengthy reports that surely would change the way we made our art.

Alone in my studio after crit, I looked at what Corydon had sent me. Her notes were comprehensive, truly excellent. I recognized the phrases. Rereading her notes over, my mind blurted out, Oh . . .

Oh, I thought, I just must be too tired to grasp wisdom's meaning. I set the comments aside for later consultation. Later consultation yielded no more wisdom for the ages. Others must have experienced this disillusion. No more careful crit notes circulating breathlessly.

CRITS CONTAINED ESSENTIAL elements. There should be at least a pretense of actually looking at the work, from a distance to get a sense of its overall composition and up close for paint handling and texture. In addition to some formal analysis, there should be commentary on the work's content and meaning and how the various pieces work together as an ensemble. It helped to mention relevant art history resonances, which usually led to the comment "You should look at . . ." followed by the name of an artist, preferably one in the art history canon or with work currently on show at a çool gallery, but in any case, not so well known as to be hackneyed.

I remembered "You should look at . . ." from Mason Gross, though I hadn't recognized its talismanic power. I knew so little back then that just hearing about artists new to me opened up my world of visual art. Teacher Hanneline suggested I look at Velásquez as a means of improving my composition. I went and looked at Velásquez, barely grasping the connection between his compositions and mine, but enjoying the exhibition at the Met.

In RISD crits, "You should look at . . ." served multiple functions: adding to the critee's "influences," the store of images to draw on and techniques to adopt; demonstrating the speaker's knowledge of art history, especially obscure art history; prolonging discussions, even competitions, with other faculty or student colleagues on hot and/or esoteric artists and galleries; and advertising exhibitions and shows currently running in New York (elsewhere didn't count so much unless it was in Berlin, and any show in New Jersey remained beneath notice).

Early on at RISD, my own ignorance appeared in a You-should-look-at . . . lesson on how to talk and whose work to heed. Looking at a piece I had made with text, someone suggested I look at the work of Ed Ruscha. I heard the student say "Roo-SHAY." I didn't recognize a name I knew only from reading, pronouncing it in my mind's ear as "ROO-shah." Chagrin. How could I not know so important a contemporary artist?! I went to the library and looked at Ruscha's work, which, yes, did suggest techniques I definitely could use. See, crit worked when my paintings interested my audience.

In one crit I showed a set of drawings that I really wanted to hear people discuss, as I was using photographs prominently for the second time. Were these drawings too slight to count as interesting? As so often in my work, there was a back story as well as surface appearance. Did the back story outweigh the work?

The drawings took off from a photograph in a book by a pioneering black art historian, Sylvia Boone, the first black PhD in art history and the first black woman to be tenured at Yale. Boone specialized in concepts of beauty in African art and published *Radiance from the Waters: Ideals of Feminine Beauty in Mende Art* in 1986. Boone and I did not overlap in Ghana in the 1960s, for she departed just before I arrived. But I followed her career and sent a copy of her book to my best friend, the Wisconsin literary scholar Nellie McKay. After Nellie's death, her daughter, a banker, dispersed her library. A Harvard colleague with whom Nellie had collaborated bought the very copy I had inscribed to Nellie. Once she had the book in hand, the colleague recognized my inscription and generously sent me the book in Providence. I made several drawings from one of the book's photographs as a gesture of thanks.

Sylvia Boone Drawings, 2009, ink on paper, each panel 10" × 8"

I selected nine of my twelve *Sylvia Boone Drawings* to show in crit. Fearing they might be too close to their photographic origin, at the same time, I liked them immensely. In crit, people found the back story interesting. But that was it. No one said anything about the images.

There was nothing said about the *Boone* drawings as artwork, not that they were visually appealing or that they were slight, not that they were intriguing, not that they might be improved if they were bigger or brighter or more or less saturated in color. Was bright color the problem?

Silence.

Silence before my *Sylvia Boone Drawings* took me by surprise, because they were figurative and colorful, united in imagery but separated by palette, touch, and support. Still untrusting of my eye, I couldn't tell whether my *Boone* drawings were bad or boring. Maybe there just was not enough to them to be interesting. Certainly silence conveys a negative reaction, and without explanation, it discouraged me from continuing with them. I should have been stronger, because pushing on with a series holds the key to development, to moving past where you begin.

I cheated myself as an artist by being discouraged by silence in crit. For a long time, not knowing whether those *Sylvia Boone Drawings* were good art, only that I liked them, I cherished them as a kind of secret indulgence, as images that I alone cared for. I ultimately concluded that what happened in crit had nothing to do with anything when it came to my *Sylvia Boone Drawings*.

MIKE'S WORK ALWAYS elicited much more commentary. His paintings were big, 84" × 48", but always pop art objectifying women and based on the same image derived from an advertisement for panty hose. Over the course of two years the work hardly changed, but it engendered extended commentary in crit, skeptical as well as positive, that sounded like conversations about real art that took the work seriously, even though in every single crit, he would show us versions of the same flat paintings of a woman's leg. In every single crit, students would decry the images as thoughtlessly sexist. Each time, Mike would protest that his work should only be judged formally, that is, on the basis of the surface appearance of the paint and composition. We'd say you can't separate the appearance from the meaning, the form from the content. Then he'd make more of the same. In crit, the teachers would discuss the work at length. Teacher David said,

You seem to be in a reductive frame of mind. You seem to be painting less and less.

Maybe the paintings were lazy.

Mike half agreed, saying he was trying to distill the real.

I asked him to say more about the real. Mike answered,

They're about so many things. They're utterly ridiculous in so many ways, but they're very telling.

Keith defended Mike's paintings as really complex.

Teacher Holly, skeptical, posed rhetorical questions: What level of thinness are you insisting on, and what are we to do with that?

Teacher David decided the minimalism of the minimalist paintings worked, that they were engaging, quiet pieces, not wondering what's not there.

Teacher Jessica agreed with Teacher Kevin, seeing Mike's leg paintings as a '60s pop-art package with a place in art history by virtue of Mike's use of primary colors.

Teacher Kevin announced that although Mike had vacated and vacated, his paintings were not emptied out.

Now there was a substantive crit.

•

BETWEEN YOU-CAN'T-DRAW-AND-YOU-CAN'T-PAINT AND evasion, my first year of graduate school ground me down into a pathetic, insecure little stump. I made a three-sided piece in plastic that encapsulated my mood. The gray ground came from architecture software. I stenciled the words in colored acrylic ink from text taken from the book of *Revelation*, all about the end of the world. More of my art of end of the world.

Three-sided *Woe* sculpture, 2009, ink and collage on plastic, each side 12" × 12"

I should have known better than to succumb, for my mentors had warned me of art graduate school as an experience in humiliation. Artist Emma Amos, for one, had visited me at the Studio School years earlier and described graduate school as one long tearing down. She meant graduate school in general, but in my days at RISD, I felt my wretchedness, my misery, to be uniquely my own. I

was wrong. Everyone I've talked to about their MFA experience—
in poetry, fiction, nonfiction, theater, and visual art, north, south,
east, and west—recognizes what I went through. It wasn't just
RISD. It was art graduate school.

During my first year of graduate crits, I couldn't tell whether
my teachers and fellow students were critiquing me, old-black-
woman-totally-out-of-place, or critiquing my work, which was not
good enough, TOTALLY NOT GOOD ENOUGH, or, as it felt,
completely, utterly, stupidly rotten. My self-confidence collapsed.

I felt perfectly awful and alienated. There was no strength in
my alienation, no saving grace. It was abject. I was P A T H E T I C.
Pathetic was precisely how I felt. Even so, misery was not all
there was to me in my first year at RISD. Some of what was much
more about me than misery was being an old person with a long history in the world. My *much more* paid off, and handsomely. With a
wide circle of contacts outside my art school, I sought education in
my own network of support. That network saved my life as an artist. I piled my paintings into my station wagon and drove down to
New Haven, where friends in the art school and art history looked
carefully at my work and talked to me about it. They gave me a crit.

In New Haven, Friends Sarah and Key Jo looked and assessed
strong points and weaknesses. I said I didn't know if the silence
indicated that my *Sylvia Boone Drawings* were too slight—they
are just small drawings, after all. No, they said, no, the drawings
were nothing at all to apologize for—as I was practically doing. My
friends recognized the silence before my drawings as a common
reluctance of non-black viewers to engage with black figuration, a
silence I shouldn't take personally or hear as a weakness in my art.
What a relief! I liked those drawings immensely and had shown
them despite my uncertainty. My friends gave me permission to
close my ears to viewers who were working off their own issues.
To hell with you-can't-draw-can't-paint.

Friend Sarah, who was teaching at Yale School of Art, recognized my frustrations as a normal part of art graduate education. She also knew from experience that so many of our fellow citizens couldn't resist the temptation to take us down a peg. Sarah and Key Jo urged me to continue with my Michael Jackson and beauty paintings, which needed work, they definitely needed work. And my friends said so. But my paintings weren't hopeless. In New Haven I heard what I needed to hear, essential advice every art student needs to hear:

Keep on.

Keep making art.

Keep making your art.

Nonetheless, I drove back to Providence from New Haven feeling I truly did need to have my head examined for starting down the long road of visual art.

IN THE SUMMER after my first, wretched year at RISD, I gave a book talk on Martha's Vineyard and stayed with friends from Paris. My artist host took me to see her friend, the painter Irving Petlin. In a half-underground studio, Irving worked on big pastel drawings inspired by the writing of W. G. Sebald, whose work I also admired—not just the prose, but also the use of images within the prose.

Irving sat with my digital portfolio and gave me a crit from his long years' experience making and teaching art. My work wasn't randomly scattered, as one RISD teacher had decreed. Irving saw a unifying hand in my work, representational and abstract, and a coherent vision of the world. On my perpetual struggle with the bane of "illustration," he advised me to speak of "visualizing" rather than "illustrating" the concepts on my mind. Like Sarah, Irving reinforced my habit of working serially, for repetition is how art finds its way. He encouraged my work on the human figure in social context, but reminded me to stay loose. Stay loose. As a tangled-up jangle of wound-up worry, I needed that advice.

Irving sent me on to his artist friend Joyce Kozloff in New York. Joyce spent good time with me, commending my industry and my self-portraits. I share her attraction to maps, which she has been painting magnificently for decades, maps and the concept of territory, plus the process of collage, place as a fertile concept for art making. Bless her, bless him, for taking good time with my work. Life could go on.

THE ALTERNATIVE CRITS that saved my life continued with Artist Friend Denyse Thomasos, who had already helped me prepare for graduate school. She examined my work closely, explaining what she found stronger and what she found weaker, and why. Denyse reminded me that visual thinking was a language new to me and different from verbal thinking. After three hours in her New York studio, I was starting to understand what she meant. It was a matter of learning rather than of some mysterious gift of talent or inherent ability. How fortunate I was to have that extraordinarily generous, individual crit, with attention paid to my particular issues.

I didn't have any crits at Brown, but friends there offered companionship around a welcoming dinner table. My old friend from Harvard graduate school and Princeton, the earth-shaking intellectual-administrator Ruth Simmons, was president of Brown at the time. Ruth, bless her heart, would invite me to dinners at her presidential residence, where I ate and drank like I did in my good old days. I chatted with other friends like Chinua, Toni, John, and Tricia, people who spoke language familiar to me and shared my concerns.

Even at RISD, all was not alienation, for I could take refuge with Claudia, Anthony, and Donna, African Americans who recognized the cultural baggage I was carrying in so blinkered an institution. Art historians in RISD's liberal arts department spoke language I recognized and encouraged me.

Looking back, I can see there was more to RISD crits for me than silence and niggling fault-finding. Teachers Holly and Donna and David approached my work openly, even though they seemed not to know what to do with it or with me. They tried. Crits everywhere are as much about the person of the artist as about the art. The person I was in art graduate school was a misfit several times over.

It was my own alternative crits that carried me through. My alternative crits conferred the crucial endowment that only crits can provide—the thoughtful, well-informed focus on your work.

16

ART SCHOOL + HISTORY HISTORY

M Y HISTORIAN'S LIFE SEEMED TO RECEDE WHILE I was in art school, disconnected from art as a foreign country with its own native tongue. Values that governed my work as a historian—clarity, coherence, and representativeness—looked all wrong in art. If not wrong, then not very useful, almost as bad as "academic." The two halves of my brain, one orderly, the other spontaneous, connected only tenuously, the remnants of connecting tissue more hindrance than help. Frowning on historical subject matter, my teachers encouraged the disconnect. Leaving history seemed like what I absolutely had to do, because history was dragging me down. I knew for certain historians' attachment to scientific truth was cramping my painting hand and misleading my eye.

Publication of my book *The History of White People* while I was in graduate school disrupted an already uneasy coexistence, for my tasks as an author competed with art school. Starting with an appearance on *The Colbert Report* the very week *The History of White People* was published, book promotion took me away from

Providence on a regular basis. In that instance, absence increased my standing, for arm wrestling Stephen Colbert gave me impressive RISD cred. What was that like? Fun, like doing improv. Undergraduate RISD students in my digital tools class watched the video together and applauded my return to Providence. RISD's hip young president posted my Colbert clip on his blog. My book had been favorably reviewed on the front page of *The New York Times Book Review*, along with a stunning graphic image of the tangled taxonomy of the idea of white people. That review awed some New York–based RISD faculty—some, hardly all—for reviews of history books didn't count for much in the art world. I certainly did not feel any increased stature in the MFA painter's club in Fletcher.

Between book-promotion talks and interviews, I drew and painted with the purposeful resolve of my inner worker bee, drawing and painting and painting and drawing with the discipline that was ever my forte. Immersion in work always transported me to a better place, a higher plane, a truer zone. I enjoyed every moment, all right, but beyond my studio, I still felt like an alien. While I bore down on my work over solitary hours in the studio, I imagined my fellow painters lolling about together, pleasuring themselves in Matisse-like *volupté*, drinking, smoking, turning up late, and schmoozing from one studio to another. They were making the work the teachers applauded, painting with knowing hands, seeing with clever eyes. They knew what I didn't. They could drink and drug without paying a price—or so I thought. They were young enough for exemption, fresh enough not to owe alcohol's tax in sleeplessness and looking totally rotten in the morning.

We weren't supposed to eat or drink in our studios, but what the hell. Eno Fine Wines and Spirits, a combination wine bar–corner liquor store on Westminster Street, facilitated our drinking. Its sophisticated decor, expensive liquors, and wine tastings gave it upscale cachet, while its long hours and stock of cheap beers made it an all-hours convenience store. I wouldn't know about *all* hours, but I wasn't the only one fueling my art with alcohol. Well, I ate, too. Tazza, a self-consciously cool art-school hangout on the corner of Eddy and Westminster Streets, projected obscure European movies on ceiling monitors with music the cognoscenti recognized. Tazza served pretty good food as well as drink. Food and drink nearby, I worked steadily in my pitiful isolation. By the time of my crit with Teacher Irma, I had too many drawings to fit on my studio walls.

For her studio visit, I had put up a score of new drawings inspired by Ingres's *Grand Odalisque*, Michael Jackson, and Apollo Belvedere, with two large paintings and some etchings. A lot was just regular drawing, regular painting, not objects of great beauty. But some was ambitious. I was trying to make paintings that exceeded my skill, drawing on art history and history history and trying to cram too much into my images. I might have been away from Providence a great deal, but I made up for it with a lot of work. No one, not even Teacher Irma, could accuse me of slackness. She did not accuse me of slackness. Quality, not quantity, was my defect.

She walked in as usual, reminding me,

You can't draw, and you can't paint.

I fell for it every time: she had plumbed the truth of the matter; she knew the real deal; I couldn't draw, and I couldn't paint. It didn't occur to me that she might be saying exactly the same thing to other students, that other students might be torturing themselves as I tortured myself. I should have grasped the possibility that it was all psychological-warfare poppycock. She was probably one of those diabolical people who can sniff out each person's particular insecurity. I had a history colleague at Penn who could do that. He'd pass on a comment impugning the teaching of one who was insecure in the classroom and whisper a critique of his book to one worried about publication. It's a gift some people have. Maybe she had it. She tortured me, and she knew it. She did it on purpose, I just know. In my pathetic insecurity, I felt her judgment applied to me alone and feared she was right. Some of it *was* just for me, because I was the one juggling so many lives. Teacher Irma hastily looked around my studio, pausing over nothing. She dismissed all but one small, light-colored print as,

The only interesting thing in here.

She wasn't there to talk about my work; she was there to complain: Why did you choose to go to graduate school when the biggest book of your career was coming out?

That's what she said.

I heard, You stupid fart! You never should have gone to art school!

The terrible painter in me flinched.

The nincompoop that I was struggled to answer.

During undergraduate art school, I managed more than one thing. I finished my book . . .

Actually, I *thought* I had finished my book. I really hadn't.

My plan had been to finish *The History of White People* before starting art school. I had made tremendous progress the year before, then Glenn broke my writing rhythm by dragging poor little me to Paris for the month of May, where I griped about how hard it was to work there. A chapter that had practically been writing itself in April bogged down in June. No one, not one single friend of mine, empathized. Oh, jeez! I'd been finishing this book for what felt like forever; it had, in fact, gone on for years and years. I wrote steadily all summer, but I started at Mason Gross with my book still in pieces and an intention to finish the following summer. My historical organization presidency disrupted my writing for an entire year.

Teacher Irma saw *THWP* as an obstacle, a fatal distraction from art school, and she was right. But she didn't know about the obstruction that had *truly* disrupted my plan to complete my book before graduate school. I tended also to sublimate the obstruction, because it was so ridiculously, agonizingly, enragingly time-consuming. My book was a screen memory repressing the real distraction in my second year at Mason Gross, the real absurd drain of time and energy that dragged me down. I was president of the Organization of American Historians—OAH, the international professional organization of scholars of American history—a test in the guise of an honor.

I had belonged to the OAH for thirty years before being elected president, as I had belonged to the Southern Historical Association, of which I was also elected president, the American Studies Association, of which I was defeated in an election for president, the Association of Black Women Historians, of which I served as director, the American Historical Association, which gave me an award for distinguished graduate teaching, the Southern Association of Women Historians, the Berkshire Conference of Women Historians, the Association for the Study of African American Life and History, and organizations you had to be elected to, such as the Society of American Historians, the American Antiquarian Society, the American Academy of Political and Social Science, and the American Academy of Arts and Sciences. I felt it was important to be active in the historical profession, so for thirty years I faithfully attended annual meetings, served on committees, and wrote my share of reports. I did not mind taking part in professional organizations, not at all. It was the right thing to do. I was a good citizen of my profession. You get the idea.

Along with my History Department and programs in African American Studies and Women's Studies, professional organizations had comprised my intellectual community, where I was known and respected. Some colleagues became close friends. We became leaders in our fields, and our students grew up to write important scholarship. The history profession, history history, was my intellectual home. This home opened the door, the jaws of a trap.

Only now do I recall the year when my book fell off schedule, for my memory had thrown out the endless conference calls, the wrangling, the verbal struggles, the hand-to-hand combat with only the dull bayonet of my presidency to fend off my adversary, the executive director, a man whom the sweetest of historians called "a sleazy son of a bitch." The saving grace of that time was the comradeship of struggle forged between me and the presidents before and after, solid historians with a sense of humor, stick-to-itiveness, and guts. We proclaimed ourselves a Gang of Three forged in combat. Thank heaven for my dear presidential comrades.

The closest metaphor I can think of to describe my OAH presidency is the boulder Sisyphus had to push up the hill every day, only to have it roll back down in the night.

Here's the morning, sunny, warm, and clear, and here's the day's boulder, a financial plan. You roll it up the hill. It rolls back down. The next day the boulder is a conference call. You roll it up the hill. It rolls back down. The next day the boulder is a mission statement. You roll it up the hill. It rolls back down. The next day the boulder is a strategic plan. You roll it up the hill. It rolls back down. The next day the boulder is another conference call. You roll it up the hill. It rolls back down. The strategic plan was no mere boulder. It was an eagle pecking out my liver every night.

In art school I didn't talk about the Organization of American Historians. No one had ever heard of it, so even if I had bragged about being OAH president, people would have rolled their eyes at me in a netherworld of No Interest Whatsoever, a totally uncool realm of squares. So I have suppressed that time of travail. My presidency ended, and with its ending, the history profession passed, I assumed, into my anterior life. For years I proclaimed myself a *former* historian, and when asked how art school influenced my thinking about history, I maintained I no longer thought about history. Which was *so very wrong*.

TONGUE-LASHED IN MY studio crit by Teacher Irma, I forgot the OAH but countered with my ability to juggle several tasks at once: I finished my book . . .

And I looked after my parents in California as my mother was dying and my father disintegrated.

That was undergraduate, Teacher Irma countered. Graduate school is different. You're hardly ever here.

This I disputed, though I had to admit to all the entanglements of my life. I felt like I'd been in Providence a lot. I knew I'd done a lot of work, more than some other painting students. Like a chump, I carried on explaining myself as though exculpation were needed in a moment of surpassing triumph. I'm embarrassed to admit that I even sent Irma an email with the abject subject line, "It Came as a Surprise." None of my other books had attracted so much attention, even though they'd been favorably reviewed in the *New York Times* and done well. At a dinner at President Ruth's at Brown, Novelist John noted my new celebrity. He said I had finally found the right people to write about. Technically this was not true, as two of my other books had been about Americans in general. But he was right in the spirit of the thing.

A total ninny with scolding Teacher Irma, I was actually achieving a height of accomplishment. I had not only survived the devilish OAH, I had parented my parents and published a book that came in at five hundred pages in hardcover and gotten the review of a lifetime. Back at Mason Gross, I had already turned my multiplicity into art, as a collage, *Chapter Revised*, based on a page of my book manuscript. The ground was a wash of dark green under a page of manuscript I had shaped according to lines of text. On top of the shaped manuscript, I had sewn by hand in thick orange thread hand-cut strips of a dark red man's tie bought at Newark's Salvation Army. Basting the tie's strips to the manuscript at angles to lines of typing, I obscured the text and created competing lines and conflicting narrative messages in lines as though to be read. The black-and-white manuscript, though edged organically, expressed the orderliness of scholarship; the strips of red tie, unraveling and adhered by an unsteady hand, talked over the type, posing the old riddle, What's black and white and red/read all over?

So, yes, I had held it all together for years now. But, just as true, I was exhausted all the time—pressed, harried, rushed, squashed,

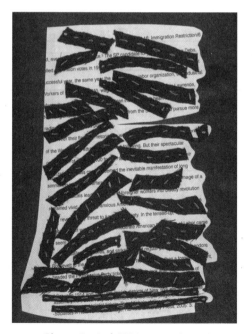

Chapter Revised, 2006, manuscript page,
fabric, and thread on paper, 12" × 9"

smashed, and impossibly stretched all over the place, barely hanging on.

Wait, now. I was also all-powerful. Omnipotent, practically. I didn't question whether I could balance book and art school. I even made a three-foot-high drawing in charcoal and pastel of myself doing both, with text from my book manuscript beside me, a brush in one hand, a book in the other, a Duchampian bicycle wheel for power, and a precisely drawn red alternator in place of a heart for converting one form of energy into another.

I had and would continue to balance book, art school, and declining parents. I'd already proven my powers. If only I had stood

Alternator Self-Portrait, 2007,
graphite and colored pencil on paper, 33" × 23 ¼"

up to Irma with the conviction of the abilities I really had! As for mollifying her, that was pissing into the wind. Even as her hostility was turning me against graduate school, she was right about at least one thing: *The History of White People*, my seventh authored book, was the biggest book of my career.

ART SCHOOL INFLUENCED *The History of White People*, but art's influence on my writing of history had originated years earlier. When did my turn toward the visual begin? When I was faced with Sojourner Truth, a biographical subject who did not read or write. My book *Sojourner Truth, A Life, A Symbol* did not turn to art history out of respect for the image. No, I was grappling with a failure of written language, a deficiency of text. The paucity of Truth's own words documenting her life, not pure attraction to pictures, led me to art. Focusing on image in its own right came later, with art school.

The History of White People is a visual book. In the first instance because human taxonomy, though fetishizing bodily measurement, usually turns on how people look. In the second instance because race scientists have used what they call science to prove racial superiority, and racial superiority often rests on the claim that the superior race is the most beautiful. Desire is all over beauty, as in the classical judgment of Paris that I have taken you through at self-indulgent length.

WHAT BECAME *The History of White People* sprang from a simple question prompted by a photograph on the front page of the *New York Times* in 2000. It showed bombed-out Grozny, the capital of Chechnya, in another round in the endless wars between Russia and the Caucasus, and looking like Berlin in 1945. Wikipedia says,

"In 2003, the United Nations called Grozny the most destroyed city on Earth." It certainly looked that way. Knowing that Chechnya was part of the Caucasus, I couldn't help connecting devastation over there to a common notation in the United States. Why on earth, I wondered, are white Americans called Chechens?

You hear the name Caucasian practically every day—maybe not every single day, because calling white people "Caucasian" is like calling your car your "vehicle." "Caucasian" proclaims an elevated purpose, like scientific truth. Medical researchers and sociologists are prime users of "Caucasian," and they don't use it sardonically. How, I wondered, did we get from the Caucasus, between the Black and Caspian Seas, just barely in Europe and thousands of miles from the Western Hemisphere, to "Caucasian" in American usage?

The great thing about having already written many books is that you can pursue whatever question sticks in your mind. So I pursued "Caucasian" as a euphemism for the too bald-faced label of white people. Answering my question took me to Göttingen, Germany, where I found Johann Friedrich Blumenbach, an eighteenth-century professor who picked out five skulls as embodiments of what he called the "varieties" (rather than the "races") of mankind.

Let me repeat that: Professor Blumenbach, working according to scientifically recognized methods, picked out five skulls—skulls from five individuals—and turned them into *varieties* of mankind. It was as though I lost my head, you boiled all the flesh off it and the brains and eyeballs out of it, and you called it "New Jersey Variety of Mankind." I would stand for all nine million people in New Jersey. My husband, Glenn, whom I love dearly and who lives in the same house with me, would not count. It would be my skull, not his, and not yours, that personified New Jerseyans as a whole.

Blumenbach's prettiest skull—no dings, all its teeth, nicely symmetrical—came from a young woman from Georgia in the Caucasus, a part of the world subject to slave raids over several millennia. Blumenbach (in translation) called hers "the really most beautiful form of skull, which my beautiful typical head of a young Georgian female always of itself attracts every eye, however little observant." The Georgian who had possessed the head that became the skull had been enslaved, brought to Moscow, and raped to death. I kid you not. Her skull, the skull of a young Georgian woman raped to death, became the emblem of white people as Caucasian.

Blumenbach's beautiful Georgian sex slave's skull stood for a figure that art history calls the *odalisque*. This is where art history and art school deeply influenced my writing. At RISD I drew by hand in colored ink a small map of the land of the odalisques, a work of conceptual rather than terrestrial geography and color.

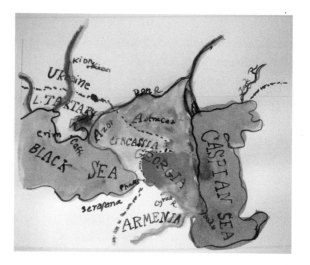

Wonky Black Sea Map, 2009, ink on paper, 14" × 17"

Violet and green made conceptual sense for the two seas, Black and Caspian. Bleached-out yellow and orange came purely from imagination.

From art history I knew the countless museum paintings of odalisques, the most famous by Jean-Auguste-Dominique Ingres, *Grande Odalisque*, who is not wearing clothes, followed by countless others, more and less clothed, by painters like Jean-Léon Gérôme and Henri Matisse. Their titles allude to slavery, slave markets, and harems, with young, mostly female beauty the constant. In the nineteenth-century United States, Hiram Powers's *The Greek Slave* allowed viewers to ogle a naked white girl in the interest of high art. There is no such thing as an ugly odalisque or an old odalisque. Tipped off by art history, I chronicled the way themes associated with the odalisque, enslavement and beauty, made their way into science. I began my chapter 5, "The White Beauty Ideal as Science," with the pioneering eighteenth-century art historian Johann Joachim Winckelmann, who established the hard, white aesthetic for the art of ancient Greece.

Having answered my original question of why white Americans are called Chechens, I needed thousands more words and nearly a decade to complete my book. In order to refute the all-too-common notion that ancient Greeks and Romans thought in the same racial terms as we use today, I began in antiquity. Yes, yes, they could see that some people had darker and lighter skin than others. But they didn't turn those distinctions into race, which wasn't invented until the Enlightenment of the eighteenth century. Upper-class ancient Greeks, who staged their manly games in the nude, derided their Persian enemies for being pale. In Greek eyes, Persians' lack of suntan presented physical evidence they spent too much time indoors; paleness impugned Persians' manhood.

After correcting errors about the ancients, my book had to come up to the present time to explain how we got to where we are now. This all took much longer than I had planned. Mounting travail exacted its toll on my own body, whose writing machine demanded peanuts and wine. I was getting fatter and fatter. My body could stand the puffing up, but the gain, oh no! made my face look its age, its old age. Either I push on with the book or I slow down, rest up, do my exercises, and, once rested up, eat right. I pushed on with everything.

During my time at Mason Gross, my own art made its way

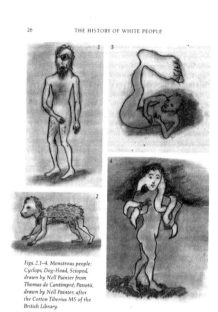

THE HISTORY OF WHITE PEOPLE

Figs. 2.1–4. Monstrous people: Cyclops, Dog-Head, Sciopod, drawn by Nell Painter from Thomas de Cantimpré; Panotii, drawn by Nell Painter, after the Cotton Tiberius MS of the British Library.

of the Roman elite from either northern Italy or southeastern France, Tacitus was an accomplished orator and author. His major works, *The Histories* and *The Annals*, tell the story of the Roman empire, and his minor works consist of *Germania*, a biography of his father-in-law,

nationalist websites, such as that of the Aryan Nations: "It's not a matter of White Supremacy it's about Racial Purity!"

Page 26 of *The History of White People*, 2010.
Four 2008 drawings are ink and graphite on Yupo, 12" × 9"

into *The History of White People* has four graphite drawings on page 26, images of the so-called monstrous races of people thought to exist in the Middle Ages.

At Mason Gross, I turned two of those drawings into lithographs, one three-dimensional in dark forest colors, one a Warhol-esque multiple in Warhol-esque brightness.

TOP: *Dog-head*, 2009, lithograph, approx. 5" × 7" × 2"
BOTTOM: *Golda's Sciopod*, 2009, lithograph, approx. 5" × 12"

History into art.

17

YOU'LL NEVER BE
AN ARTIST

YOU KNOW NOW THAT TEACHER HENRY PROCLAIMED
his truth that

I may show my work.

I may have a gallery.

I may sell my work.

I may have collectors.

But I would never be an artist.

And you know my retort,

Henry, that's bullshit.

Ontology or epistemology? The twentieth-century German Bauhaus notion that art cannot be taught held on until right down to Henry at RISD. Within that mystic ideology of the ontological An Artist, education cannot really help make art. As someone who had been in academia her entire life, I clung to my belief in education, whether my teachers did or not. Thank heaven Artist Friend Denyse reassured me that the language of visual art could be learned.

I figured out that "You'll never be an artist!" was meant

mean-spiritedly, as a way to take me down a peg—knock me off my high horse, put me back in my place, something like what that drunken Harvard lawyer at dinner in the Berkshires tried to do. That realization came only later, as I felt my own way into making my own art. Friends suspect I may have threatened my teachers, who may have been struggling against misgivings over their own status as An Artist artists. I don't know. Be that as it may, Henry's comment both enraged me, as I recognized it as criminally bad teaching, and humiliated me, by feeding into my colossal graduate-student insecurity. His comment doubtless said more about him than about me, which was of absolutely no help whatever. I was only thinking about me.

I WASN'T FEELING appreciated for my real strengths—intellectual sophistication and visual ambition. To the contrary, my strengths felt like impediments. Better to make abject images of toasters and trash bags or paintings in which accidents conveyed enigmatic meaning. Recognizable meaning seemed embarrassing to the painters around me, and, I suppose, if I had been a more acceptable painter, meaning would have embarrassed me, too. But it didn't embarrass me, and I persisted along my own singular path. That path brought recognition in the world I had come from, in the form of commissions for book and journal covers. *Signs* reproduced details from two panels of my Harriet Tubman series. *Fierce Departures* and *Chronicles*, by the poet Dionne Brand, used abstract drawings I had made by hand and then digitally recomposed in colors that were bright and subdued. For the cover of My Dear Friend Thadious Davis's book *Southscapes*, the designer used two searingly colored drawings I had made from a black-and-white 1930s southern photograph. My artwork was circulating outside my art school.

It was a wonder I didn't lose my mind, or maybe I did. On

TOP LEFT: Cover, *SIGNS*, 2010

TOP RIGHT: Cover, *Fierce Departures*, by Dionne Brand, 2009

BOTTOM LEFT: Cover, *Chronicles: Early Works*, 2011

BOTTOM RIGHT: Cover, *Southscapes: Geographies of Race, Region, and Literature*, 2011

some level I knew myself to be a super-duper intellectual, author of a blockbuster book, an Argonaut venturing where few dared to tread, et cetera, et cetera, Superwoman but not in such tight skimpy clothes. I was a star and a dud, simultaneously.

SO WHO THE hell is An Artist? Joseph Beuys said everyone is an artist, which is manifestly not true, either potentially or in terms of how you spend your time. It does seem that anything can be art, not only Marcel Duchamp's urinal and bicycle wheel, but also the contents of your dorm room or a list in a tent of everyone you've ever slept with. Arthur Danto supplied an answer that still serves: art is what is shown in the context of art, that is, what's put on a pedestal in galleries (is my living room a gallery?) and exhibited in a museum (what's a museum?). A value judgment suspended between market value and aesthetic imagination. Add what the art world calls the *critical consensus*, what critics agree is the right stuff, along with three queries: Who counts as a critic? Where does the criticism appear? When do you take your snapshot to capture consensus?

I wish I could say this reasoning comforted me on a daily basis—it did not. I didn't have to contend with the armies of negativity every day. But those armies bivouacked right nearby, ready at any time to defeat me. Just holding them in their barracks exhausted me.

I didn't know whether my fellow painters were struggling against armies of their own, even whether they were hearing criticism that made them question if they should or could stick it out. One rule about being An Artist is never to voice doubts, about yourself or about your work. "They" will use your doubts against you, especially if you are a black artist. That rule seemed to hold even among white artists, who even before so much as a hello were always touting where they had just gotten off the plane from and the places their work was being shown.

My fellows could have been doubled over in psychic pain in their studios or enjoying their Narragansett beers in serene self-assurance, leaving me as the only one hanging on the precipice of quitting. Intellectually I knew I was not the only one in the world harboring doubts. Later on when I would tell that story, someone would reply with their version of discouragement, their or a friend's leaving art school decades ago in the bad old days or only yesterday, often a woman, but sometimes a man, usually white, because non-white students in art school are rare. At the time I *felt* alone in my miserable alienation. Conflicting thoughts, confounding emotions as my everyday situation.

I held yet another set of thoughts at the exact same time. Sure, I might not be good enough, but many artists, An Artist artists, aren't good enough in other people's eyes. The curator of MoMA's PS1 told Dana Schutz, one of the leading painters of our time, "You must be the worst painter I've ever met." If you didn't know Amy Sillman and Nicole Eisenman were huge successes, you might question whether their draftsmanship was "good enough." I had overheard students belittle the painting skills of Kehinde Wiley, President Obama's official portraitist. And I knew my own surprise at Jackie Gendel's artist's talk, where she showed the progression of her art as she made figurative paintings. A lot of them were badly drawn and badly painted. But she had people on her side as she kept at it. Jackie Gendel is An Artist with gallery representation. Another cool visiting artist, Trenton Doyle Hancock, sent RISD students into raptures with work on a mythological scale, pulp culture, cartoons, imaginary fantasy worlds, text, personal and biblical narrative, all rooted in the art history of Hieronymus Bosch, George Grosz, Philip Guston, and R. Crumb and carried off with faux naive craftsmanship. His work exceeds judgments of "good" or "bad." I saw his work in his gallery in Chelsea. Definitely An Artist.

GALLERY REPRESENTATION, I quickly learned, is the main criterion for who counts as An Artist. I once filled out a questionnaire for artists that divided us into two categories: those with gallery representation and those without—the better class and the lumpen. Even if you thought Gendel's paintings weren't very good or Hancock's were childlike, you had to admit they were An Artist artists because of gallery representation. How do you get a gallery? You make work that counts as interesting in the eyes of An Artist with a gallery. Who are artists with galleries? Your teachers, your peers, your friends. They persuade the gallery director to visit your studio and concur that your work is interesting. There are so many galleries and so many ways of making art and so many good artists, even, and a whole lot of even bad artists have gallery representation. How do you tell what art is "interesting"? It looks like art. What is art? Art is what's in galleries. Now you know.

I learned another way to recognize An Artist artists. We graduate students would visit their studios to admire their process or at least recognize theirs as ways An Artist artists make art. There was the artist who poured acrylic paint on plastic sheets, let it dry, and glued it to canvas. There was the artist who projected pages from old IKEA catalogs and painted them mimetically in large format. There was the artist who put her paper on the floor and walked on it to make her marks. There was the professionally trained British artist who purposefully painted like a child. Clearly there were hundreds, thousands of ways to make art and to be An Artist.

RISD Teacher Kevin and Mason Gross student Keith used gallery representation as taglines of artists' identity, as though their galleries were their last names. (Some annoying writers do this to size up other writers according to the prestige of their publishers.) You rank galleries along a scale of coolness, so that attaching Pierogi to an artist's name would definitely sound good. Not just any gallery—not just any Chelsea gallery on the ground floor—could make an artist An Artist or a cool An Artist.

Gallery representation, as one sign you are An Artist, connects to two other criteria: selling your work and having collectors, two different things. I sold a little of my work even before going to art school, to friends and occasionally to colleagues. I know painters in Newark who haven't gone to art school who have sold way more art than I have or ever will. Plein air painters, cowboy painters, painters of pop star portraits and horses in sunsets can all sell circles around me. After all, who was the bestselling contemporary painter? Thomas Kinkade ("Painter of Light™"), with his nostalgic, kitschy scenes of Victorian mansions all lit up in the kind of deep snow that global warming has extinguished. Selling like crazy, but hardly An Artist artist.

Selling their work is a criterion very few artists can fulfill, even An Artist artists with gallery representation, solo shows, and work in public collections. Some years ago the painter Susan Crile won her Internal Revenue Service appeal that was all about sales and professional status. Because she listed very few sales, the IRS sued her for back taxes, reclassifying her art as a hobby rather than a business. This counts financially, because you can't deduct hobby expenses; business expenses are tax deductible. Crile hadn't sold enough art to make a steady profit, even though her work was in museums. She won her case in tax court, vindication for us all, for very few artists, even An Artist artists, make enough money to live on through sales of their work. Those who do are—this won't surprise you—disproportionately white and overwhelmingly male.

To be recognized as a serious artist, An Artist artist today, you need an art degree, an MFA, not just a BFA, though the essential graduate degree won't pay your bills. Even artists well enough credentialed to teach in higher education aren't making much money. Nowadays most artists teaching in colleges and art schools are adjuncts who either scrape by financially or teach in several institutions at the same time. I should say *and/or* teach in several institutions. Art and sustenance often conflict, for earning a living will prove fatal to your art if you have to spend too much time on the road chasing from gig to gig to paint. I didn't have to take a day job in order to live, thanks to my Rutgers professor husband. My financial well-being may have counted against the possibility of my being An Artist. To explain, I need to return you to my studio for another studio visit from Teacher Irma.

She was razzing me about wrong painting, and I, pathetic as usual, was trying to propitiate her. I riffled through the computer in my studio, desperately hunting for a work I hoped would meet her approval. She glowered. I searched. I couldn't find the image I was searching for. I apologized.

It must be in my laptop in my apartment, I stammered.

You own two laptops? Irma shrieked.

Yes, I owned more than one computer, I confessed. But one was just a dinky little white plastic laptop! (All right, it was a MacBook.) Another demerit on my record, another obstacle between me and An Artist artists. And I hadn't even begun to approach the collector criterion.

Collectors. When people in The Art World say "collector," they mean rich people. Really rich people who own more art than they can put on their walls at one time, even though they have lots of walls in multiple houses. They fly private jets from one international art fair to another, rotating between glitzy parties in exotic rooms. These big-name collectors, like François Pinault, Alice Walton, Walter Evans, the Rubells, David Driskell, the Broads, Dakis Joannou, Nancy Lane, the Chenaults, and Agnes Gund, are known for owning the work of superstar artists like Koons, Warhol, and Basquiat, mostly male New York artists. Hardly any of the big collectors are black, as are few of the artists they collect. This is changing to a certain degree as society desegregates, but there's still a very long way to go.

Big-name collectors serve on the boards of museums and contribute dollars, euros, and, increasingly, United Arab Emirates dirham and Chinese renminbi in the six and seven figures. They donate art from their personal collections to their pet museums, public and private, that turn the artists from their collections into "museum artists," attractive to other collectors. At auction, museum artists' work can sell for millions; in galleries, for hundreds of thousands and more. Collectors sometimes stand in line to buy work that hot artists haven't even made yet. Those hot artists are clearly museum artists, An Artist artists. I could see that museums, like galleries, were ranked according to wealth, status, and coolness. Obviously New York museums—MoMA and the Met and the Whitney and PS1 and the New Museum—sit at the top of the heap. Through the sponsorship of wealthy philanthropists, the Studio Museum in Harlem comes in close behind, having moved up in a generation from scrappy alternative space to premier destination for collectors and for hot young artists trained at Yale.

Henry was right that I would never be that kind of An Artist artist, though, as he conceded, I may sell my work; I may be represented by a gallery; I may have collectors. In fact, I already have collectors in New Jersey. But do collectors in New Jersey count? Oh my, I had so many deficits: no gallery, few sales, and New Jersey.

YOU KNOW, BACK in graduate school, I should have ignored my deficits. Even better, I should have flaunted them, making art according to my own bad-artist's hand, and lots of it, like a woman in the undergraduate painting class I had to take in the winter session of my first year. Sulking over my punishment, I envied her freedom over in the large corner she had commandeered and turned into her own personal studio.

Mary wasn't a regular RISD student. She was on the staff, taking a painting class just for the hell of it. No one was telling *her* to work on her skills. She fenced off her corner with piles of the work she made with a cadmium-red-hot-furious, total disregard. She made tons of work, most of it junk. But some of it grabbed you and would not let loose of your eyes. Some of it exploded with all the energy she threw—and I do mean threw—into her paintings.

The rest of us in the class, mostly undergraduates, were dutifully painting studio set-ups with models and a collection of miscellaneous objects—tires, fishnet, pots, chairs, and fabrics—things famously hard to depict. I hated every last damned painting I made there, so stinking were they of art-school set-ups. There I was, laboring like an undergraduate over verisimilitude, striving to capture the set-up, when I should have been, like Mary, painting what my hand was seeing. I was trying to paint as I thought I was supposed to in order to improve my skills. I hated hated hated every fucking moment in the studio in that class. Mary loved it with matching fervor.

Over in her corner, she painted, tore up her paintings, pasted them together in every which way, assignments be damned. To hell with the assignments! To hell with the blasted set-ups! Meanwhile, boring old me painted my stupid paintings by the rules. I'd never be an artist, never be An Artist. What would I be?

A TOTAL FAILURE

Hey! Not so fast. Not a total failure. One assignment, tapping into my old habit of painting myself, suited my eye and my hand. Sitting at the kitchen table in my apartment, I freely drew, painted, and collaged myself. We were to paint ten self-portraits, 12" × 12". I made twenty-five. I made them on paper and on board, as drawings, collages, and monoprints, in colors bright and subdued. They were all close-ups, but with varied backgrounds: landscapes, patterns, collage, and abstract. Okay. Twenty-five instead of ten of me me me. Best things ever at RISD. Who cares if I'm never An Artist artist?

I have never tried to make my self-portraits look like me, for issues of beauty and skin color and all the other judgment-laden markers of race and gender threaten to trip me up. I'm a nice-looking woman. What does it say if I paint myself as beautiful? My

TOP LEFT: *Self-Portrait 3*, 2010, acrylic on board, 12" × 12"
TOP MIDDLE: *Self-Portrait 5*, 2010, acrylic and collage on paper, 12" × 12"
TOP RIGHT: *Self-Portrait 10*, 2010, acrylic and collage on paper, 12" × 12"
BOTTOM LEFT: *Self-Portrait 11*, 2010, acrylic and collage on paper, 12" × 12"
BOTTOM MIDDLE: *Self-Portrait 12*, 2010, acrylic and collage on paper, 12" × 12"
BOTTOM RIGHT: *Self-Portrait 16*, 2010, acrylic and collage on paper, 12" × 12"

skin is dark. What if I made myself too dark or too light? What even counts as *too* dark or light?

Here lie snares for every black artist, for issues of skin color and nose shape and lip size and thickness and hair texture all carry positive and negative connotations in the aesthetics of race. They aren't just appearance, not just how things look. Every single line or volume carries social meaning. If I made my lips too thin or my color not dark enough, it could speak a lack of race pride. What about my hair? What a chore to try to depict it in its variegated nappiness, but how to capture it? Every single decision about self-representation could tip me into a racial morass.

My self-portraits wouldn't be just paintings of a particular individual rendered in a particular painting style. They entered a field of black-woman visual representation encompassing the beauty of Beyoncé and Michelle Obama, in which the light skin of the former fits easily into American tastes and the dark skin of the latter awakens new understandings while also attracting bigotry. "The black body" as minefield.

Black artists have myriad strategies for dealing with "the black body," for each individual black person's body, in this case, my own, exists within a visual field of pre-existing imagery, be it negative or positive. I had seen this firsthand with my parents, who were seen differently with the passage of time. And I don't mean this in terms of age, but with regards to skin color and evolving beauty ideals.

My father had always been considered handsome—still was, deep into his nineties, his light skin according with American beauty standards, his good health and personal charm further heightening his attractiveness. My mother, a different story, and not only because for years she was so shy. Because of her dark skin, my mother never felt beautiful, even though she always was beautiful. Only in her maturity was she widely complimented, due not to a change in her appearance, but to a broadening of American beauty ideals. She was in her eighties when she quoted what people said to her as the title of her memoir: *I Hope I Look That Good When I'm That Old.* After black became beautiful in the 1960s, my mother's beauty became obvious. I watched that change, and it inspired my work on physical beauty, manifested in my Michael Jackson and Apollo Belvedere paintings. So, yes, when you see my paintings and my self-portraits, you're seeing reflections of my mother's emergence into beauty and my awareness of a nimbus of images and appearances around "the black body," mine as well as hers. Prominent artists have tackled the challenge of racial expectations in various ways.

Emma Amos and Robert Colescott, two light-skinned African American painters, solved the color conundrum by depicting themselves in their paintings with darker skin to signal their racial identity. Colescott painted himself as dark-skinned in his art history paintings, where a light-skinned figure of the artist would complicate, even obscure their ironic cultural message.

Contemporary artists' depictions of dark skin avoid mimesis entirely. Toyin Odutola draws with multicolored ballpoint pens so her dark figures shine with countless colors. Amy Sherald, Michelle Obama's portraitist, paints African American subjects' skin a flat gray reminiscent of black-and-white photographs. Derrick Adams fragments faces into collage-like blocks of bright, unrealistic color. Kerry James Marshall solves the skin-color conundrum by painting his black figures a dense, matte black to reclaim the "power of blackness." His paintings are ironic and otherworldly, allegorical rather than naturalistic. Deep black figures in suburban settings transport viewers into an idyllic fantasy realm. Yet this means of rendering dark skin can confuse viewers, can even pique black viewers more accustomed to seeing work in public by white artists, and, given American history, accustomed to seeing black figures depicted in ways that denigrate us. The traps awaiting black artists can encourage a turning away from figuration. I braved adoring crowds to query abstract painters Julie Mehretu, in Providence, and Mark Bradford, in New Haven. I asked whether the racial politics around depictions of black people played any role in their choices of genre. Both said yes, that by working abstractly they sidestepped controversies of figurative representation that would distract from their art. Mehretu and Bradford do not approach figuration in their painting, and seldom in their titles. Jack Whitten, an abstract painter of great distinction, splits the difference. He captioned an abstract painting *Self-portrait*, and his titles often refer to black history. I came to painting too late to meet Alma Thomas, who rarely attached political titles to her abstract painting, one reason her work was so hard for such a long time for critics and collectors to value.

HENRY'S CONCEPT OF being An Artist brings me back to ontological thinking, this time about race. You *are* An Artist in the way you *are* your race. Both race and art can be envisioned as some quality beyond words that inheres within the person, a quality that can't reliably be measured. You can be dark-skinned, but still not be black enough. You can have gallery representation but still not be An Artist. It's more than skin color, more than sales, more than geographical origin, more than gallery representation, more than hair texture, more than collectors. According to this kind of logic, art and race reside in something as slippery as your temperament and the way you perform your identity of black person or artist; you can't change them, by this common line of thought, for they cannot be taught or learned. Being An Artist has little stable meaning, and its definition and the criteria you use to define it depend, as with race, on who's speaking to whom, when, where, and for what purpose.

Easy enough for you to say, oh lofty voice of reason. But impossible to hear down here on the ground in the muck and the confusion of the studio and the crit room, down here where An Artist mythology strode the halls as ideal. Impossible to avoid, so just run away.

18

DISCOVERY

BOMB-THROWING LURKED IN THE HEART FLEEING Providence, a pathetic, pissed-off, self-pitying, dioxazine purple ball of exhausted confusion stumble-driving from the first year of graduate school. I would have quit school, burned the goddam place down, and slit my wrists, but there was no giving RISD the satisfaction of defeating me, a price too steep to pay. Off I went, from Rhode Island toward the Adirondacks, staggering—in a diesel-station-wagon stagger—into the southern Massachusetts asphalt jungle where Route 146 meets the Mass Pike at I-395. Beyond the tangle, a congested snarl on the Mass Pike pierced remote distance in one-point perspective.

Rerouting.

The Mass Pike was meant to replace two-lane US 20, doubtless to improve it by diverting cars from the charming, run-down hamlets where every house was selling something and every building looked ruined. The Mass Pike took you into controlled-access fleetness. But not this time. Where the Mass Pike was a clogged artery, Route 20 flowed openly. Rural settlements with hardly any stoplights lined this federal highway. Good driving—until I rounded a curve, looked up to my right at large hand lettering:

Impeach Obama
His Mission is to destroy America

Now I know full well this sign had naught, nada, zero, *assolutamente niente* to do with my art-school agony. But on that road in that place, that foul Massachusetts video-gaming, blackness-hating, conspiracy-minded, gun-slinging militarist salted my wound. RISD. Obama-hater. RISD. Obama-hater. All the same southern New England cussedness.

Once safe in the mountains of northern New York State, I got some rest, and Obama evaded impeachment. The pull toward art returned; pain I felt as uniquely my own subsided. I recalled Friend Sarah's assurances, wisdom that had escaped me when my misery seemed strictly personal and heavily permanent. Now, in the Adirondacks in the early summer, I could hear her narrative of painters entering art school, their first-year despair, then their recuperation over the summer between their first and second years. In their second year, they would make art their own way.

MY NEIGHBOR ARTIST Friend Frank Owen looked at the work I tacked to my studio walls. In an afternoon of long looking and talking, Frank glimpsed my ambition as well as my shortfall. Noting my interest in the world, he lent me R. B. Kitaj's *Second Diasporist Manifesto*. On my first look, its untamed monomania blew me back. On second look, I settled into its omnidirectional nuttiness. Kitaj knew his book was all mixed up, and he dove deeply into piebald obsession. Kitaj's weirdness, even though it cost him his reputation as a painter for many years, inspirited me. Intellectually—though not in my heart's gut—I had known all along I wasn't the only one juggling history, group identity, individual proclivities, and visual art. For heaven's sake, that's what much of black and feminist art is all about—and has been for decades. Yet here was a visceral painter of pungent, acid palette, of people twisting through Chinese perspectives of his life's history in colors weird and bold. I lapped up the painting, but Kitaj's gift to me was writing.

Kitaj wrote a book—a combination of image and text. For now, though, I couldn't relate what I used to do, writing history, to what R. B. Kitaj had done, and what I was doing now in art.

I rested a little longer.

Before mind and body had fully recovered, my reptilian brain connected to my hand and recommenced pushing me around and back into painting. It sent me, with my two tabby cats, down the hill from the house a little ways to a long, narrow burnt-umber wooden outbuilding that had been a rabbit hutch and now entered service as the Rabbit Hutch Studio. About ten feet wide and thirty feet long, the Rabbit Hutch Studio has windows along one long side, low rafters—no ceiling—and a softly uneven faded linoleum floor directly on the ground. Insect life, flying and crawling and abundant, stayed right at home. No reason to vacate just because I was tacking up unfinished work.

Insects were a nuisance, especially the spiders that from me elicit a mixed reaction. I'm not good with spiders. Even middling ones bring back the terror of a gigantic spider-monster in its chain-link web blocking my garage door in Ghana. How did I ever get to my car? But ever since Ghana, spiders have been more than monsters. I've half regarded them as Ananse, my ancestors. I cannot kill a spider, repulsive though they be. Hero Glenn came to expel—not to kill—the Rabbit Hutch Studio's spiders.

On the long wall facing the windows of the Rabbit Hutch Studio, I put up my 60" × 60" acrylic paintings on unstretched canvas of Michael Jackson and Apollo Belvedere, the ones that had been alternately disparaged and ignored. I continued working on them in thinned-down paint and ink, each one with more than one figure.

LEFT: *Beauty + the Sublime: Jackson*, 2010, acrylic on unstretched canvas, 60" × 60"
RIGHT: *Sublime: Apollo*, 2010, acrylic on unstretched canvas, 60" × 60"

Painting standing up, except for the lower sections requiring me to sit on the floor or on a chair, I quit, hot and weary, only after five. Many excellent studio sessions turned my problem paintings' corner. They were finally looking like real paintings. With no crit looming, I just followed my hand, painting, looking and painting until the paintings said, Okay, we're done.

Once other work left over from the spring semester declared itself finished, I started new work inspired by Maira Kalman.

Maira Kalman is not usually considered a painter. She's called an illustrator, because her paintings accompany narratives, and she publishes in books. Books. There I was again, cozying up to an artist writing and making books. Even though art school told me real artists do not make books, I kept coming back to artists writing and making books. Bookmaking, with its everlasting pull. My teachers would talk me out of using text, maybe to break me of a bad old habit, maybe to teach me new tricks. Maybe I wasn't good enough to use text the right way (as though there were a right way). If one of their favorite artists, like Patricia Cronin, used research and narrative and text, that was allowed, even admired. But she was *good enough* to do it *right*. Research and narrative were only admitted on a one-time, case-by-case basis. Cronin could do it. My RISD peer Anna could do it and garner teachers' praise. But bookmaking, narrative, and text for me were to be discouraged. This prohibition frustrated me into response. For an art criticism class I wrote a paper entitled "Maira Kalman Is a Painter," meaning Maira Kalman *is so* a painter.

Maira Kalman grew up in Israel and New York knowing life to be "un-figure-out-able." As a student of literature at New York University, she met a self-appointed young revolutionary, Tibor Kalman, whom she married. Before his death at forty-nine in 1999, Tibor Kalman prospered as a designer. Maira taught herself to make art. And her drawing shows it. When I first saw her work in the *New York Times*, I thought, stiff-neckedly, that she could not draw. I quickly recovered from that conceit.

Kalman published twelve children's books in the 1980s and 1990s. In the early 2000s she made poignant adult books. Using line to delineate shape and perspective to define space, she employed an innocent palette of Hansa yellow, pink, and cerulean blue in *The Elements of Style*. In *The Principles of Uncertainty*, magenta, earth tones, and many shades of green joined her familiar pink. Though her books contain images of both cake and genocide, she is more likely to speak of the former than the latter.

Kalman, thank you, refuses to choose sides in the commonplace distinction between art and idea. Asked why she makes art, she replies:

It is a desire to tell a story.

Telling a story makes sense to me. It allows for a benevolent relationship to the world.

For her, the image does not come first, as it's supposed to in fine art.

I quoted her, They both come first.

I identified with Kalman out of my stake in the never-ending distinctions between design and art, between illustration and painting. Maira Kalman helped me place myself on the more prestigious art and painting sides of the judgment. I was, after all, a student of painting, not of graphic design. My imagery still felt constrained, too closely tied to narrative, but Maira Kalman was making me more comfortable telling stories visually.

WORKING LONG, SWEATY days in the Rabbit Hutch with my little tabby cat Gerda (Ro didn't like being so far from his house), I inched toward developing my own process. I began by drawing, initially copying, parts of photographs in *(un)Fashion*, a book by Tibor and Maira Kalman on the ways people around the world adorn themselves. Colorful people in colorful photographs wore a panoply of colorful costumes, for dressing up and for working in even the most wretched work sites. These photographs put me in a warm, 1950s Brotherhood-of-Man frame of mind, a balmy mood after the man's inhumanity to man I felt in art graduate school.

As I drew and painted, I inserted collage, scanned my hand-made drawings, and recomposed them in Adobe Photoshop. The collages incorporated torn strips of the *History of White People*'s manuscript, still present in my head and whispering my other life. Alternating with other-life-voice, also speaking practically out loud, came commands to "Loosen up! Let go! Stop making sense!" Glenn and I believed in coherence, in making sense of the world.

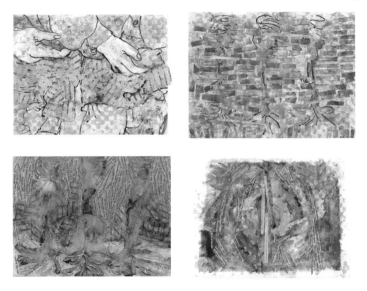

TOP LEFT: *Unfashion drawing 5*, 2010, colored ink and collage on Yupo, 9" × 12"

TOP RIGHT: *Unfashion drawing 8*, 2010, colored ink and collage on Yupo, 9" × 12"

BOTTOM LEFT: *Unfashion drawing 9*, 2010, colored ink and collage on Yupo, 9" × 12"

BOTTOM RIGHT: *Unfashion drawing 11*, 2010, colored ink and collage
on Yupo, 9" × 12"

But now I was telling myself—was it my reptilian brain again?—let up on the coherence. Okay.

To unscrew my attachment to coherence, I discovered my means in the music other RISD students listened to, especially the Black Eyed Peas, those phenomenal, omnipresent musicians I had first encountered during Barack Obama's 2008 presidential campaign. I was probably the last person in the world to discover them, but better late than never. The BEP spelled for me the difference between acoustic music and music made post-recording through mixing in the studio. Their message to me said music need not sound acoustic—like the classical music I used to listen to. Better not to even try to sound acoustic. You didn't have to get as close as possible to the sound of live music being played in your living room. Music could be gleefully unnatural, music I was liking.

My peers' music moved me from Schubert to techno, from analog to digital, from traces of the artist's hand to the unabashedly technological. From earth colors of yellow ochre, umber (raw and burnt), and sienna (raw and burnt) to chemical colors of Naphthol red, Phthalo blue, and Diarylide yellow. Digital manipulation had already begun loosening me up during the spring semester. The summer offered unlimited time to wander around in my computer in Photoshop.

The great thing—one of many great things—about Photoshop is its lack of brain. It thinks it has memory, but not like people. Pixels don't have any narrative sense; they don't care what's next to them or whether proximity makes meaning. What Photoshop calls "history" is so drastically foreshortened that it relates solely to what you did before you turned off your computer. Rather than use Photoshop to improve the appearance of photographs—to take away pimples or brighten a sunset—I could just go crazy. I could work purely according to my eye and my hand on my mouse or tablet. Photoshop was my post-production studio, my move from analog to digital. Perfect for me, in such dire need of haphazard.

In Photoshop I chopped up my drawings that I had scanned in a process of repetition, recomposing, and recoloring that went on for days. Photoshopped layers and fractured, meaningless images transported me into purer visuality. I projected my Photoshopped images onto canvas and painted by hand. Taking further steps, I photographed my paintings and played with them again in Photoshop, to project and paint—again—by hand. In this way, in this endless toggling back and forth between my computer and my hand, I found my own manual + digital way to make art.

Yes, my own manual + digital process.

Halfway through the summer, coherence was softening up;

anxiety's grip was loosening. That trap that held wild-animal me was opening, freeing up the paw, the hand I used for art making. I could still make out the trap's saw-teeth marks. But I was able to move my hand. I still beat myself up for lack of confidence, for my self-confidence hung back until someone I thought knew something about art (e.g., Critic Friend Sarah, Artist Friend Frank) corroborated my feeling that a thing I'd made and liked was really any good. I still didn't fully trust my own eye, though I knew what I liked and didn't like in my work. What a dumb way to be an artist! I knew that. Could I get past that? *Really* get past that?

Not yet.

Make more work.

MY DAYS DOWN in the Rabbit Hutch Studio were returning me to art-sanity, when came bodeful calls and emails from my father's friends.

My poor father.

There in Oakland, moldering in his bed of sorrows, he needed me.

Still depressed, still self-pitying. Inertness had sagged him back after a burst of outgoing pleasure several months after Dona's death.

Depression clawed him back. Wretchedness ruled. Again. How could I, in good conscience, devote day after day to joyous visual discovery, to the freedom of incoherent pursuit, when my poor father rotted in his bed, moaning, I'm all alone.

My poor father.

I can't make it by myself.

My poor, dear father.

Depression is the cruelest disease, as cruel as cancer, crueler than dementia, drilling its pain deep within soul, brain, and body. And, for my father, depression overruled medication. Depression sucked his energy, nailing him to his bed with railroad spikes of mean, rusty iron. Emptied of his good humor, my father could not smile, for pleasure exceeded the reach of his heart and his memory. The jaunty man in a beret who used to stride from Oakland to Albany and grin as he came up your walk could barely take himself to the bathroom. Immobilized physically and mentally, he felt nothing but sorry for himself.

On the phone, I'd counter that he wasn't by himself, he was hardly alone, that he had so many friends who loved him and that Salem's conscientious caregivers looked in on him regularly to make sure he was safe. At Kaiser Permanente he had the best possible health care. I reassured myself, tried to, that he really wasn't alone.

No good, my line of argument. No use whatever. My father allowed no salvation. His sight, he cried, was worsening. Everything was closing down. Darkness. What would he do when he could no longer see? His life would be naught. He and Dona had been married for seventy years; they had become one person; without her he was ruined; he was "alone," completely, devastatingly alone, because neither Dona nor I was there with him. I had to come to Oakland. Now.

I went to Oakland.

I took my art supplies.

I stayed a week, sitting beside my father weeping in his bed because I would be leaving. I read him Manning Marable's *Malcolm X: A Life of Reinvention* and my positive review of it in the *Boston Globe*. When my father was not even able to abide Malcolm, I pulled out my art supplies and made a series of small abstract drawings on paper in colored ink and collage from art magazines. Most were smaller than 8" × 12". I called them *Bedside Collages*.

My anguished father draped his pain and his suffering over me. How could I mitigate his agony? My helplessness before his helplessness thwarted my impulse to comfort him.

But he did not snuff out my art. He failed to make me quit art

TOP: *Bedside Collage 2*, 2010, colored ink and collage on paper, 7" × 10"
MIDDLE: *Bedside Collage 5*, 2010, colored ink and collage on paper, 7" × 10"
BOTTOM: *Bedside Collage 1*, 2010, colored ink and collage on paper, 7" × 10"

school, or to leave my husband, or to move to Oakland to take care of him forever. But, boy, did he ever try.

BY THE END of the Adirondack summer, I had found myself again, my real, pre-graduate-school me, I mean. I no longer mourned my mother gut-wrenchingly, heart-searingly. I had new confidence in my art and the feeling I had made a decent start in finding my way to make *my* art. Alternate crits with people liking what I liked and doubting what I doubted had lessened my distrust of my own eyes. I had gained a footing, found a perch, discovered a place where I could stand or hang on to make my work. A toehold in *my* process. After the pieces inspired by *(un)Fashion* and the *Bedside Collages*, I made a series of abstract ink drawings on Yupo with collaged pieces of the *History of White People* manuscript. In vivid hues and sinuous drawing, they rounded out my break.

At the end of the summer in a gesture of self-confidence, I opened the Rabbit Hutch Studio to friends and neighbors, some of them painters and art historians. They stayed around and talked about my paintings and took note of my growth, occasionally marveling, as I had heard before, over how far I had come in so short a period. My visitors made it feel like a real art opening by dwelling on my art. There's nothing like the massage of approval to unclench the gut. Open studio over, gut unclenched, I wrapped up my work to take back to RISD for my second and last year of graduate school.

I COULD NOT attend the traditional RISD painters' kick-off barbecue at Teacher David's house before the start of classes. Instead I traveled to Durham, North Carolina, for the opening of my archive—*my archive*—in the John Hope Franklin Center in the Duke

TOP: *Lake Clear Drawing Ecclefechan*, 2010, colored ink,
gouache, and collage on Yupo, 11" × 14"

MIDDLE: *Lake Clear Drawing Lapouge's Anthroposociology*, 2010, colored ink,
gouache, and collage on Yupo, 11" × 14"

BOTTOM: *Lake Clear Drawing 1*, 2010, colored ink,
gouache, and collage on Yupo, 11" × 14"

University Library. In place of meeting the incoming class of RISD painters, the new boys and girls in town, I savored the official unveiling of this archive of my personal and professional papers. Though my archive mainly documents my stature as historian, it holds artwork going back to high school. The Ghana drawings in this book come from my archive at Duke.

Being feted at Duke as a Person of Importance, seeing items from my archive laid out as artifacts, talking about my quarter-century-long correspondence with Nellie McKay, felt awfully good. For the first time, I spoke publicly about my individual singularity, for I was feeling exceedingly singular.

Singular was me, wallowing, glowing in appreciation of my scholarship. I loved it all, unabashedly. Even so, and for all my scholarly shining, the real high point of my Durham visit was an onstage interview with the Duke art historian Richard Powell. Sitting beside me onstage, Professor Powell gave a close reading of my Apollo painting, one that fell flat in Providence. He recognized the art historical allusions—Apollo Belvedere, Caspar David Friedrich, and the Harriet Tubman figure walking through Harlem on the lower right. Here was the crit from heaven, my painting critiqued according to composition, palette, and art-historical resonance.

Sharing a stage with Rick Powell gratified me personally, for years earlier, as I began researching art for *Creating Black Americans*, he had widened my way into the history of black artists. Powell pointed me toward scores of works by black artists, only a few I already knew, and scores of artists I never knew existed. Art historical discovery is what Rick Powell meant to me.

For the world, Powell was a pioneering art historian specializing in black art. He made known the extraordinary and ultimately tragic artist William H. Johnson, a genius painter in Europe whose art changed—had to change?—when he returned to the United

States, where a black artist who painted like a modern artist—not like a *black* artist—found no audience. It's as though the few eyes at the time aware of black artists could not see his art as art, or if they did see his work, they didn't like it. Noting young Jacob Lawrence's extraordinary success, Johnson figured things out. He switched to a faux-naïf style and recognizably southern black subject matter, turning out work that found its audience. Those faux-naïf paintings are still the work Americans associate with his name. The earlier work is only slowly gaining a following.

In the Q and A after Rick Powell's crit from heaven, I giddily quoted the immortal Santana:

I am free! I am free! I am freeeeeee!

Okay, okay. I wasn't exactly free, for one more RISD year lay coiled to bite me back in Providence. But I was no longer the pathetic little ninny of the spring. For the second-year walk-through I put up the work I had made over the summer, filing a whole wall of my big second-year studio. The teachers came in, David and Donna first, astonished, they said, to be praising the magnitude of my output. How fine that I had continued to work on my big paintings from last year! How much better they were now than they were then. Teachers Holly, Dennis, Kevin, Jessica, and Duane came in later, all totally astonished by what they saw. Teacher Holly even suspected there might be some good painting somewhere in the Michael Jackson painting, which I heard as approval. Expressing the sense of the group, Kevin said the plantain paintings were pretty good: The best painting I've seen from you.

High praise. High praise.

I had made these paintings in the digital + manual process I had figured out in midsummer, digitally juxtaposing and repeating a detail of a figure from *(un)Fashion* with the scan of the miniature dragon toy of Former Student Crystal's son. I made the layered composition in Photoshop, projected it onto canvases, and painted each one separately, varying the colors in opacity and saturation. It felt like a good way for me to work over the long haul.

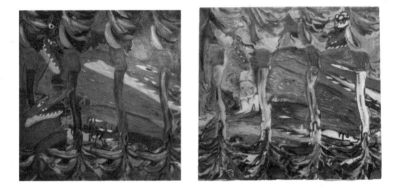

LEFT: *Plantains 1*, hand-painted acrylic on digital archival print on canvas, 36" × 36"
RIGHT: *Plantains 2*, hand-painted acrylic on digital archival print on canvas, 40" × 40"

By fall's midterm crit, I was practically home free. Kevin and David saw the first four of my Brooklyn paintings as testimonials to my continuing progress. Liking my *Second Man* paintings a month later, Teacher Kevin was stunned by our positive, sophisticated, extended discussion of my work. How could this be? How could this be *my* work he was liking?

He just could not, totally could not see how this could be happening, having questioned the very possibility of improvement in my painting, but here it was. How could this have happened? Of his astonishment, I said,

I know, Kevin, I know.

Kevin wondered what earthly power could explain my progress, but it was no secret to me. My answer? My old standbys: education and hard work.

Education and hard work?

Maybe painters weren't supposed to work as hard as I did. And if artists were born, not made, as in Henry's ontological-not-epistemological concept of An Artist, how could education make so much of a difference? How could last year's bad painter turn into this year's good—okay—promising painter? Remembering Friend Denyse of the generous alternative crits, I rejected ontological reasoning. Education and hard work made all the difference in the world.

IN THE FALL there came a broadcast email announcement of artists' studio residencies in Gallery Aferro in Newark, New Jersey. My colleagues, all bent on moving to Brooklyn after graduation to become An Artist artists in New York, turned up their noses and trashed a flyer from New Jersey. Not me. I was going back to Newark, so Gallery Aferro was pertinent. Glenn and I had attended art events on Market Street and knew Gallery Aferro. A six-month residency with a big studio for $225/month sounded excellent. Perfect, in fact.

I applied.

I made the first cut.

I was accepted for a residency to start at the end of the summer after my graduation. Hunky-dory. I glimpsed a life after art school. Only my MFA thesis, written and painted, stood between me and graduation.

19

MFA THESIS

WORKING IN MY STUDIO EXPANDED TIME AND SPACE: the space, one of the large second-year painting studios, the time, limitless. The studio had windows on the south and west— bright and good for seeing colors, but hot, not good for so sweaty a person as me. Fix that, and soon, even though the remedy proved strenuous. Glenn bought me long curtains and climbed high on a ladder, up, down, up, down, to install brackets and hang curtains. Thank you, Dear Glenn, for perilous labor that turned my studio into a work site for the duration. Big walls for painting and for hanging. I installed my work from the summer, work that passed muster in fall crits.

Not just my summer's work, but I also passed muster, bolstered by conversations with artists far from Providence who noted my productivity and called productivity a strength, not a quality beneath notice. They told me productivity was a crucial ability—a talent even, as precious a *talent* as the talent considered inborn for An Artist artists. Yes, productivity was a skill for the long haul, not some dun-colored, dogged clotting. In my outside crits, my

ambition, even when falling short in execution, merited acknowledgment as a unifying vision binding the many kinds of work I was
trying out. My outside crits of the summer said what I needed most
to hear:

Keep going.

Keep on making *your* work.

I had acquired defenses against silence and too-hasty turnings
away.

No, this is not fair to my RISD teachers and student colleagues
who were now trying to find words for my work, even to sound encouraging. Too late. We were on different wavelengths, maybe even
on different spectra, distanced not only in measurement but also in
meaning. In any case, I was now less susceptible to the discrepancy
between what I was trying to do—to say something about the state
of the world and about history, not striving for the aesthetic of
uninhabited objects without further meaning. My paintings were
inhabited reflections of my mental world.

This second fall, now, I disengaged, not completely, not success-
fully, not definitively, but sufficiently to figure out that this was not
my place, and these were not my people. To say I was transcending
RISD sounds too lofty and way too resolved. I still fell prey to painful bouts of self-doubt and visual thrashings. Even so, I established
distance from my milieu. I didn't know exactly where I was, but I
was searching for my work, *my* work, on a map or in a place apart
from theirs.

Part of my problem was wanting to engage issues that came up
in class at greater length and depth than my fellow students considered seemly. Part was plain old disagreement. For example. Visiting Critic Bob lectured us on conceptual artists, taking as a case
in point Adrian Piper, who in the streets of New York City in the
1970s and 1980s challenged people to examine their assumptions
about race and gender. I'm not sure my colleagues had known of

Piper, and I was glad Critic Bob talked about her work. (I should have been more grateful to him for mentioning a black artist, for I didn't give sufficient thanks.) In any case, I couldn't let pass his assertion that Piper was the first artist to address issues of black identity.

What the hell!

I could not let pass that lump of sheer, complete, glaring, even insulting unadulterated ignorance. I mentioned the Black Arts Movement of the 1960s, the very least of what needed to be said at a moment when my time for lecturing was circumscribed. No one picked up on my comments, whether what I had said seemed like TMI or simple irrelevance. I hadn't said much, but it felt like too much. It was as though the Black Arts Movement belonged to another world—a world away from here, a world foreign to The Art World as I was encountering it. Luckily for me, other experiences weren't so frustrating.

I was taking an art criticism class with Teacher Debra that I looked forward to every week. Teacher Debra was a Canadian, an eerily white-skinned blonde dressed in art-world black and vivid crimson lipstick that accentuated her whiteness. No matter. In her chairs-everywhere, obstructed-view-of-the-screen, windowless classroom with the temperamental projector, we read and discussed not just Clement Greenberg, but also Harold Rosenberg and Arthur Danto, and we turned over perennial questions of what constitutes good art and who decides. One painting student expressed blithe confidence in the market as an efficient arbitrator of the good and the bad. Others of us stayed after class to keep talking. I loved that class and was coming to adore Teacher Debra.

If you enlarge your definition to suit art-school demography, I wasn't the only old person in Debra's class. Within the usual RISD range of ages, people in their thirties felt old. My fellow old people in Debra's class were two photographers, one from South Korea, the other from Portugal, both in their forties. I could practically be their mother. Still, we shared a kind of we've-seen-this-before firmness beside the inexperience of our younger peers. We old folks sat around after class with Teacher Debra (herself between the photographers and me in age), free to turn over our reading and our lives at greater length. We discovered one another's art practice, paying one another studio visits, beers in hand. Talk about a balm, Debra's class was Gilead balm, a salve for my hurt. Well, come now. Let's not exaggerate. My RISD world beyond Debra's class wasn't all cruelty. It just felt like that a lot of the time. Her class, with its occasions for fruitful, friendly conversation and studio visits, was downright enjoyable.

GLENN AND I were soon on our way to Oakland to spend the holidays with my father, who hardly got out of his pajamas or his apartment. While we were there, he managed to get up to talk to his visitors, but mainly he complained of being all alone, despite helpers and friends. His complaint conveyed a new message, no longer that I should leave New Jersey and move to Oakland to care for him. Now he was saying he wanted to move to New Jersey to be with family. That was, to be with me.

What about all his friends here in Oakland? All the experts say friends are crucial to successful aging. What about his Kaiser Permanente doctors in one of the best health care systems in the country? Everybody knows good health care is essential. Apart from one former College of Chemistry graduate student from the 1960s, my father lacked friends in New Jersey. And Kaiser Permanente doesn't operate there. But my father would have family in New Jersey, that is, he would have me. I spent my winter break scouring northern New Jersey for assisted-living facilities.

My investigation revealed contradictions of race and class that had not appeared so starkly in the Bay Area. In Oakland, my father, a well-educated and moderately prosperous man, lived in Salem Lutheran Home among other well-educated and moderately prosperous people, a quorum of whom were also black, two of whom he had known for many decades. A perfect place.

Was the likes of Salem Lutheran Home in Oakland to be found in northern New Jersey? Not that I could see, at least not at that time. The well-educated, moderately prosperous places were way too white for a man who grew up in the segregated South and who still, after all these years and despite individual white friends, regarded large masses of strange white people as a condition to be avoided. Certainly not something to pay for in the tens, even hundreds of thousands of dollars. At the same time, the places with enough black residents weren't comfortable enough and didn't have well-enough educated people. My father, no longer always agile in his chatting, couldn't just start a lunchtime conversation asking what his tablemate did at the university.

My father was already wavering. First he was feeling better, getting out of his apartment and once again walking Salem's grounds. He was going to be okay in Oakland. My weeks of research seemed wasted, but better he remain in Oakland. The prospect of moving my father and his medications and his incontinence across the continent made my head ache. Fingers crossed for his staying on the up and up.

My father stayed up.

I returned to Providence for my last semester.

I FACED MY MFA thesis with a confidence as sublime as it was unmerited. The sublime: having already located the photographic

Studio Postcard, digital media, 4 ¼" × 6"

archive that was inspiring my paintings, I had pinned the photo archive on my studio wall and gone to work manually + digitally.

At first my images came along slowly, but the process was its own reward. I used Photoshop to reimagine Lucille Fornasieri-Gold's photos of Brooklyn in the 1970s and 1980s, figurative images that I edited in composition and turned from black and white into color according to my own inspiration. I was getting ready to paint when my father called, weeping, moaning, wailing that he was losing his eyesight. He couldn't see. His sight failing, whatever would become of him when he could no longer see?! Sob, sob.

My father's eyesight had been failing for years—for decades— from glaucoma. His first ophthalmologist had told him when she diagnosed his glaucoma he would be blind in fifteen years. That was in the 1960s. Over the decades and into the new century, he took his drops faithfully and preserved sufficient sight to drive (until recent years), read, and walk. He lived with his disability in the recognition that it had a psychological as well as a physical dimension.

Once as I was driving him to his bank in San Leandro, we talked about glaucoma, which I am likely to inherit. My father could still see a stop sign and surveil my driving. Every now and then he felt the need to remind me of who was the father and who the daughter. Between overseeing my driving—totally unnecessary as I am an excellent driver, I want you to know—he related an encounter with a man who was completely blind. My father said he had asked this blind man how he could enjoy life even though he couldn't see.

The blind man said,

It's all in the spirit of the thing, not in the physical disability.

It's all mind over matter.

If you don't mind, it doesn't matter.

My father, a great positive thinker back in the day and even later in San Leandro, resolved to face his "challenges," as my parents termed disasters, in a positive frame of mind.

That was then. Now, in his bed in his room, he lay at the edge of perdition, crying his eyes out, so to speak. His sight, he cried, really was failing, for his current ophthalmologist had now declared him legally blind. At the same time, the ophthalmologist assured my father that he could preserve what little sight remained if he continued his drops—which he did thanks to the aides at Salem—went outside, and exercised regularly. Which my father only did for a while. He walked around the Salem grounds and could read the time from the clock on the far wall of his apartment. For a time that was his objective situation. Then depression knocked him back into his bed, his vale, of tears.

He wept for two weeks in the season that coincided with the

anniversary of my mother's death. Angry and wretched, he cried and complained. My thoughts were not generous in his regard. I cursed the fate that had taken away my plucky little mother and left me with him. She, with so much to live for. He, a disconsolate, self-pitying mess taking me down with him, his depression a contagion infecting me through the phone. Somehow, from a source that may also have been him, I found my way to paint and broach my written thesis.

FROM THE PHOTOGRAPHS on my studio wall, I picked one to start with, a black-and-white dogfight, for its action. My two paintings added color and stuttered the original image, adding a horizon line for distance, and, from another photograph, graffiti and a partial figure. In recognition of my images' digital origins, I painted the pixels. I made two versions of my image, one in warm, saturated colors, the other desaturated.

In both these paintings the dogfight photo origins are clearly discernible. Years later on, after leaving RISD, I kept painting from the Brooklyn photographs, returning to the dogfight image. After several alternations between hand-painted works and digital manipulation, the dogs slipped into abstraction, as in *New Dogs Symmetrical*.

In my RISD studio, I reviewed Lucille's photos one after another, trying to resist her strong sense of narrative, seeking out her multiracial scenes, and trying to reconfigure them as my own, not wanting merely to repeat a play Lucille had already staged. From a photo with strong interaction between three men and a little dog, a piece contrasting figures from conflicting classes and generations, the little dog's aggression enacting social conflict, I extracted just one figure I called "2nd man." Leaving out the other two men and

LEFT: *Nature of Life April*, 2010, acrylic on canvas on panel, 30" × 36"
RIGHT: *Nature of Life*, 2010, acrylic on canvas on panel, 36" × 36"

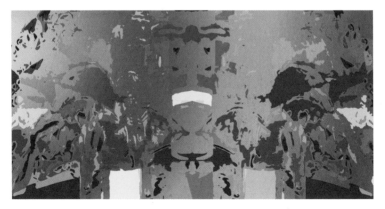

New Dogs Symmetrical, 2015, digital collage on paper, 48" × 96"

LEFT: *Second Man Walled and Windowed*, 2011, acrylic on canvas on panel, 40" × 40"
RIGHT: *Second Man Drawn*, 2011, acrylic on canvas on panel, 40" × 40"

the little dog, but working with 2nd man, I experimented with his image in my *2nd Man* paintings.

I recombined motifs freely, painting in series in order to try different ways of making images and applying paint. A pair of lifeguards showed through a window over 2nd man. What a joy, this time for experimentation and imagination.

And so it went, day after day, in the luxury graduate school grants its fortunate inhabitants: the gift of time. The gift of time to concentrate on your own work, to try out new approaches, new techniques, new visual moods as unhurriedly as possible in American life. I painted steadily, not wanting to stop at the end of the day or the end of my evening. Just a touch of acrylic here, of varnish there, painting no longer a test I was constantly failing.

Once I had made fourteen paintings, I had extinguished RISD Painting's dragon's breath. My last manual + digital painting combined imagery from three of Lucille's photographs, plus collage of a little bootlegged text. The colors, chemical rather than organic, declared their departure from nature. I titled this 40" × 40" painting, with the lifeguards I had used in a *2nd Man* painting, *Back Man 1*.

It was *Back Man* because I extracted this figure with his back to the viewer from the far background of one of Lucille's photographs. Back Man spoke to me as a gesture as well as an image, for in his fuck-you little hat, he turned his back to you, to graduate school, to all its pathetic groping bewilderment. Later on, Back Man would reappear several times in my paintings, but no longer as a mood, simply as a motif, an arresting figure wearing a hat.

Back Man 1 was *1* because I expected to paint others inspired by the motif. In my studio I addressed it familiarly as *My Last RISD Painting*, or *MLRP*: my emblem of survival. It was, in fact, the last painting I made at RISD, and I showed it in the MFA Thesis Show.

Back Man 1, 2011, acrylic, oil stick, and collage on canvas, 40" × 40"

In the event, the painting side of my MFA thesis unrolled straightforwardly, even though initially it was the more intimidating. The written thesis was another thing. The concept came easily as the elaboration of my transit from historian to painter by comparing how I used archives as historian and as visual artist. I titled it "Archive to Brush." Surely a snap for me, the author of seven books. I wasn't afraid of words. I knew I could write. I loved to write. The only problem I envisioned would be stanching a flood of words.

A Skype with Teacher Roger in charge of our written theses envisioned fifteen hundred to two thousand words. Fifteen hundred to two thousand words! I could write that in a weekend! I had written more words than that for Teacher Debra's term paper. I made a start on my thesis, quickly up to 525 words, and I was only warming up.

Please, Roger, give me at least twenty-five hundred words.

Was word limit my major obstacle?

NO NO NO NO NO

Two huge boulders, one discursive, one emotional. The discursive seemed easier to overcome, a matter of approach, of style. I had to write at length about how things looked, not what they meant. What they were made of—medium, composition, palette—and how they were made, meaning process. This entailed a refocusing, and that I could manage.

The emotional obstacle was much bigger and harder to finagle, for I began by expressing my conviction, which I still hold today, that the art world—rather, The Art World—had no firm criteria beyond the market for deciding what is good art. Scholarship isn't innocent of bias, but it has peer review and the expectation of respect for the archive. The market, in contrast, relates to social constructs of race and gender and to who can be an interesting artist according to society's values. I knew from Critic Rob and Artist Stanley that social exchange—who wants to spend time with whom, who feels comfortable in the studio with whom, which studios curators visit, which artist is young and cute enough to create buzz—all that influenced gallery representation, sales, and collecting. Yes, yes, there is definitely such a thing as the quality of the work. But there's too much good work in the world to explain in terms of quality alone who counts as an artist worth noting and who gets ignored. I could see that who counted had to do with race and gender and class and place (New York, yes; New Jersey, no). What I considered discrimination pissed me off, still pisses me off, this art-historical-canon-making a reflection of fashion, not some free-floating quality of intrinsic worth or artistic genius, all the while pretending that objective criteria exist.

I knew from my own book *Creating Black Americans* that there existed entire bodies of work, entire worlds of interesting art that were not visible in the art history I studied at Rutgers and that RISD took for granted. My Artist Mentors Mildred Howard and Camille Billops said it plainly and right out loud:

The Art World is racist as hell and unashamed of it.

This was why Romare Bearden, the avatar of collage, did not even appear in a book on collage and why Robert Colescott, my patron saint of painting, only came up if I mentioned him.

Experienced women painters I knew, Pat Steir and Faith Ringgold, told me stories of disregard, of keeping on with their work out of "sheer spite." Howardena Pindell stated much the same thing. I knew the visual art world I was writing about and entering was rigged and rigged against me, even before factoring in my own personal fatal flaw of age. These things pissed me off, and I wrote as with ten tiny penises pissing through my fingers.

There was piss all over the draft I read to my colleagues, the part about art's lack of standards. They were aghast. How could I be so self-righteous about scholarship and dismissive of visual art?

NO NO NO NO NO

How could I be so sanctimonious about scholarship's weighing of evidence and application of professional standards? Whose side was I on, anyway? What was I? Princeton historian or RISD painter? I had to choose.

Here's how it came down: I wasn't qualified to write a thesis in visual art. Gotta get expert help. I took my draft to the writing center. Yes, *I* went for help in writing. I sat down with Teacher Jen; I ate humble pie. I went home. I revised. I consulted with Teacher Jen some more. More humility. I revised. I consulted. I revised. I purged the anger from my written thesis, deleted self-righteousness and wrung out the piss—tried to, at least.

My thesis as well as my paintings met their deadlines, ready for visits from our two outside readers, Mira and Helen. I met productively with Reader Mira, who noted my citation of her work. She liked *Back Man 1* and urged me to paint more like that and not be diverted into books, even artist's books. But when Reader Helen was scheduled to come to Providence, I could not be there.

I could not be in Providence when Reader Helen came because the Harvard Graduate School of Arts and Sciences was giving me a Centennial Medal at commencement that very day. An honor of a lifetime. What about the scheduling conflict? There was no way in hell or in heaven or purgatory that I would skip Harvard commencement and my Centennial Medal to meet Reader Helen in Providence. Not even a teensy twinge of divided loyalties between my second reader and my Centennial Medal. I would have to see her some other time, and I was willing to come to Boston in order to see her. I emailed Reader Helen to explain my predicament and to ask please please to let me bring JPGs of my paintings to her at her convenience.

Reader Helen did not reply. I waited another week before re-sending my message, figuring my email might have gotten buried or accidentally deleted. Making the enormous request for half an hour of her eyes on my painting and my written thesis, now down to only twenty-eight hundred words, I was exceedingly humble in tone. Would she please please let me know when would be convenient for her to let me come to Boston, just not at the same time as Harvard commencement?

Reader Helen never responded. I don't know why, can't even begin to guess what happened on her end, for I know what it's like to be overwhelmed and to fall behind in my email. In Reader Helen's unbroken silence, Teacher Duane scolded me for harassment. His accusation spewed out of my email, as though I had mugged Reader Helen and run off with her things. In Reader Helen's absence, a young visiting artist signed on as my second reader so I could graduate alongside my colleagues.

NOW THAT WAS a very good day! My Dear Friend Thad came from Philadelphia, and my former Princeton student Crystal and her family came from New Haven. Duhirwe and I graduated. In a mass of black robes, I wore my bright (though faded) crimson Harvard PhD robe, unable to resist that final gesture of personal vanity. I patted myself on the back for perseverance. For survival. For simply getting through.

Everything was copacetic, even after the program revealed that all seven other MFA painters, including Mike, whose painting had hardly progressed in two years, that all seven of them had graduated with honors. Only one painter of the eight lacked honors.

20

AND NOW?

Now what?
All done with formal study, MFA in hand, a body of work still groping for its own way of seeing but a body of work nonetheless. That wave of crimson-robe-clad exultation receded, revealing conundrums both familiar and strange. I was a new painter, in the parlance of the day, an "emerging artist," but in an old body, a body old enough for an emerging artist's mother or grandmother who would have had more mother's or grandmother's skills. Artists who were actually my age—assuming they were still working—many were retired, even already dead—were so much more accomplished than I. My chronological age disqualified me for benefits intended for new painters, and many prizes outright rejected artists over thirty or forty. Other enthusiasms wordlessly discounted artists with more than a few miles on them. My lying eyes had moved into the twenty-first century, but I still couldn't make *right nowness*'s grade.

I still had to push down that feeling of being superannuated, of suspecting people wanted me to go away, to disappear along with my disproportioned combination of new and old. Was I making this up? Exaggerating, if not inventing my incongruity? Very possibly. No matter how exposed I felt, there was good fortune in my now. In actual fact I was not homeless as an artist. A residency at Aferro Gallery in Newark offered me a studio to work among new colleagues. Thank heaven for Aferro, this new artist's new home, with its mix of ages and ways of making work.

Aferro Gallery, a nonprofit, artist-run institution, sits in an enormous former furniture store on Market Street in downtown Newark in a block of stores between the former Bamberger department store, Essex County College, and the Essex County courthouse, with its statue of seated Abraham Lincoln. Some of the stores are still selling furniture to other people's taste, but most of them are empty, one recently re-darkened after the closing of a new business, a trendy fluorescent-lit clothing store selling tight, short, low-cut dresses for the club, pointy-toed shoes for men, and accessories for giggly women who called themselves girls. Another newly re-darkened furniture store had previously reopened as an art gallery featuring up-to-date installations, huge paintings on unstretched canvas, and iconic sculptures of men's manly parts. Glenn and I had attended this gallery's openings before it closed for lack of sales on Market Street and moved to an even bigger space in Paterson.

At one of the old-time furniture stores still operating, the salesman stood in the doorway, regular and friendly, greeting me with his one lazy eye looking the other way. Artists coming and going to Aferro diversified a crowd of Newarkers waiting for the bus. On the other side of Aferro and beyond the huge former art gallery, a mannequin of President Obama sat smiling at passersby, sufficiently lifelike to demand a second look the first time you saw him. Here's still there now, sitting on his bench, his paint nicked and peeling, a smile still on his face.

Aferro's space is so long you can't see the back from the front.

The ground and second floors are exhibition space, with bathrooms and water on the second floor. Studios on the third and fourth floors. From my third-floor studio, I had to come down to the second floor to pee or wash my brushes. Dahlia, an experienced artist whose work I admired, was installed in apparent permanence on the fourth floor. Her ironic paintings used text and many shades of blue, making her, in her settled studio, my role model.

The third floor's five studios connected, so that to reach mine in the windowless front of the building, I walked through two other artists' spaces. If I turned toward the back as I came up the stairs, I would walk through two other studios. This configuration kept me abreast of my comrades' work, but not in a New-York-y spirit of competition. We talked. We attended one another's openings at Aferro and elsewhere. We organized artists' talks and the most attentive of crits, going down the line of the third-floor studios: Katrina's charcoal drawings. Ken's dismembered stretcher bars. Vikki's prints and drawings. Marcy's tiny figures made of dryer lint. My paintings.

Aferro crits and conversations felt good, like belonging to a community of artists, something I missed at RISD despite the declaration that our MFA painting classmates would stay community now and forever. Maybe for them. It was actually happening for me at Aferro, in daily exchanges on the third floor, in artists' talks, in shows where the public came to see our work and talk with us, and, in one instance, to ask me how old I was. Former Aferro residents like Artist Jerry Gant, dean of Newark street artists, showed work there and met me as a comrade.

After Glenn built me a closet for my valuables—this was still the city, after all—I made my first post-RISD paintings, eight 12" × 15" works, acrylic ink on unstretched canvas, inspired by text text text!, such as a poem by my Poet Friend Meena, "When Asked What Sort of Book I Wish I Could Make," perfect for me still

Meena's Book, Grandmother's, 2011, acrylic on canvas, 12 ¼" × 15 ¼"

with books in my blood and in my eyes. These were painterly little paintings, lush in subtle color and sweetness. Maybe too much sweetness.

After my art-school slaps on the hand for bookishness, my fondness for words broke free. And ran all over my studio. Call it abandon. Call it belated defiance. Felt good at Aferro. Felt very very good, even a little naughty-child-beyond-teachers'-oversight.

Rolling around in text felt great for a month, then the Brooklyn paintings tugged back at me, calling me back to my digital + manual process and to larger formats. I sketched out a couple of 40" × 70" drawings on heavy watercolor paper repurposed from amateurish drawings I had made years earlier at the Studio School Drawing and Painting Marathon, then four canvases on stretcher bars. After the sketches, I went as a short-term Fulbright scholar to the United Kingdom, where I lectured in Edinburgh and Newcastle. I intended to complete these pieces in color on my return.

While I was in Britain, my paintings absorbed the spirit of Aferro's third floor, where Katrina and Vikki were working in charcoal, no color. By the time I got back to Newark, my sketches were full of themselves in the palette they had learned from the other artists on my floor. My drawings had joined the third-floor club and wanted to belong in the company they were keeping. They said they did not want color. While I was away they had been plotting with other Aferro artists' work in charcoal and gray dryer lint to get me in line in grisaille.

At first I resisted. Who was the painter here, and who the painted? The sketches held firm. I tried bargaining with them to let me use just a little color. Ooooo-kay. The first result was a disaster, an ornery, sullen image of muddied, grudging color that looked like the compromise that had produced it. I pulled it off its stretcher bars, rolled it up, and hid it behind the one ineffectual radiator in the far corner of my studio. Its only title was (and remains) lowercase *bad painting*, as in bad dog. A couple of others weren't so awful, just paintings for other people to like. Only when I gave in to grisaille did the work start living. My Aferro neighbors' charcoal drawings were conspiring with the gray figurative works of Gerhard Richter, the German painter whose work I had been looking at in Providence.

Richter has been a Very Big Deal as a painter for longer than I've been susceptible to art-world enthusiasms. It wasn't his subject matter of German politicians and the Baader-Meinhof Gang of leftwing German terrorists in the 1970s and 1980s that intrigued me. It was his process and his palette.

Richter came back to me at Aferro as my paintings demanded grisaille. (Using a squeegee, he also makes colored "abstract pictures" he calls simply *Abstraktes Bilder*. These do not interest me.) On my way to his process I hardly paused over his subjects, banal scenes and ordinary people. It was his gray paintings' use of photographs that pulled me into his work. Some digging on my part revealed his route to verisimilitude: he projected photographs onto his canvas, traced the photographs with charcoal, and painted the tracings.

Voilà! Another drawing technique that was perfectly acceptable when done in German.

I adjusted Richter's process so that the images I projected were my own handmade drawings and paintings, hence "manual," plus images created from them with Photoshop, hence "digital." I had already named this way of working—my process—manual + digital. But it was really becoming more established as a process of repeated toggling back and forth and back and forth between my hand and my computer, a manual + digital + manual + digital + manual process. Settling into grisaille, I made big drawings, one I called *Back Man + Cook 1*. I laid down a ground in powdered graphite over a masking-tape grid, erased to create pixelated lines, and went back in with charcoal for volume and texture.

Back Man + Cook Drawing 1, 2012, graphite and acrylic on paper, 30" × 60"

"Cook" came from one of Lucille's photographs that I had not used at RISD, though "back man" survived from my last RISD painting. Some of the paintings were very dark, others very light. None looked like anything I had made before. I could work this way for a very long time, varying my mediums and tones.

•

AS I WAS making a series of *Back Man + Cook* drawings and welcoming a stream of visitors to my studio, there came another Oakland crisis. Once again, my father was in Kaiser's ER with elevated blood pressure and confusion, having fallen on his way to the bathroom. After a few hours in the ER, his blood pressure had subsided, and he was sent home. Was there anything else wrong with him? Evidently not. This was turning into a familiar circuit, from Salem to ER with elevated, then normal blood pressure, and home to Salem. Home to his complaints about one thing to the next. For gouging him on price. For aides treating him roughly. I couldn't know which complaint was merited, the matter of price gouging most certainly not.

There was more. He was lonely; again, loneliness. No family around him. His eyesight was failing him, and what would he do when there was nothing left? Friends signed him up for lowsight workshops that his depression prevented his attending. They brought him audiobooks he wouldn't listen to and apparatuses requiring more initiative than he could muster. He lay immobilized in his heartbreak hotel.

NEWARK WAS ANNOYING me now. I waited for my 27 bus on the crowded corner of Market and Broad Streets, Newark's fabled "Four Corners" of the olden days when Newark was New Jersey's booming retail, manufacturing, and distribution hub. That was before Paramus's malls snatched away retail, before manufacturing went overseas, and before Exit 8A on the New Jersey Turnpike captured warehousing. So many empty offices testifying Newark's loss.

The evening darkened, the now strictly working-class crowd at Market and Broad was thinning; yet enough foot traffic remained to prompt an amplified orator to set up below the police surveillance tower. The orator stood before five Fruit-of-Islam-looking protectors, young men so clean-cut as to appear menacing. As the light faded, the orator addressed Latinos in the no-longer-dense crowd:

You Latinos think you better than the black man because you have light skin.

You no better.

You bastards. Bastards of the white man.

You only closer to our European oppressors.

Wake up, you Europeanized bastards!

The orator was preaching black-brown unity through a detour of insult. My Newark didn't usually seem so hostile to me. Maybe it was the season, the holidays with their impending visit to Oakland. There was Christmas music's aggravating cheeriness. Even Nat King Cole roasting chestnuts over an open fire sounded futile in globally warmed New Jersey. We hardly had winter anymore, except for catastrophic dumps of twelve inches of snow that shut everything down for days of excavation. Did anyone roast chestnuts or even know what they were?

Oakland for the holidays just made things worse. My father, bitter in his bed, accused me of doing "nothing" for him, alternating with thanks for reading him Sherwin Nuland's *The Art of Aging*. But mostly my father muttered and griped and circled back to renewing his demand to move to New Jersey.

Move him to New Jersey! What a huge, expensive, impossible undertaking! My stomach ached at the thought. The dressing and undressing. The baggage. The medications. My indentured servitude for the rest of his days.

After we left he got better. He perked up to tell his friends that moving to New Jersey was my idea, that he was only going along for my sake.

Okay, I said to him by phone. Are you ready to move?

I had found the place.

Are you ready to move to New Jersey?

Not yet.

I put my moving-my-father-preparations on hold and went to New Haven for an artist-scholar residency at Yale.

THE ENTHUSIASM OF my Yale welcome stunned me, even after the warmth of my Newark world of artists and my community at Aferro, for I hadn't completely overcome my felt identity as the worst painter in the world. Yale people didn't care. They embraced, even celebrated the genius of the new project I called *Odalisque Atlas*. Yale people, unlike my recent art-school contingent, applauded its growth out of history and art history and current events. My turning the figure of the odalisque—the beautiful, young, sexually available slave girl at the root of the term "Caucasian" for white people—into visual art seemed absolutely original and positively inspired in New Haven. They didn't mind at all that the research came out of my book *The History of White People*. What a productive notion!

Yale was my Elysian Fields, my hog heaven. I could take books out of the Haas Family Arts Library. The Beinecke Rare Book and Manuscript Library let me examine pictures and manuscripts on the world's many slave trades. Teacher Sam in the Yale School of Art invited me to pit crits and a presentation of drawings at the Yale Center for British Art. In Sterling Library I plodded through the details—and I do mean the *details*—of a multivolume history of Ukraine from Soviet times full of analysis of institutions and categories of objects, all mercifully translated into English. I presented a first draft of my odalisque project to the Gilder Lehrman Center for the Study of Slavery, Resistance, and Abolition to an appreciative audience of graduate students and faculty. They told me,

We're so glad you're here.

I luxuriated in Yale's embrace, ready to render my thoughts as images. I set up in an unused faculty office, tacked paper to the wall, and pulled out my graphite and ink. I had time and space and the encouragement to take advantage of all Yale offered me. Who could ask for anything more?

MY FATHER CALLED me in tears. Again. It must have been 8:00 a.m. in Oakland, him crying,

I can't live alone any longer.

His call jerked me back from anticipation to my real life, from shining promise to bleak depression. From expectation to responsibility, eagerness to duty, self-centeredness to empathy.

By now I had heard "can't live alone" many times before and knew how to interpret it. It meant I should move to Oakland. I should, as family, answer to his needs and care for him full-time. He knew by now this would not happen. That yearning was in vain and totally not to be. It meant his moving to New Jersey, even though he said he wasn't ready, and even though his concept of moving from Oakland to New Jersey was on the order of traveling up to the Oregon border.

Okay, was he ready to move right now?

No, not yet.

I returned to my project at Yale, met my friends, ate and drank and talked. I made drawings inspired by Harriet Jacobs's *Incidents in the Life of a Slave Girl*, whose Penguin Classics edition I had edited a decade earlier. Jacobs's observation on beauty in slave girls had stayed with me over the years:

> If God has bestowed beauty upon her [the slave girl], it will prove her greatest curse. That which

commands admiration in the white woman only hastens the degradation of the female slave.

Jacobs was writing about her North Carolina, but she knew she shared a condition with thousands of others. She was from the American South, but her words applied to Georgia in the Caucasus, the home of the odalisque.

I included Jacobs's words in my *Odalisque Atlas*, even though enslaved black girls weren't ordinarily considered odalisques. I wanted to make connections, to emphasize the kindredness of women's experiences, of women's vulnerability despite color-line habits of thought that would separate them. Youth, beauty, plus subjugation imperil a girl, no matter where she lives and no matter who enslaves her.

I rewrote Jacobs's words in graphite exactly as they appeared on page 46. Then I scanned my writing. Using Photoshop, I rescaled and recomposed the image, superimposing layers of different

If God Has Bestowed Beauty, 2012, conté crayon and graphite on paper, 24" × 18"

sizes. I projected my new composition and redrew it in conté crayon and powdered graphite on paper.

In a technique I repeated later in images I made using projection, my Harriet Jacobs drawing depicted the icons at the bottom of the projected frame: "Rotate," "Slideshow," "Return." Unlike sneaky Gerhard Richter, I was candid about projection as one step in my process and a feature of my sense of composition.

In addition to my drawings from *Incidents in the Life of a Slave Girl*, I was envisioning an *Odalisque Atlas* of imaginary maps to pull together many slave trades, starting with the Caucasus and Georgia and Ukraine, the sources of the millennia-old Black Sea slave trade that was already so old that Herodotus, writing in the fifth century BCE, couldn't trace its origins, a slave trade into the eastern Mediterranean that didn't end until about 1900. There was also Thailand, with its present-day sex slavery, and western and central Africa, of the Atlantic slave trade to the Western Hemisphere's islands of the Caribbean Sea and the U.S. American South.

I would invent a new geography of submission, taking apart and reassembling the lands of the odalisque around a reconfigured Black Sea. I couldn't wait to start drawing, to get back to painting. Another phone call.

A family friend in Oakland was in a drugstore buying the ACE bandage my father wanted for his wrist, sore and swollen after a fall. I called my father, who offered an explanation. He had fallen, he said, walking outside by the railroad tracks in Texas. Railroad tracks in his hometown in Texas. Yes, he had been a boy beside the railroad tracks in his Texas hometown. In the 1920s.

Now add the railroad tracks in Texas to the territory my family life needed to administer:

Newark. New Haven. Oakland. Texas.

While I ricocheted between my places, the *New York Times* asked me to write an op-ed column on poor white people, who were becoming a hot topic. In succeeding years they got even hotter, and as the author of *The History of White People*, I became an expert on white people. My *Times* op-ed appeared while I ran between my places, now adding West Orange, New Jersey, where we were preparing to move my father with his constant need for my presence. Oakland, Texas, Newark, West Orange.

New Haven?

New Haven was ceding place to my father. His mind had moved on from walking and falling along the railroad in Texas to a series of lurid, pitiful, enraged fantasies about his wife, my mother, who had died three years earlier. She had had a baby by another man. The baby was white. She was riding on a bicycle holding the white baby. She was riding on a bicycle down Piedmont Avenue with the white baby from the Key System's bus terminal at 40th Street. The baby was female. The baby was dead. I tried not to encounter myself in his fantasies.

Worried for my father's life and, given his imagination, for my own, I went to Oakland. A move to New Jersey would have to come now, not later, or I would have to return to Oakland every single week.

Goodbye, New Haven. Farewell, Elysian Fields. Au revoir, hog heaven.

It seemed like forever that my father had been emotionally impaired. For the last seven years or more, never-ending scenes of tears, accusations, anger, and self-pity, but interspersed with returns to the sweet generosity of spirit, of openness, of attention to others that had made my father universally beloved.

Now depression enfeebled his physical body. He no longer walked Salem's grounds, didn't even go down to the dining room to eat with the tablemates he had cherished. His physical appearance degraded. His hands looked dead, doughy-colored and scrawny, with all the veins standing out over the bones, the deadly colorlessness a defect of light-colored skin. My mother's dark-skinned hands never looked lifeless in that way, even in her mortal illness. It was as though my father's hands had been butchered and all the blood drained away.

In Oakland with my father about to move, I was tired tired tired to death, emotionally wrung out and flattened by his complaints. The generous soul he remained glimpsed my fatigue intermittently and tried to do his part toward his move. There was so little he could manage to do that his gestures saddened me further. How to recover from his move to New Jersey? I was already so tired, and so many tasks remained. No way could I reconnect with my project in New Haven.

My spring semester's project was moving my father, not my *Odalisque Atlas*. Arrangements, money, arrangements, more money, more and more and more money, starting with a check for $8,000 to my father's New Jersey assisted-living facility. The money coursed out a Mississippi River through countless delta channels.

Saintly Husband Glenn was to fly overnight with my father from San Francisco to Newark. On our drive from Oakland across the Bay Bridge to SFO, Glenn remarked to my father that he was leaving the Bay Area after seventy years. My concentration on details had blocked that ending from my mind. Sure enough, I realized, crossing the Bay, my father was leaving the Bay Area to die in New Jersey. He knew that. The point—half the point of his move—was not to die alone. The other half was having me close at hand for trips to the ER, though Glenn, too, did major ER duty in New Jersey.

Glenn's comment on my father's departure from his adopted home after seventy years meant I was doing something of the same thing. For decades after my move east for graduate school and faculty appointments, my parents had anchored me in the Bay Area for at least two visits a year, more, for increasingly frequent emergencies. I'd see my parents' old friends, my old friends, and my new

Bay Area artist friends like Mildred and Anna. This was a goodbye for me as well, a kind of an ending.

After Glenn and my father left for New Jersey, I returned to his apartment. In my father's definitive absence, a decision I had made years earlier came back to me. I was with my mother at Salem as my father was undergoing electroconvulsive therapy. In the course of ECT, his heart stopped. My father had a do-not-resuscitate order, but the doctors called my mother to ask whether they should honor it or restart my father's heart. My mother froze and handed the phone to me. Was she afraid of what she might answer? Phone in hand, I hesitated a moment, figuring he was healthy except for having a heart that had stopped beating. I didn't figure in his depression, which had sent him to ECT in the first place. I said, Restart his heart.

Which they did. But the heart stopping set out-of-bounds the only therapy that fixed my father's depression, even temporarily. He was alive. He was still depressed.

That was years ago.

It was my mother who died.

Now she was dead, and he was alive and on his way to New Jersey. I made the wrong wrong wrong decision, I said to myself in his empty room. If only I could take it back and spare my father this misery. My mother, after grieving, would be a happy widow, emancipated from her husband's depressed negativity, free to pursue her writing and play bingo in the Salem living room as often and as long as she wanted. When I had that phone in my hand, I should have taken another moment to think what "healthy" meant for someone so severely depressed. Would that I had thought more before making that wrong wrong wrong decision. The wrong parent was living, I thought now. The wrong parent had died.

•

EMPTYING MY FATHER'S apartment at Salem, I acted on his permission to give away cherished possessions he had held on to for years. He still had friends, good and old friends in Oakland who could share his belongings. One friend brought her teenage granddaughter, who delighted in my father's fountain pens and a notebook whose wooden cover he had carved. Her pleasure gave me pleasure, though my pleasure was burnt-umber sadness in the darkness of earth tones.

Still, delight in a young person's discovery of the unknown: fountain pens drawing ink from a bottle! Woodworking made by someone right there in Oakland! The pens had been instruments of my father's pride in calligraphy and the notebook a product of his art before glaucoma compromised his eyesight and depression drained his creative spirit.

Departure changed my father's feelings toward money. Although he had always been generous financially as well as helpful to family and friends, he had always hedged his generosity with judgments as to his recipients' ability to use his gifts wisely. He always preferred a thrifty receiver to a spendthrift, educational expenses to consumption. And he let his preferences be known.

Now he judged less, gave more, musing on the irony of having saved more money than he could spend in the time remaining to him. That irony proved vain, for his life in New Jersey cost money by the fistfuls, even for non-Alzheimer's care. He had probably expected lower expenses—his notions of what things cost aligned with 1970s and 1980s prices. In his mid-nineties, he was living longer than any of us expected, himself included. He had enough money for assisted living in New Jersey, but there would hardly be leftover fortunes for him ruefully to enjoy giving away.

YALE OVER. AFERRO ended. What to do now? In Newark's Ironbound district, I rented a studio of my own whose outfitting brought back my father as he used to be, before depression, before frailty. He offered—dear old man—to help me cart a flat file weighing five hundred pounds from Frenchtown on the Delaware River to my Newark studio. That offer was my father's old impulse speaking, his love of pitching in. By now he was too weak to manage even the few steps down to my basement studio. Back when he was only eighty-five, he could actually have helped me; he actually had helped move us to the Adirondacks from Vermont. No longer. Still, in his nineties, a sweet recall of how he used to be.

21

NEWARK ARTIST

OKAY. MY FATHER SETTLED BUT UNHAPPY IN WEST Orange, New Jersey. Me moving into my own studio in the Ironbound. Newark artist. From home in North Newark, I took my 27 bus to Market Street and walked the opposite direction on Market Street from Aferro, a few blocks east toward and through Newark Penn Station to my studio. I wore work clothes like what I was wearing six years earlier at Mason Gross on that day at Rutgers when I first heard the refrain of my art education, How old are you?

Same clothes, but no question.

On the 27 bus I sat among my fellow Newarkers, but just now seeing Artist Jerry coming on board. As Jerry walked down the bus's center aisle, I spoke to him from my seat. My greeting brought him into awareness.

I didn't know that was you, he said.

You blend right in, he added.

And I did blend right in, something I love about Newark. I blend right in. No need to explain my presence or answer questions or present my credentials to prove who I am or justify my being there. I'm not a curiosity or a presence to be appreciated or avoided. I blend right in.

I blend right in. That's what I said back to Jerry, who gave me a high five right there on the 27 bus on my way to my studio.

Art in Newark is a nonprofit undertaking dependent on auctions to raise money for worthy causes. One sign you're a Newark artist is requests to donate your art for auction. I donated a *History Does Not* print to Aferro for auction, a small black-and-white lithograph inspired by an antebellum photograph of an enslaved young musician with vacant eyes and my comment on the absence of his name. Only the name of his owner, Robert E. Lee, is known. This very plain lithograph worked better as an image than a concept in undergraduate crit, because the students thought the musician's name must be Robert E. Lee. The Newark Public Library's Dane Fine Print Collection bought this piece. My first public collection.

An artist's residency in the Newark Public Library let me investigate a little-known, unexpectedly rich visual collection, browsing

History Does Not, 2008, lithograph on BFK Rives paper, 8" × 8"

at leisure as I had in Yale's repositories. The Newark Public Library can't match Yale's libraries, the latter engorged by gifts from the wealthy over centuries. But characteristic of Newark's institutions, the Newark Public Library has more than you might assume. And the 27 bus stops right there.

There came an emergency call—not about my father, thank heaven—but from the Friends of the Newark Public Library. Glenn and I belonged to the Friends of the Newark Public Library, having joined on moving to Newark from Princeton. I had presented book talks on the Friends' behalf. This call wasn't about my books. This was an emergency need to resolve a crisis caused by what would seem great good fortune. Great good fortune complicated by the history of American politics of visual representation. A wealthy New York collector had lent the Newark Public Library a very large drawing by Kara Walker, the famous, legendary, superstar international artist Kara Walker, which the Newark Public Library director had installed, wisely, far from the rooms frequented by children. Indeed, it is a drawing for grown-up eyes.

The charcoal drawing in black and white, reminiscent of Picasso's *Guernica*, is huge, truly monumental in its artistry and sheer size, 6' × 9 ½', entitled *The moral arc of history ideally bends towards justice but just as soon as not curves back around toward barbarism, sadism, and unrestricted chaos* (2010). The title is apt. Beautifully drawn with Walker's expert draftsmanship, the piece embodies the second part of the title in scenes of atrocity.

A black body lynched over the flames.

Beatings of black people, some naked, some clothed.

A cross burning.

The small figure of candidate Barack Obama delivering his speech on race in America, dwarfed by a naked black figure sucking off a gigantic white man as an older black woman looks on.

Yes, these are recognizable scenes from the iconography of

American history. At the same time, this is not an assemblage to make you feel good about being black. It's more a reminder to white people that American history is more than Diarylide-yellow enterprise and democracy in viridian green.

Revolt ensued.

One of the Newark Public Library's librarians, an organizer who had convened meetings of Newark artists that I had attended, told the Newark *Star-Ledger*,

It can go back where it came from. I really don't like to see my people like this.

She had a good point, and she spoke for masses of African Americans who needed to see something less distressing. Once again, art-world enthusiasm confronted African American tastes. The Newark Public Library worker expressed what so many had so deeply felt for so long, that black people had been cruelly stereotyped as stupid and ugly, when not exiled entirely from American visual culture, that we needed to see not more ugliness, but a corrective that showed our beauty.

In the face of uproar, the Newark Public Library director had panicked, covering the drawing with a drape. Obviously, in an institution serving a majority black city, a large work by a major black artist could not remain shrouded. To deal with the crisis, the Friends of the Newark Public Library called an emergency session. We talked to Kara Walker.

Kara Walker to the rescue!

She came to Newark with her images, her assistant, her gallerist, and her gallerist's assistant, all without charging the Newark Public Library a cent. A cent the Newark Public Library didn't have but would somehow have found if necessary. Walker sat with me on a raised platform in Centennial Hall to show her work and answer first my, then the audience's, questions, the audience, rapt, overflowing, and full of Newark artists thrilled to be in the presence of so renowned an artist. Walker charmed Newark artists who were already her fans. Artists, after all, were not protesting her work. Artists weren't her critics.

She showed slides of the drawing as she made it in her studio as part of a larger exhibition, *Dust Jackets for the Niggerati.* Walker spoke softly—she said she felt a little anxious. She explained that her work expressed the "too-muchness" of race in America. When she said her images of racial terrorism "should be horrible to behold" and "should feel both familiar and uncomfortable," was she thinking of black viewers? I don't know that she convinced those hungering for something uplifting. After Walker's visit, the drape came down.

IN THE FALL I had another residency, at Yaddo in Saratoga Springs, New York, where I resumed the *Odalisque Atlas* I had begun at Yale in the spring before my father's needs superseded my own.

Maps have always intrigued me as visual images and as representations of human and geographical presence. They depict at once physical space and cultural significance. At Yaddo I used my atlas to draw regions of enslavement on tracing paper, arranged them according to my plan, and scanned the assembled tracings as an imaginary geographic template. Most of the tracing paper disappeared in the scan, but the rectangle around Puerto Rico showed up, purely an artifact of my process. Liking the way it looked, I kept it in my paintings. Viewers could interpret its meaning as they wished, especially if their roots lay in Puerto Rico. It could be a cobalt-green rectangle as a green rectangle or a cobalt-green rectangle of Puerto Rican innuendo. I forgot to show Cuba, an oversight that also prompted political interpretation.

I projected the template on 26" × 40" sheets of Yupo, traced the projection in charcoal, and applied acrylic paint and ink thickly on some and thinly on others. I painted eight maps that contrasted visually, though all derived from the same template. One looked like it might be a real map, with local names in the right local places, but the places where slave girls came from jumbled together. Haiti scrunched up by Crimea. Thailand abutted Russia and Ukraine. New Orleans and the Mississippi River delta stuck out into the Black Sea. West Africa turned around to face east. Istanbul lay near Moldova. The Caucasus occupied a prominent place at the top. One map in whited-out color had no place names. Place names on another bore no relation to actual geography, so that the rivers on the turned-around shape of West Africa bore European names. One map was splotchy angry red and blue. Two were gray, with textures I made with different kinds of erasers.

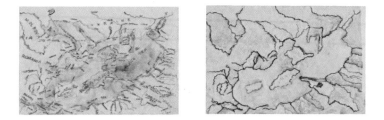

LEFT: *Black Sea Composite Map 4 Historic Map*, 2012, acrylic on Yupo, 26" x 40"
RIGHT: *Black Sea Composite Map 7 Washed Away*, 2012, acrylic on Yupo, 26" x 40"

With a freedom unavailable to me as a historian, my imagination was feeding off history that I had written. After my eight maps, I turned to two new paintings, repeating a figure I took from a New Orleans brothel photograph in the Beinecke. The backgrounds of these two paintings were from detailed maps, one of West Africa, one of the Caucasus. I was relishing my work, savoring it as a kind of secret pleasure, for I still lacked confidence in my own eye. If I liked something I had made, I couldn't be sure it was truly any good.

So dumb to still be so insecure! One evening in the library (the only place with internet connection), I confessed to Richard, another Yaddo guest—at Yaddo, residents are called "guests." Richard was a composer nearly as old as me, but with a long list of prestigious achievements befitting his age. The world had listened to Richard's work and applauded it. In the library I confessed to him that I had asked a more experienced artist friend to stop by and look over my new work on her way up to the Adirondacks. She could tell me if my *Odalisque Atlas* was actually okay. Or not. I was so fucking self-doubting.

Richard of the long experience and impressive achievements made a confession of his own:

I'm still insecure.

Now that was good to hear.

My artist friend rightly skipped Yaddo, leaving me to trust my own eyes. Eventually that trust crept into me. Eventually. But more as I-don't-care-if-this-is-good-or-not-I-like-it than as certainty as to the objective value—*objective value?*—of my work.

RIGHT THEN THE longtime partner of my Dear Cousin Diana called me from Oakland. Devastating news. Diana had liver cancer. Liver cancer kills, kills fast. It would kill her before my next visit to the Bay Area. And now, with my father in New Jersey, when would that be? If I wanted to see Diana alive, I would have to suspend my work and leave Yaddo to go see her now. Once again, family won out over art.

But there was no going to see her now, as Superstorm Sandy shut down air travel. I was stuck; Diana was dying. I spoke to her by phone, both of us choking up, both of us crying. She said she really wanted to see me, with an emphasis stronger and deeper than the usual afternoon visits I would pay her whenever I was in Oakland. This wasn't whenever-you're-in-Oakland. This was now. She *really* wanted to see me urgently. This meant now. A *now* feeling more urgent than my father's nows, which belonged to a series. Please, Diana, hold on. Hold on. Diana's *now* would expire.

I felt that *now*, that impending ending as a muddy gray mashing down, the green-tinged brown on an unwashed palette, the same heaviness as in my mother's death. Diana's dying seemed like my dying, too.

Growing up we had been like sisters, close in age—she a little older—and sharing much of the looks of my father's mother's side of my family, but not his pale skin. Same braids. Same composed expression. My parents drove us around California with the abandon of southerners finally allowed the freedom of the out-of-doors that had been denied them in the South. California was ours, experience was new, and we drove all over. Both generations experienced California with the freshness of first time, before repetition and familiarity dulled the edges of our delight. As adolescents, Diana and I diverged. We became less sisterly while remaining close cousins. She went to Hayward State. I went to Berkeley. I visited her every time I came to California, year after year.

Stuck at Yaddo until the Superstorm passed and I could travel, I called my friends and cried to them for consolation. Finally in California, I sat with Diana in convalescent care, where a woman down the hall cried out ceaselessly, Help me! Help me! Help me! Diana, weakened and in pain, was not yet moribund, but I saw death coming for her. This took her partner totally and unaccountably by surprise. He was determined she would recover, and, bent on recovery, he refused her hospice care. Shortly after I departed, Diana died, hooked up to machines intended for cure.

My return flight east traced, no, retraced, a gorgeous transit I had made countless times over nearly countless decades, over the Phthalo-blue San Francisco Bay, over the yellow ochre hills of the Coast Range, over the Jenkins green fields of the Central Valley with its aqueducts, over the now sepia, not yet *nevada*-snowy Sierra Nevada to the arid neutral gray flats of Nevada where you can hardly see any roads.

From the Bay to Nevada I wept over losing Diana, the sister of my girlhood, and the shutting down, the closing out of even the memory of my youth in my hometown and home state. When Glenn remarked to my father on leaving after seventy years, I had sensed an ending, but as more a thought than a sensation. I had become the parent of my parent, and I was bringing him home to me. His was an ending, yes, but an ending as a transition opening to a continuation elsewhere and in that way an opening to something new.

Losing Diana meant an ending as transition only in that New Age denial of the finality of death. My ending flying over California this time leaving Diana did not open onto new. This was chopping off a root, the closing down of the time when I was learning my way around for the first time, not as the constant readjusting of age to keep up with change over time, a severing of the connection to the personal deep past of my geographical history.

FROM MY YADDO residency I took a yield of eight maps and two paintings of my *Odalisque Atlas*. My early years as a painter, in Providence, New Haven, and Saratoga Springs, felt as much about family and loss as about art making. But how else could it be for a grown-up with a grown-up's attachments? After a certain age, you're responsible for your family, and family means crisis; family means loss.

•

BACK IN WEST Orange, New Jersey, I was reading my father Toni Morrison's new novel *Home*. He was praising it, savoring Morrison's language, following her plot. Then he weakened. Suddenly he couldn't sit up in his wheelchair or keep his eyes open. Uh-oh, he was sinking. He had seemed terminal before, actually several times before. But he had always bounced back. Still, I had never before seen him this unresponsive. I fetched the nurse to check on him, and she called hospice. Someone would come the very next day.

The hospice nurse came the next day, but, she said, she couldn't find the right room. The man in the room she'd been sent to was sitting at his table eating peanuts. Wrong room? Wrong person? No. That was my father at the table eating peanuts. He was back in life again.

22

ART HISTORY BY NELL PAINTER

O NE EVENING AFTER YADDO, AFTER COUSIN DIANA'S death, I had dinner in the Village with Friends Michele and Charlie from the Adirondacks. An agreeable evening, talking mostly about art and artists we knew. In the most innocuous way, Charlie asked me if I was expecting to have a career as an artist. Charlie is a real artist, making work and selling through a gallery for years, my definition of a real artist. Was I expecting a *real* art career?

He didn't say it like that, of course. His words, his tone, all were totally innocent. But here's what I heard:

Is so baby a painter as you expecting really to succeed as an artist?

Is so crummy a painter and as old a person as you going to get anywhere in art?

Probably he was just curious about the prospects of a newly minted MFA painter as old as I was.

Charlie didn't know my exact age, or maybe he did, as my age was not only an object of curiosity, but also public knowledge, as I discovered at Jerry's art supply store in West Orange.

I was standing in line for a demonstration of art printing papers. Printing paper is a hot topic, so the audience exceeded the seating around the expert and his printer. We stood in line fifteen minutes and more, time to strike up a conversation about our art with the woman next to me. She wanted to see my work, so I pulled out my cell phone and Googled myself.

Usually when I Google myself, my own website comes up first without my having to type in the URL, and there's my art on it. Not this time. Not noticing a change, I clicked on the first link. What came up was a simple site with the photo from my own website—a nice photo—and a few lines of text.

The first line read, simply, age 70.

The second line, born in 1942.

I was mortified.

MORTIFIED

There were my age and my date of birth proclaimed for all to see, clear as the sun, stark as death. I hadn't been able to acknowledge my birthday, so strong my consternation on turning seventy. I didn't go as far as Jacques Derrida, who called seventy hell and wished for some way to un-age. Still . . .

What? Who? is a woman in her seventies? She is, I was, indisputably *old*. You can pass for middle-aged in your sixties. And I was looking forward to my eighties.

A woman in her eighties is a sage. She is dignity and wisdom. She inspires the world. She has gravitas. She is elegant. She is Maya Angelou, all eloquence and sagesse.

Eighties? Yeah!

Seventies? Arghhhhhh!

Knowing I couldn't remove or even bury that page, I left Jerry's stripped naked and feeling sad. The first thing anyone looking for my work would see was my age. Not that I had ever lied about my age or even fudged it by leaving dates off my CV. No lying for me. If you visit my own website you'll see that I graduated from Berkeley in 1964. Do the math, and you'll know how old I am. But you would have to do the math that Google had now pre-done for you.

MORTIFICATION

In the morning I felt a whole lot better. Google, in blurting out my age, broke down my chagrin. I felt like my mother once she overcame her reluctance to use a cane (a.k.a. walking stick), because then people would know she was old. Just as her walking stick had restored her confidence, Google's revelation gave me freedom something akin to the freedom I'd experienced years earlier when I'd stopped dying my hair and let show my gray. Then I had freed myself from the tyranny of youth—or the tyranny of the appearance of youth, of its simulacrum—over physical attractiveness. That gesture was long years behind me, now so comfortably gray haired.

The freedom produced by the bald announcement of my age was one just as precious, a freedom that I had edged up to repeatedly but failed to grasp securely: the freedom to disregard the career path that art graduate school had laid out for all of us. You could have a past, but it had to be in art. You couldn't have responsibilities to aged parents or children or attachment to a spouse with work of his own. The fact of children had complicated the education and career path of Keith among my RISD colleagues. Keith tortured himself over his selfishness, as he felt it, for dedicating himself to the exalted-but-iffy future of a visual artist instead of providing for his family through a reliable vocation.

Assuming youthfulness, that path was hard for me. But lacking an alternative, I kept trying to walk that path, stayed attuned to that narrative. Google's announcement of my age made me examine that path and query that narrative, both intended for youth's lack of obstruction. For me there was family, most starkly in the person of my father, with his alternating confusion, weakness, and great good spirits. He would telephone me in high dudgeon to demand my presence right now. Then the very next day or days later and recuperated from cataclysm, he would hold an unperturbed conversation about the state of the world or his memories of the University of California College of Chemistry or his youth in Texas. He could blast me with flaming anger or thank me tenderly for his care. I never knew what each day would bring, which version of my father I'd encounter, only hoping for no fall and no emergency room.

EASY AS IT was to recognize the part family played in my past that was still with me, it was harder to see how art school had redefined my relation to history. What I heard in art school soundly rejected my history and what history meant in me.

Academic.

Academic as bad.

Academic as what things meant rather than how things looked.

Fussiness.

Tired images.

Technique in place of freshness.

Me with my lying twentieth-century eyes and my attachment to meaning.

I TAMPED DOWN that part of my past and tried to believe it no longer connected to me as something I actively thought about. This misconception ensnared me at Yale.

While I was at Yale, my Host Elizabeth chaired an interview between me and Crystal, one of my favorite former graduate students who was on the faculty. Crystal asked how art school had changed my thinking about history. Not how history entered my art, but how art entered my history.

I said I no longer thought about history.

What I meant was I no longer conducted research in historical archives and no longer wrote scholarly books. I wasn't agile enough to give this explanation, so my answer to Crystal's question was basically,

Duh.

Key Jo, one of the smart art history graduate students, tried to help me out by pointing to my odalisque project, so rooted in history. But for myself, I couldn't see the connection between the images forming in my imagination and what I thought of as history, an undertaking in scholarly research that took no liberties with the archive. I felt dumb, and I sounded dumb. A few weeks later, after my talk at the Beinecke, Friends Laura and Rob posed questions much like Crystal's. Once again, I lacked a good response. Finding that answer, I mean being able to formulate it in words, took me years. But find it I did through talking about history.

ART SCHOOL HASTENED, not initiated, my move beyond straight history. I had already embraced new tools like psychology's attachment theory while writing on the Georgia plantation mistress Gertrude Thomas[8] and the New Yorker Sojourner Truth. I was already less interested in generalities and representativeness. I was already going deeper into particularities, even where conventional historical sources failed. Now, with images in my eyes, I wanted to ask

8. Nell Irvin Painter, introduction to *The Secret Eye: The Journal of Ella Gertrude Clanton Thomas, 1848–1889*, edited by Virginia Ingraham Burr (Chapel Hill: University of North Carolina Press, 1990).

questions even when I knew I could not answer them, but when the mere asking let me focus my attention on particular individuals in the past.

In a talk in Germany I concentrated on the individuals whose skulls Blumenbach turned into the embodiments of the varieties of humanity we call races: American, African, Malay, European, and Asian. Who were these people in their own lives, I wondered. In *The History of White People* I had delved into the Georgian slave background of the woman whose skull made white people "Caucasian." But what of the others? Only one, the Siberian warrior who became the Asian, had a name, Tschewin Amureew. The Malay had fallen victim to Captain Cook's men in Tahiti. The American was a Carib chief whom Englishmen had sacrificed to empire. I said this in my German talk, taking the skull with the name only of "Ethiopian" as one example.

I knew from the archive that the skull had belonged to a woman from present-day Ghana who had died at twenty-seven in Amsterdam, where she lived with a Dutch seaman. Her missing teeth said she was a mother.[9] The Dutch professor who had sent her skull to Germany called her a concubine. Was she a concubine? Was she a wife? Was she a slave? I didn't know the answers, for the archive did not offer the information I sought. Even so, I was asking the questions in public.

Painting had taught me to slow down, to tarry over details that might seem insignificant. I lacked answers, for archival documentation failed me. But I could heed painting's prompt to pause over what I could not know and imagine this individual woman's

---

9. Pregnancy changes hormonal balance and saps calcium from the mother's body to nourish the growing fetus. Unless the mother is well nourished enough to replace the calcium in her body, pregnancy's cost to the mother is paid by her teeth and bones.

existence. Making images to accompany my German lecture accorded her historical resonance that words alone withheld.

DURING THE YEARS I needed to find an answer to Crystal, Laura, and Rob about art school and history, I enjoyed myself reprising my former occupation of making books. Not in the way I had written books for other people to publish, but with little books I drew and painted in the spirit of narrative, of one thing after another, even when the narrative wasn't apparent or coherent.

At Jerry's—the same art supply store where Google outed me as seventy—I bought little blank accordion books that I drew and painted on just for the hell of it. I made one in colors and collaged roads with writing on them to celebrate the birthday of my Dear Friend Thad and our years together. Thad's birthday book stretches landscape textures and lighthearted, non-landscape colors across accordion pages, with roads of text recalling places she has been and we have shared. The road strips of text trace the lengths of this friendship.

Happy Birthday Thadious Davis, 2014, accordion artist book on paper, 6" × 38 ½"

I made a simpleminded little book with text to congratulate myself for swimming thirty-three laps in the pool of the Newark Y, to say in image and repeat for emphasis that this happened on this particular day.

Thirty-three Laps Book, 2014, accordion artist book on paper, 6" × 38 ½"

And I made one in graphite and collage from the shadows in my downstairs bathroom for Poet Friend Meena. *Bathroom Book for Meena* has no meaning beyond the visual presentation of the daily passage of time. Only later did I connect my little book to Jun'ichirō Tanizaki's 1933 essay "In Praise of Shadows," a meditation on classic Japanese aesthetics that value the interplay of light and shadow. My book as a physical gift appreciates Meena's presence as I move through the visual contrasts of my everyday life.

Bathroom Book for Meena, 2014, accordion artist book on paper, 6" × 38 ½"

I gave them away.

Around the same time I was making my little books, the *New York Times* once again brought me back to writing about white people. It felt very good to reach a large audience, but I couldn't yet put together my writing history and my art. Two books in particular helped me along, reminding me of my fondness for the combination of text and image and for the drawn books of Maira Kalman, who, I had argued back at RISD, is yes indeed a painter.

One book I pulled out of my Dear Friend Thad's bookshelf, *Lose Your Mother: A Journey Along the Atlantic Slave Route*, by her eloquent English professor colleague, Saidiya Hartman. A poignant travel account by a gifted writer, *Lose Your Mother* traces Hartman's trip to Ghana in search of the Atlantic slave trade that had ensnared her ancestors—some of them, for like most black Americans, her ancestor tangle included some who had not been enslaved and some of European descent. All by itself, Hartman's language makes her book memorable. What caught my eyes were the photographs.

Hartman scattered photographs throughout her pages, some of her family, others of places she had been. The photographs did their work, more autonomous than simple illustration that said, "This is what that looked like." In silent call-and-response with the text, her images sang their own song, not exactly telling their own story, but not exactly telling Hartman's text's, either. Oh my god! I said to myself. These images are making visual meaning apart from, but from within the covers of the book. *Lose Your Mother* demonstrated the possibilities of juxtaposition of text and image to make larger, broader, deeper meaning than scholarship alone.

My other text-plus-image guidebook was W. G. Sebald's *Austerlitz*, also presenting a traveler, European this time, exploring another historical trauma, the Holocaust/Shoah. Photographs appear throughout the book, unexplained and conveying their own indeterminate meaning. Fictional Jacques Austerlitz, like nonfictional Saidiya Hartman, fails to find his ancestors. *Austerlitz* reaped rewards denied *Lose Your Mother*. But these two books projected a contiguity of image and text that I might use.

I COULDN'T YET imagine making such a book on my own, for *Odalisque Atlas* remained tethered to the text of *The History of*

White People in a spirit of illustration, as in illustration = bad. An invitation from the Metropolitan Museum of Art offered just the opportunity, just the prompt that I needed. I was invited as Nell Irvin Painter the historian to comment on "African Art, New York, and the Avant-Garde," a small exhibit in one of the Met's galleries, an invitation that of course I accepted. Of course, if I were going to present at the Met, I would show my own artwork. But what to show? Neither of my two bodies of work, my Brooklyn MFA paintings or my *Odalisque Atlas*, related to the topic at hand. What could I make to show on African art and the New York avant-garde? How about African art in the Harlem Renaissance?

Though hardly a specialist, I had already made a start with my general knowledge of U.S. history and my research for *Creating Black Americans*. A Pyrrole-orange flash took me down to Princeton to Marquand Library for research. I discovered a German source for European primitivism, that early-twentieth-century conviction that over-civilization had sapped Europeans' vitality (often phrased as their virility) and that a remedy lay in art made by non-Europeans deemed "primitive."

Primitivism conveyed Leo Frobenius's photographs and drawings and Karl Einstein's book of African sculpture into the studios of Pablo Picasso, Henri Matisse, and Amedeo Modigliani via the Parisian art dealer Paul Guillaume, and from Guillaume to the rich white collector from Pennsylvania, Albert Barnes. In Marquand Library I found the German graphic artist Winold Reiss, illustrator of the Harlem issue of *Survey Graphic* and *The New Negro*, and mentor of the quintessential Harlem Renaissance artist Aaron Douglas.

My research revealed that while Alain Locke, a Howard University philosopher and a godfather of the Harlem Renaissance, sought to endow black American art with the ancient pedigree of

African art as the "ancestral arts" of African American artists, black artists did not necessarily go along. For one thing, the African art Locke touted was sculpture, while most black American artists of the time were painters. In Marquand I was looking at what artists were actually painting, not merely heeding an idealized theory of the role, in the parlance of the era, of "the Negro artist."

I paid attention to individual proclivities, going past notions of what black people or black artists represented as an undifferentiated mass. In the work of two pioneering, prizewinning painters, Palmer Hayden and Hale Woodruff, I found art in the tradition of Western art. Woodruff collected African art, but he painted like an American painter of his time. Hayden made one painting on African motifs but said he preferred to paint the people around him, his people. Aaron Douglas's success in incorporating African motifs, Locke's "ancestral arts," appeared as only one way, one of many, of making art while black. In Marquand I found controversy, and I incorporated controversy into illustrations of my talk at the Met.

I loved this work.

I loved the research.

I loved making the art that went with the research.

In my Met presentation I showed my own digital collages along with my art history research. I reworked Winold Reiss's drawing of Alain Locke to put Locke into a suit (my husband's), filling in the blank space in Reiss's portrait to stress Locke's identity as a sophisticated Howard University professor, as contrasted with "the Negro" working-class figure of the southern migrant to the North. I set Locke in his/Glenn's suit before Romare Bearden's *The Block*, a twentieth-century Harlem scene. I showed Palmer Hayden and Hale Woodruff within their own paintings, which resembled Western painting of their time. I showed Aaron Douglas's Africanity.

After my Met presentation I continued to work on the images I had created for my talk, elaborating some, jettisoning others. Images too closely tied to the work of illustration fell away. Others survived, becoming an artist's book I called *Art History by Nell Painter Volume XXVII Ancestral Arts*. There was no volume XXVI; I began with XXVII. I had it printed at Staples, hence the "Staples Edition."

LEFT: *Art History by Nell Painter Volume XXVII #10 Frobinius*, 2015, digital collage, 48" × 34"

MIDDLE: *Locke Ancestral Arts*, 2015, digital collage, 48" × 35"

RIGHT: *New Negro Stomps Fuller*, 2015, digital collage, 48" × 32"

One digital collage began with my reworking and coloring a page of Leo Frobenius's sketchbook and his drawing of a Congo sculpture. Another inserted Alain Locke's text on ancestral arts into his mouth in a close-up photographic portrait. Another put together an African piece from Albert Barnes's collection with the cover of Locke's *The New Negro* anthology stomping on a sculpture by Meta Warrick Fuller, an older woman artist whom Locke virtually ignored, even though African imagery inspired her.

A year later I returned to images from *Volume XXVII* and created new ones from Leo Frobenius's photographs. The new series became *Art History by Nell Painter Volume XXVIII*. One of the Palmer Hayden drawings that I had already simplified from the Met talk into *Art History by Nell Painter Volume XXVII* underwent further alteration. The *Volume XXVII* version placed Hayden with a looming silhouette of the philanthropist William Harmon in the dark background and Mary Beattie Brady, the administrator of the Harmon Foundation, in the lower right. In *Volume XXVIII* a fractured image of Brady swamped a fractured Hayden on one page, and on another page, a simplified Hayden repeated in negative in a tint of alizarin crimson and cerulean blue.

Palmer Hayden + Harmon, 2015, digital collage, 48" × 38 ½"

Art History by Nell Painter Volume XXVIII, page 6, 2015, 12" × 12"

and

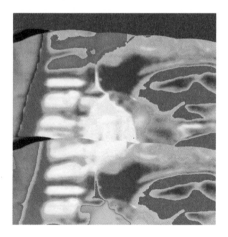

Art History by Nell Painter Volume XXVIII, page 3, 2015, 12" × 12"

After *Volume XXVII*, with its cast of characters at the end, text lost its purchase. No such guidance in *Volume XXVIII*.

Art History by Nell Painter melds history and image in ways that feel right to me and that let me answer the question that Crystal, Laura, and Rob had posed in New Haven. Image lets me concentrate on detail and particularity, on what makes a person or an event or an image unique unto itself. For viewers in search of corroboration—consolation? comfort?—in declarations of community, my stress on singularity can feel wrong, even suspect. An embrace of individual uniqueness can also disappoint the American audience that asks black artists to speak for black people as a whole and to show art whose main role is black identity. To speak to individuality can even seem anti-black within constructions of American identity that equate blackness with community and individuality with whiteness.

In my history books I have already had my say in clear language and discursive meaning about community. Now what history means to me in images is freedom from coherence, clarity, and collective representation. My images carry their own visual meaning, which may or may not explicate history usefully or unequivocally. For me now, image works as particularity, not as generalization. That is how art school changed my thinking about history and how visual art set me free.

Coda

HAPPY ENDING

So, YES, I DID FINALLY TRANSCEND MY ART-SCHOOL unsettling and move past pathetic insecurity. When others overlook or turn away from my art I no longer feel belittled. But transcendence has not come once and for all. So many times I had freed myself from the gaze of others, from their judgments and expectations of an artist so ill-suited as me, only to lose sight of myself as I am and return to self-doubt. Thanks to an interview with Journalist Zahra, I grasped a solution that still works.

Zahra joined a stream of visitors to my Newark Ironbound studio. We talked for hours in a conversation that turned, as such conversations do, from my talking about me and my work to my listening to her talk about herself. I'm not eighty years old yet, but younger women already consult me for advice on getting through this life. Lamenting American society's hostility toward black women, in particular toward black women with dark skin, like hers and mine, Zahra trembled distress. She judged herself a little darker than me, a difference I could not see. Zahra, with roots in the Caribbean Islands, was able to calibrate fine gradations of skin color, an ability I missed out on growing up in California. I recognized her anguish, though my own version replaced skin color with age. I sought to assuage her pain.

I gave Zahra advice against my own wisdom. I usually don't give people advice before they ask for it specifically, because people don't usually want advice. They want to complain. I gave Zahra advice anyway. I told her she absolutely must not see herself through other people's eyes. Great advice.

Zahra needed that advice. She might even have heeded it. But let's be candid here. The person who needed to hear and to heed that advice was me.

I did hear. I did heed. I grew up into who I am as no other. This is not something I could do just one time and have it work forever. Like artists the world over, my bayoneted, hand-to-hand struggle against insecurity and for self-confidence never ends. I have to take my own advice and shoulder my armament every single day. Every single day, not only to close the eyes of disparagement, but also to stop my ears against adulation.

Not to see myself through other people's eyes.

To remain what the gurus call *centered*. When practiced every day, this works, more or less, with regard to myself and my own artwork of artist's books so far outside popularity. And also to accept as part of my practice my day job of talking and commenting that grows out of my career as a historian.

I'm an artist who lives and works in Newark, New Jersey, an artist whose other—not, as I once said, former—lives as a historian and as a daughter are still crucial parts of me. I am a wise old person, not a hot young artist, not a young anybody with a young anybody's future before me. I know the value of doing my work, *my work*, and keeping at it. I do keep at it—in the pleasure of the process of making the art only I can make.

Serious artist? Yes. I make and show my work regularly. Professional artist? Yes, I get paid for my work. An Artist artist? Probably not, probably never, because I still do other things. Do I miss not being An Artist artist? Yes, a little. But not enough to live my life any other way.

Princeton Self-Portrait, 2015, charcoal on paper, 10 ¼" × 8"

As for my father, so integral a part of my art-school experience, turning ninety-five brought transformation as his depression lifted. He and I could sit and talk like old times. My father had support beyond what Glenn and I could offer: monthly visits from the deacons of Bethany Baptist Church, mature black men in dark suits and dignity. The Bethany deacons reconnected my father to men like himself as no others could, and they reminded him of truth from his youth, that god is good. During my father's last years in assisted living in West Orange, New Jersey, life was good.

My father died as I was finishing up this book, a peaceful passing after years of turmoil. He could not last forever, though almost ninety-eight meant a very long life, nearly forever. He had always said he wanted to die in his sleep in his bed, to which my mother expressed horror at the thought of waking up next to a dead body. She died first, so no such waking up. He died alone very early in the morning. Dead in his bed, my father looked as he had looked transitioning, eyes closed, mouth open, only no longer breathing. Was that how death looked? Later, on a slab in Perry Funeral Home, we saw the real, the colorless, closed-mouth look of death, the soul departed.

My father, like my mother, wanted to be cremated. I respected his wishes, so Perry Funeral Home sent him to the crematorium wrapped up with a copy of his favorite painting, *The Banjo Lesson*, Henry O. Tanner's tender chiaroscuro depiction in lemon yellow and cerulean blue of a grandfather teaching his young grandson to make music. My father's ashes rest in peace along with his beloved Tanner.

My father had seemed to have died several times before rebounding. Every time he seemed to be leaving, we grieved. Each time his recovery allowed us a reprieve, again and again and again. Surely, by the time he died and did not recover, we were pre-grieved. In the first weeks of after-death paperwork, that almost seemed to be so. Then it was so not the case.

Glenn and I fell into absence's pit whenever my father crossed our minds, whenever we passed Exit 10 to West Orange, when one of his favorite sayings came to mind or something that particularly pleased or annoyed him turned up. My father's death drained my strength and ruined my voice. It knocked me down for a month before I could get off my couch and resume my life.

I resumed my life. I made art again. With art school behind me and my father safely dead—safe with my mother—I live and work in Newark, New Jersey.

ACKNOWLEDGMENTS

Throughout art school and the writing of this memoir—hell, throughout my entire life—I've been fortunate and felt grateful for my parents and my friends and my good luck. It's as though a shielding cover, a protective quilt of family and friends, saved me from misfortunes that might easily have come my way. To protectors beyond the edges of this work, I thank you.

I could not have thrown myself into art school without women, older women, who knew both the snares and the means of escape. Some were already friends, others I just knew that they existed and that they would help me. They did. Thank you.

Some names have escaped me, but many I gratefully recall: Elizabeth Alexander, Russell Ames, Emma Amos, Ellen Few Anderson, Jared Ash, Katrina Bello, Mary Bergstein, Bethany Baptist Church Deacons, Dawoud Bey, Kevin Bewersdorf, Camille Billops, Elena Borstein, Dionne Brand, Judith Brodsky, Marcia Brown, the late Donna Bruton, Abena Busia, Mary Ellen Capek, Hazel Carby, Barbara Chase-Riboud, Marcy Chevali, Susanna Coffee, Stephen Colbert, Dennis Congdon, Cicely Cottingham, Cathy Gaines Crump,

Evonne Davis, Victor Davson, Jeanette Démeestère, Jessica Dickinson, Greg Drasler, Anna Edwards, Ottmar Ette, Lauren Ewing, Rochelle Feinstein, Diane Fine, Claudia Ford, the late Lucille Fornasieri-Gold, Terri Francis, David Frazier, Henry Ferreira, Jerry Gant, Bill Gaskins, Judy Glantzman, Sarah Granett, Farah Jasmine Griffin, Brooks Hagan, Sue Hallgarth, Daniel Harkett, Mildred Howard, Holly Hughes, the Irvins' Family Folks, Erica James, Brian Jermusyk, Anthony Johnson, Jeremy Johnson, Tayari Jones, Mary Lu Kirsty, Joyce Kozloff, Key Jo Lee, Cyra Levenson, Jennifer Liese, Barbara Madsen, Sam Messer, Vikki Michalios, Katherine Min, Carrie Moyer, Mansa Musa, Randa Newland, Linwood Oglesby, Ferris Olin, Coleen Gutwein O'Neal, Frank Owen, Irving Petlin, Anna Plesset, Madeleine Polymeropoulos, Richard Powell, the late Clement Price, Mary Sue Sweeney Price, Andrew Raftery, Charles Ramsburg, Faith Ringgold, Carin Rodenborn, Hanneline Røgeberg, Joseph Ruck, Nicholaas Rupke, Duhirwe Rushemeza, Charles Russell, Leslie Sanders, Joe Scanlon, Mira Schor, Deborah Schwartz, Janet Shafer, Ruth Simmons, Duane Slick, Jacqueline Bryant Smith, Jeffrey Stewart, Robert Storr, the late Denise Thomasos, Angola Thomson, William Villalongo, Kara Walker, Michele Wallace, Paul Andrew Wandless, Ken Weathersby, Alison Weld, Anker West, Stephen Westfall, Laura Wexler, Adrienne Wheeler, Roger White, Iain Whitecross, Stanley Whitney, Emma Wilcox, Didier William, Deborah Willis, Alexi Worth, Michele Zachheim, and Kevin Zucker.

My work—this book, especially—needed its sheltered time at Yaddo, the Ucross Foundation, and the MacDowell Colony. Once the book was done, the ebullient team at Counterpoint Press, notably my editor Jennifer Alton and Lena Moses-Schmitt, Sarah Baline, and Wah-Ming Chang, turned the processes of publication into pleasure. Jacqueline Ko remains indispensable.

I would have self-destructed without my Very Special People.

Sarah Lewis, Sarah Chalfant, Meena Alexander, Debra Balken, Thadious Davis, and Glenn Shafer deserve outsize appreciation for helping me survive art school and learn a new way of writing. Thank you for standing beside me over many years of everything.

LIST OF IMAGES

1. *I Hope I Look That Good When I'm That Old*, 2002, Dona Irvin photo by Ron Carter, 9" × 6"
2. *Ghana Drawing of Girl*, 1964–1965, graphite on paper, approx. 10" × 8"
3. *Ghana Drawing of Man*, 1964–1965, graphite on paper, approx. 10 ¼" × 7 ½"
4. *Ghana Drawing 3*, 1964–1965, graphite on paper, approx. 7 ½" × 10 ¼"
5. *Red Hat*, 2003, oil on canvas, approx. 12" × 16"
6. *Gray Scale*, 2003, oil on canvas, approx. 24" × 18"
7. *Blue Boxes*, 2003, oil on canvas, approx. 24" × 18"
8. *Still Life with Red Pot*, 2004, oil on canvas, 9" × 12"
9. *Figure with Shadow*, 2004, oil on canvas, 12" × 9"
10. *Newark Penn Station*, 2006, paper collage, approx. 18" × 24"
11. *Faux Chinese Scroll*, 2006, oil on canvas in two pieces, each 12" × 48"
12. *Positive Historical Silhouette*, 2006, paper collage, approx. 8" × 10"
13. *Negative Historical Silhouette*, 2006, paper collage, approx. 8" × 10"
14. *Sojourner Truth + Franz Schubert Territory / Wein York City and Rivers*, 2003, felt pen and collage on paper, approx. 8" × 8"
15. *My Neel's Ringgold*, 2007, oil on canvas, approx. 24" × 18"

327

NELL IRVIN PAINTER is the Edwards Professor of American History, Emerita, at Princeton University. Her acclaimed works of history include *Standing at Armageddon*, *Sojourner Truth*, and the *New York Times* bestseller *The History of White People*, which have received widespread attention for their insights into how we have historically viewed and translated ideas of value, hierarchy, race, and gender. She holds an MFA from the Rhode Island School of Design and a BFA from Mason Gross School of the Arts. Her visual artwork has been shown at numerous galleries and in collections, including the San Angelo Museum of Fine Art, the Brooklyn Historical Society, and the Smith College Museum of Art. She lives in Newark, New Jersey, and the Adirondacks.